S0-CAB-329

Items in an Access Database

Item	Description
Tables	Lists of records containing the information that you want to store in the database
Queries	Selection of fields and records from one or more tables in the database (a *select query*); other types of queries can add records to a table, modify the records in a table, or create a new table
Forms	On-screen arrangement of information from a table or query; you use forms for entering, editing, and looking at information in the database
Reports	Printed arrangement of information from a table or query
Macros	Programs using the Access macro programming language
Modules	Programs using the Access Basic programming language

Getting Around in a Form

To Move Here	Press These Keys
Next field	Tab or Enter
Previous field	Shift+Tab
First field	Home
Last field	End
Next record	Ctrl+PgDn
Previous record	Ctrl+PgUp
First record	Ctrl+↑
Last record	Ctrl+↓

The Navigation Bar

Record Number   Total Number of Records

First Record   Last Record

Record: I◀ ◀ | 1 | ▶ ▶I ▶* of 100

Previous Record   New Record

Next Record

Progress Check

Unit 1: Starting Out in Access

❏ Lesson 1-1: Running Access

❏ Lesson 1-2: Seeing What's in the Database

❏ Lesson 1-3: Looking at the Records in a Table

❏ Lesson 1-4: Using Menu Commands and Toolbar Buttons

❏ Lesson 1-5: Exiting Access

Unit 2: Creating Your Own Database

❏ Lesson 2-1: Creating an Address Book

❏ Lesson 2-2: Entering Records Using a Form

❏ Lesson 2-3: Another Way into Your Database

❏ Lesson 2-4: Printing Reports

Unit 3: Editing, Finding, and Deleting Records

❏ Lesson 3-1: Editing and Copying Entries

❏ Lesson 3-2: Stupid Data-Entry Tricks

❏ Lesson 3-3: Fixing Mistakes

❏ Lesson 3-4: Deleting Stuff

❏ Lesson 3-5: Finding Records

Unit 4: Slicing and Dicing Your Data

❏ Lesson 4-1: Getting Answers with Queries

❏ Lesson 4-2: Looking at Selected Records

❏ Lesson 4-3: Designing a Query from Scratch

❏ Lesson 4-4: Sorting the Results of a Query

Unit 5: Importing Information into Access

❏ Lesson 5-1: Importing Data from Another Access Database

❏ Lesson 5-2: Importing Data from Web Pages

❏ Lesson 5-3: Importing Text Files into Access

❏ Lesson 5-4: Combining Data from Two Tables

Accessing the CD-ROM Files
CHEAT SHEET

The CD-ROM does not contain the Access 97 program (Microsoft would never allow it!). You must already have Access 97 installed on your computer to use the exercise files on the CD-ROM.

Follow the installation instructions in the Introduction or Appendix B to copy the exercise files to your hard disk. To open an exercise file after you've installed them, follow these steps:

1. **With Access 97 running, choose File⇨Open Database from the menu.**

   You see the Open dialog box.

2. **Click in the Look in box and move to the drive and folder in which you installed the exercise files.**

   Unless you specified otherwise, the exercise files are in the C:\My Documents\Dummies 101 Access 97 folder.

3. **Click the filename of the file you want to open and then click the Open button.**

   Access opens the database file. Don't make changes to exercise files until instructed to do so in the lessons in this book.

Important Commands

Command	What It Does
File⇨Open	Opens an existing Access database
Edit⇨Undo	When editing, undoes changes to the current field or record
File⇨Print Preview	Displays on-screen the selected or open table, query, form, or report as it will appear when printed
File⇨Print	Prints the selected or open table, query, form, or report
Edit⇨Find	Displays the Find window
Tools⇨Relationships	Displays the Relationships window
File⇨Exit	Exits Access

 ®

COMPUTER BOOK SERIES FROM IDG

References for the Rest of Us! ®

Are you intimidated and confused by computers? Do you find that traditional manuals are overloaded with technical details you'll never use? Do your friends and family always call you to fix simple problems on their PCs? Then the *...For Dummies*® computer book series from IDG Books Worldwide is for you.

...For Dummies books are written for those frustrated computer users who know they aren't really dumb but find that PC hardware, software, and indeed the unique vocabulary of computing make them feel helpless. *...For Dummies* books use a lighthearted approach, a down-to-earth style, and even cartoons and humorous icons to diffuse computer novices' fears and build their confidence. Lighthearted but not lightweight, these books are a perfect survival guide for anyone forced to use a computer.

> *"I like my copy so much I told friends; now they bought copies."*
>
> **Irene C., Orwell, Ohio**

> *"Quick, concise, nontechnical, and humorous."*
>
> **Jay A., Elburn, Illinois**

> *"Thanks, I needed this book. Now I can sleep at night."*
>
> **Robin F., British Columbia, Canada**

Already, hundreds of thousands of satisfied readers agree. They have made *...For Dummies* books the #1 introductory level computer book series and have written asking for more. So, if you're looking for the most fun and easy way to learn about computers, look to *...For Dummies* books to give you a helping hand.

IDG BOOKS WORLDWIDE ™

7/96r

DUMMIES 101™: ACCESS 97 FOR WINDOWS®

by Margaret Levine Young
and Rodney Lowe

IDG Books Worldwide, Inc.
An International Data Group Company

Foster City, CA ✦ Chicago, IL ✦ Indianapolis, IN ✦ Southlake, TX

Dummies 101™: Access 97 For Windows®

Published by
IDG Books Worldwide, Inc.
An International Data Group Company
919 E. Hillsdale Blvd.
Suite 400 Foster City, CA 94404
www.idgbooks.com (IDG Books Worldwide Web site)
http://www.dummies.com (Dummies Press Web site)

Library of Congress Catalog Card No.: 96-80234

ISBN: 0-7645-0095-3

Printed in the United States of America

10 9 8 7 6 5 4 3 2 1

1M/RV/QR/ZX/IN

Distributed in the United States by IDG Books Worldwide, Inc.

Distributed by Macmillan Canada for Canada; by Transworld Publishers Limited in the United Kingdom and Europe; by WoodsLane Pty. Ltd. for Australia; by WoodsLane Enterprises Ltd. for New Zealand; by Longman Singapore Publishers Ltd. for Singapore, Malaysia, Thailand, and Indonesia; by Simron Pty. Ltd. for South Africa; by Toppan Company Ltd. for Japan; by Distribuidora Cuspide for Argentina; by Livraria Cultura for Brazil; by Ediciencia S.A. for Ecuador; by Addison-Wesley Publishing Company for Korea; by Ediciones ZETA S.C.R. Ltda. for Peru; by WS Computer Publishing Company, Inc., for the Philippines; by Unalis Corporation for Taiwan; by Contemporanea de Ediciones for Venezuela. Authorized Sales Agent: Anthony Rudkin Associates for the Middle East and North Africa.

For general information on IDG Books Worldwide's books in the U.S., please call our Consumer Customer Service department at 800-762-2974. For reseller information, including discounts and premium sales, please call our Reseller Customer Service department at 800-434-3422.

For information on where to purchase IDG Books Worldwide's books outside the U.S., please contact our International Sales department at 415-655-3172 or fax 415-655-3295.

For information on foreign language translations, please contact our Foreign & Subsidiary Rights department at 415-655-3021 or fax 415-655-3281.

For sales inquiries and special prices for bulk quantities, please contact our Sales department at 415-655-3200 or write to the address above.

For information on using IDG Books Worldwide's books in the classroom or for ordering examination copies, please contact our Educational Sales department at 800-434-2086 or fax 817-251-8174.

For press review copies, author interviews, or other publicity information, please contact our Public Relations department at 415-655-3000 or fax 415-655-3299.

For authorization to photocopy items for corporate, personal, or educational use, please contact Copyright Clearance Center, 222 Rosewood Drive, Danvers, MA 01923, or fax 508-750-4470.

 is a trademark under exclusive license to IDG Books Worldwide, Inc., from International Data Group, Inc.

About the Authors

Margaret Levine Young: Unlike her peers in that 30-something bracket, Margaret Levine Young was exposed to computers at an early age. In high school, she got into a computer club known as the R.E.S.I.S.T.O.R.S., a group of kids who spent Saturdays in a barn fooling around with three antiquated computers. She stayed in the field through college against her better judgment and despite her brother John's presence as a graduate student in the Computer Science department. Margy graduated from Yale and went on to become one of the first microcomputer managers in the early 1980s at Columbia Pictures, where she rode the elevator with Paul Newman, Bill Murray, and Jeff Goldblum.

Since then, Margy has co-authored over 15 computer books on the topics of the Internet, UNIX, WordPerfect, Microsoft Access, and (stab from the past) PC-File and Javelin, including *Dummies 101: The Internet for Windows 95*, *The Internet For Dummies*, 3rd Edition (with her brother John), *Internet FAQs: Answers to Frequently Asked Questions*, and *UNIX For Dummies* (all published by IDG Books Worldwide, Inc.). She met her future husband Jordan in the R.E.S.I.S.T.O.R.S., and her other passion is her children, Meg and Zac. She loves gardening, chickens, reading, and anything to do with eating, and she lives near Middlebury, Vermont.

Rodney Lowe: Rodney graduated from the University of Newcastle-upon-Tyne, England (his home town), with a degree in Zoology, at which point he wondered what he was going to do with his life. He is eternally grateful to a nameless career counselor who advised him to check out a career in the world of computers. He took a job with an engineering firm willing to offer a job to someone who had nothing but potential to offer. His first programs were converted into punched cards and fed into a monolithic IBM mainframe. After graduating to minicomputers and becoming more of an analyst than a programmer, he took up the offer of a job in Bermuda (he actually thought about turning it down, but sanity prevailed).

While working in Bermuda he fell in love with an American tourist, moved to Massachusetts, and married her. Sally and he now live in Lexington, Massachusetts, with Chris, his stepson, and Bethany, his daughter. It was there that his family became good friends with Margy and her family after meeting them at their local Unitarian Universalist church.

Since moving to the U.S., he has used PCs at home and at work as a toolbox to help get the job done. Access has been one of his favorite tools in the toolbox since it was first released. He believes that the only asset that is a greater waste than an unemployed worker is unused software. There are millions of computers in the world and probably 95 percent of the software sitting on them is unused, because of lack of training and education. That's why he was glad to get involved with the writing of this book.

ABOUT IDG BOOKS WORLDWIDE

Welcome to the world of IDG Books Worldwide.

IDG Books Worldwide, Inc., is a subsidiary of International Data Group, the world's largest publisher of computer-related information and the leading global provider of information services on information technology. IDG was founded more than 25 years ago and now employs more than 8,500 people worldwide. IDG publishes more than 275 computer publications in over 75 countries (see listing below). More than 60 million people read one or more IDG publications each month.

Launched in 1990, IDG Books Worldwide is today the #1 publisher of best-selling computer books in the United States. We are proud to have received eight awards from the Computer Press Association in recognition of editorial excellence and three from *Computer Currents'* First Annual Readers' Choice Awards. Our best-selling *...For Dummies®* series has more than 30 million copies in print with translations in 30 languages. IDG Books Worldwide, through a joint venture with IDG's Hi-Tech Beijing, became the first U.S. publisher to publish a computer book in the People's Republic of China. In record time, IDG Books Worldwide has become the first choice for millions of readers around the world who want to learn how to better manage their businesses.

Our mission is simple: Every one of our books is designed to bring extra value and skill-building instructions to the reader. Our books are written by experts who understand and care about our readers. The knowledge base of our editorial staff comes from years of experience in publishing, education, and journalism — experience we use to produce books for the '90s. In short, we care about books, so we attract the best people. We devote special attention to details such as audience, interior design, use of icons, and illustrations. And because we use an efficient process of authoring, editing, and desktop publishing our books electronically, we can spend more time ensuring superior content and spend less time on the technicalities of making books.

You can count on our commitment to deliver high-quality books at competitive prices on topics you want to read about. At IDG Books Worldwide, we continue in the IDG tradition of delivering quality for more than 25 years. You'll find no better book on a subject than one from IDG Books Worldwide.

John J. Kilcullen

John Kilcullen
President and CEO
IDG Books Worldwide, Inc.

Eighth Annual
Computer Press
Awards ≥1992

Ninth Annual
Computer Press
Awards ≥1993

Tenth Annual
Computer Press
Awards ≥1994

Eleventh Annual
Computer Press
Awards ≥1995

IDG Books Worldwide, Inc., is a subsidiary of International Data Group, the world's largest publisher of computer-related information and the leading global provider of information services on information technology. International Data Group publishes over 275 computer publications in over 75 countries. Sixty million people read one or more International Data Group publications each month. International Data Group's publications include: **ARGENTINA:** Buyer's Guide, Computerworld Argentina, PC World Argentina; **AUSTRALIA:** Australian Macworld, Australian PC World, Australian Reseller News, Computerworld, IT Casebook, Network World, Publish, Webmaster; **AUSTRIA:** Computerwelt Osterreich, Networks Austria, PC Tip Austria; **BANGLADESH:** PC World Bangladesh; **BELARUS:** PC World Belarus; **BELGIUM:** Data News; **BRAZIL:** Annuario de Informática, Computerworld, Connections, Macworld, PC Player, PC World, Publish, Reseller News, Supergamepower; **BULGARIA:** Computerworld Bulgaria, Network World Bulgaria, PC & MacWorld Bulgaria; **CANADA:** CIO Canada, Client/Server World, ComputerWorld Canada, InfoWorld Canada, NetworkWorld Canada, WebWorld; **CHILE:** Computerworld Chile, PC World Chile; **COLOMBIA:** Computerworld Colombia, PC World Colombia; **COSTA RICA:** PC World Centro America; **THE CZECH AND SLOVAK REPUBLICS:** Computerworld Czechoslovakia, Macworld Czech Republic, PC World Czechoslovakia; **DENMARK:** Communications World Danmark, Computerworld Danmark, Macworld Danmark, PC World Danmark, Techworld Denmark; **DOMINICAN REPUBLIC:** PC World Republica Dominicana; **ECUADOR:** PC World Ecuador; **EGYPT:** Computerworld Middle East, PC World Middle East; **EL SALVADOR:** PC World Centro America; **FINLAND:** MikroPC, Tietoverkko, Tietoviikko; **FRANCE:** Distributique, Hebdo, Info PC, Le Monde Informatique, Macworld, Reseaux & Telecoms, WebMaster France; **GERMANY:** Computer Partner, Computerwoche, Computerwoche Extra, Computerwoche FOCUS, Global Online, Macwelt, PC Welt; **GREECE:** Amiga Computing, GamePro Greece, Multimedia World; **GUATEMALA:** PC World Centro America; **HONDURAS:** PC World Centro America; **HONG KONG:** Computerworld Hong Kong, PC World Hong Kong, Publish in Asia; **HUNGARY:** ABCD CD-ROM, Computerworld Szamitastechnika, Internetto online Magazine, PC World Hungary, PC-X Magazin Hungary; **ICELAND:** Tolvuheimur PC World Island; **INDIA:** Information Communications World, Information Systems Computerworld, PC World India, Publish in Asia; **INDONESIA:** InfoKomputer PC World, Komputek Computerworld, Publish in Asia; **IRELAND:** ComputerScope, PC Live!; **ISRAEL:** Macworld Israel, People & Computers/Computerworld; **ITALY:** Computerworld Italia, Macworld Italia, Networking Italia, PC World Italia; **JAPAN:** DTP World, Macworld Japan, Nikkei Personal Computing, OS/2 World Japan, SunWorld Japan, Windows NT World, Windows World Japan; **KENYA:** PC World East African; **KOREA:** Hi-Tech Information, Macworld Korea, PC World Korea; **MACEDONIA:** PC World Macedonia; **MALAYSIA:** Computerworld Malaysia, PC World Malaysia, Publish in Asia; **MALTA:** PC World Malta; **MEXICO:** Computerworld Mexico, PC World Mexico; **MYANMAR:** PC World Myanmar; **NETHERLANDS:** Computer! Totaal, LAN Internetworking Magazine, LAN World Buyers Guide, Macworld Netherlands, Net, WebWereld; **NEW ZEALAND:** Absolute Beginners Guide and Plain & Simple Series, Computer Buyer, Computer Industry Directory, Computerworld New Zealand, MTB, Network World, PC World New Zealand; **NICARAGUA:** PC World Centro America; **NORWAY:** Computerworld Norge, CW Rapport, Datamagasinet, Financial Rapport, Kursguide Norge, Macworld Norge, Multimediaworld Norge, PC World Ekspress Norge, PC World Nettverk, PC World Norge, PC World ProduktGuide Norge; **PAKISTAN:** Computerworld Pakistan; **PANAMA:** PC World Panama; **PEOPLE'S REPUBLIC OF CHINA:** China Computer Users, China Computerworld, China InfoWorld, China Telecom World Weekly, Computer & Communication, Electronic Design China, Electronics Today, Electronics Weekly, Game Software, PC World China, Popular Computer Week, Software Weekly, Software World, Telecom World; **PERU:** Computerworld Peru, PC World Profesional Peru, PC World SoHo Peru; **PHILIPPINES:** Click!, Computerworld Philippines, PC World Philippines, Publish in Asia; **POLAND:** Computerworld Poland, Computerworld Special Report Poland, Cyber, Macworld Poland, Networld Poland, PC World Komputer; **PORTUGAL:** Cerebro/PC World, Computerworld/Correio Informático, Dealer World Portugal, Mac*In/PC*In Portugal, Multimedia World; **PUERTO RICO:** PC World Puerto Rico; **ROMANIA:** Computerworld Romania, PC World Romania, Telecom Romania; **RUSSIA:** Computerworld Russia, Mir PK, Publish, Seti; **SINGAPORE:** Computerworld Singapore, PC World Singapore, Publish in Asia; **SLOVENIA:** Monitor; **SOUTH AFRICA:** Computing SA, Network World SA, Software World SA; **SPAIN:** Communicaciones World España, Computerworld España, Dealer World España, Macworld España, PC World España; **SRI LANKA:** Infolink PC World; **SWEDEN:** CAP&Design, Computer Sweden, Corporate Computing Sweden, Internetworld Sweden, it.branschen, Macworld Sweden, MaxiData Sweden, MikroDatorn, Nätverk & Kommunikation, PC World Sweden, PCaktiv, Windows World Sweden; **SWITZERLAND:** Computerworld Schweiz, Macworld Schweiz, PCtip; **TAIWAN:** Computerworld Taiwan, Macworld Taiwan, NEW ViSiON/Publish, PC World Taiwan, Windows World Taiwan; **THAILAND:** Publish in Asia, Thai Computerworld; **TURKEY:** Computerworld Turkiye, Macworld Turkiye, Network World Turkiye, PC World Turkiye; **UKRAINE:** Computerworld Kiev, Multimedia World Ukraine, PC World Ukraine; **UNITED KINGDOM:** Acorn User UK, Amiga Action UK, Amiga Computing UK, Apple Talk UK, Computing, Macworld, Parents and Computers UK, PC Advisor, PC Home, PSX Pro, The WEB; **UNITED STATES:** Cable in the Classroom, CIO Magazine, Computerworld, DOS World, Federal Computer Week, GamePro Magazine, InfoWorld, I-Way, Macworld, Network World, PC Games, PC World, Publish, Video Event, THE WEB Magazine, and WebMaster; online webzines: JavaWorld, NetscapeWorld, and SunWorld Online; **URUGUAY:** InfoWorld Uruguay; **VENEZUELA:** Computerworld Venezuela, PC World Venezuela; and **VIETNAM:** PC World Vietnam.   10/22/96

Dedication

Margy lovingly dedicates this book to the celebration of her daughter Margaret Virginia Young's sixth birthday.

Rodney dedicates this book to Sally, who willingly agreed to become a single parent while it was being written, and to Chris and Bethany, who became semi-orphans without being given the option to agree or disagree.

Rodney and Margy both also dedicate this book to First Parish Church Unitarian Universalist in Lexington, Massachusetts, which is where their families became friends.

Author's Acknowledgments

We would like to acknowledge the care of Mary Goodwin and Kelly Ewing as they shepherded this book through the editing and production process, as well as all the folks listed on the Publisher's Acknowledgments page (right after this page) who worked on the book. IDG Books Worldwide, Inc., is a wonderful and talented group!

Margy thanks Jordan Young and the Cornwall Elementary School for making it possible for her to get any work done, and Susan Arnold, Don Arnold, Kate Tilton, Jim Arnold, and Monica McKenna for providing housing.

Rodney thanks Margy, for risking her good reputation by offering him the chance to work with her on this book, and Sally, who was more help than she will ever know.

Publisher's Acknowledgments

We're proud of this book; please send us your comments about it by using the Reader Response Card at the back of the book or by e-mailing us at feedback/dummies@idgbooks.com. Some of the people who helped bring this book to market include the following:

Acquisitions, Development, and Editorial

Project Editors: Mary Goodwin, Kelly Ewing

Acquisitions Editor: Gareth Hancock

Product Development Director: Mary Bednarek

Permissions Editor: Joyce Pepple

Copy Editors: Susan Diane Smith, Diane L. Giangrossi, Patricia Yuu Pan

Technical Editor: Publication Services, Inc.

Editorial Manager: Seta K. Frantz

Editorial Assistant: Heather H. Dismore

Production

Project Coordinator: Valery Bourke

Layout and Graphics: Brett Black, Cameron Booker, J. Tyler Conner, Dominique DeFelice, Maridee V. Ennis, Angela F. Hunckler, Jane E. Martin, Brent Savage, Kate Snell

Proofreaders: Joel Draper, Sandra Profant, Rachel Garvey, Robert Springer

Indexer: Anne Leach

Special Help: Stephanie Koutek, Proof Editor

General and Administrative

IDG Books Worldwide, Inc.: John Kilcullen, CEO; Steven Berkowitz, President and Publisher

IDG Books Technology Publishing: Brenda McLaughlin, Senior Vice President and Group Publisher

Dummies Technology Press and Dummies Editorial: Diane Graves Steele, Vice President and Associate Publisher; Judith A. Taylor, Brand Manager

Dummies Trade Press: Kathleen A. Welton, Vice President and Publisher; Stacy S. Collins, Brand Manager

IDG Books Production for Dummies Press: Beth Jenkins, Production Director; Cindy L. Phipps, Supervisor of Project Coordination; Kathie S. Schutte, Supervisor of Page Layout; Shelley Lea, Supervisor of Graphics and Design; Debbie J. Gates, Production Systems Specialist; Tony Augsburger, Reprint Coordinator; Leslie Popplewell, Media Archive Coordinator

Dummies Packaging and Book Design: Patti Sandez, Packaging Specialist; Kavish+Kavish, Cover Design

◆

The publisher would like to give special thanks to Patrick J. McGovern, without whom this book would not have been possible.

◆

Files at a Glance

Files at a Glance

Here's a listing of all the CD files and where in the book you can find more information about them. See Appendix B for instructions about installing the files from the CD on your computer. Please go to the appropriate lesson or appendix for further instructions about the particular file.

Part I

Lessons 1-1 through 1-4 and Unit 1 Exercise	Starting Out in Access	Middlebury Tours.mdb
Lessons 2-3 and 2-4	Another Way into Your Database and Printing Reports	Dickens Address Book 2.mdb

Part II

Lessons 3-1 through 3-5 and Unit 3 Exercise	Editing, Finding, and Deleting Records	Middlebury Tours.mdb
Lessons 4-1 through 4-4 and Unit 4 Exercise	Slicing and Dicing Your Data	Dickens Address Book 4.mdb
Lesson 5-1	Importing Data from Another Access Database	Dickens Address Book 4.mdb, Dickens Extras.mdb
Lesson 5-2	Importing Data from Web Pages	Dickens Address Book 4.mdb, Dickens Extras.htm
Lesson 5-3	Importing Text Files into Access	Dickens Address Book 4.mdb, Dickens Extras.txt
Lesson 5-4	Combining Data from Two Tables	Dickens Address Book 5.mdb

Contents at a Glance

Table of Contents

Introduction

Welcome to *Dummies 101: Access 97 For Windows,* part of the new hands-on tutorial series from IDG Books Worldwide, Inc.

Database programs are a little different from other programs you may have learned to use. Before you can do much with a database program, you must learn about databases themselves, including some terminology. This stuff isn't complicated, but if you don't understand how databases work, Access isn't going to make much sense. And when it comes to databases, you've got to learn by doing.

If you're new to Access and databases, the best way to learn about it is to take a course, with step-by-step instructions that build up your expertise lesson by lesson. That's just what this book does. This book is a series of lessons that takes you through the basics of creating a database in Access (or using one that exists already), entering information, and creating reports. As you read the book, follow along at your own computer, using the sample databases we supply. The tutorials in this book take the place of a class, complete with lessons, exercises, quizzes, and tests. (If you need to look up specific tasks in more of a reference format, you may want to buy *Access 97 For Dummies* by John Kaufeld (IDG Books Worldwide, Inc.), which covers a broad range of Access topics.)

If you've ever read any of our *...For Dummies* books, you probably already know that this book will give you a great deal of information in a form you can understand, without taking computers and software too seriously. This book is for you if:

- ◆ You want to use a database program but are daunted by all the incomprehensible technical terms in software manuals.

- ◆ You must learn to use Access for a project.

- ◆ You want to take a class so that you can learn all the important features of Access, but you just don't have time.

- ◆ You want to learn all the basic tasks of running a database program — such as entering information, editing information, and printing reports — so that you don't have to run for help every time you need to get some work done.

This book includes a CD-ROM containing Access databases that you will use as you follow the lessons in this book. Later in this introduction, we tell you how to install the Access files to your hard disk so that you can easily open them when necessary.

Notes:

Who Are You?

This book is designed for the beginning or intermediate computer user who wants more than just techno-speak about Access. We have to make some assumptions about you in order to make the course work for you. We assume that:

- Windows 95 is installed on your machine.

- Microsoft Access Version 8.0 or Microsoft Office 97 Professional is installed on your computer.

- Your computer has a CD-ROM player that you can use to install the *Dummies 101* CD-ROM that is stuck inside the back cover of this book.

- You have a basic understanding of how to use Windows 95. If you don't, check out *Dummies 101: Windows 95* by Andy Rathbone (IDG Books Worldwide, Inc.).

- You have a wild urge to use Access.

How the Book Works

This book contains a course in Microsoft Access 97 (also known as Access Version 8.0, but we'll just call the program Access). The step-by-step approach leads you through each basic Access feature by telling you exactly what to do and what your computer should do in response. Each unit offers hands-on procedures to follow as you learn the basics and then an additional exercise at the end of the unit that you can use to review what you've learned. At first you use databases that we set up for you, and then you learn to build your own.

After you learn the basics, you can skip to the units that cover what you need to know right away. Each unit indicates what you need to know to begin the unit, in case you are skipping around, as well as what you'll learn in the unit. A progress check is even included at the end of each lesson so that you can gauge how you are doing.

We don't take Access (or computers, for that matter) very seriously. After all, there's more to life than running a database program (or so we hear)! So don't be surprised if you run across some trick or joke questions in our quizzes!

Here's how to follow the lessons in this book:

- The course contains ten *units,* each starting with an introduction to the topic to be covered. Then you'll get to the *lessons* that delve into the topic with step-by-step instructions for what to do. Most lessons guide you through database work using a database included on the *Dummies 101* CD-ROM at the back of this book.

♦ Topics that are more complicated or less widely used are covered in *Extra Credit* sidebars. These topics aren't necessary for your learning but may contain just the information you need to make your Access database dance.

♦ When we tell you something important to remember, we summarize the information in a note in the margin (such as the one in this margin).

♦ A *Recess* section indicates a good place to stop and take a breather. (Perhaps a walk around the block — or the cubicles — will help clear your head.) When you reach a Recess section, we tell you how to stop what you're doing and how to get started again when you come back.

♦ At the end of each unit, a quiz provides a way for you to review what you've learned and adds some comic relief. If a question stumps you, flip back through the unit to find the point you missed. You'll also find an exercise that lets you practice what you've learned, using the databases included on the *Dummies 101* CD-ROM. At the end of each part of the book is a review of all the units in that part, along with a grueling test. (Well, maybe it's not so grueling, considering that the answers are in the back of the book.)

In the text, stuff you type appears in **boldface**. When you have to press more than one key at a time, we show the names of the keys connected with a plus sign, like this: Ctrl+C. Hold down the first key (Ctrl, in this example), press the second key (C), and then let them both up.

When we tell you to choose a command from the menu bar, little arrows appear between the parts of the command, like this: File⇨Open. Click the first part of the command (File, in this example) on the menu bar, and then click the second part of the command (Open) on the menu that appears. The underlined letters are *hot keys* for the command; simply hold down the Alt key while you press the hot key to access that menu.

use margins for taking notes (or doodling)

File→Open means click File on menu bar, then Open on menu that appears

How the Book Is Organized

This book is divided into four parts.

Part I: Database Basics

This part of the book tells you how to run Access from Windows 95, how to open a database, and how to see what's in it. After you are comfortable with Access, you learn how to create your own database.

Part II: Getting Data into Your Database

In Part II, you learn how to type information into a table in Access, how to correct mistakes, and how to find a record you entered earlier. You learn how to select groups of similar records from a table, such as people who haven't

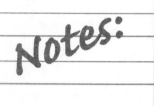

paid their bills or people who live in Wisconsin. You also find out how to copy information from other types of files — such as spreadsheets and text files — into your Access database.

Part III: Printing Reports and Creating Web Pages

Part III covers the ways that you can get information out of your Access database and onto sheets of paper, including printing datasheets, reports, and mailing labels and publishing tables and queries as Web pages.

Part IV: Creating and Using Multitable Databases

This part of the book introduces advanced topics, such as creating databases with more than one table (in which the tables are related). You create your own multitable databases by using the Database Wizard that comes with Access. Finally, you learn how to make changes to a database, such as adding tables, adding or deleting fields from a table, and making the necessary changes to queries, forms, and reports.

Icons Used in This Book

This icon tells you when you need to use a file that comes on the *Dummies 101* CD-ROM. You install the files from the CD-ROM onto your hard disk in the next section of this Introduction. Appendix B describes the contents of the CD-ROM in detail.

Here's an item that you're going to need to know when you get to the quiz at the end of this unit or the test at the end of this part of the book. If it's on the test, it must be important!

Descriptions of advanced topics appear in sidebars highlighted with this icon.

Heads up! Here's a piece of information that will make your life easier or help you avert disaster.

Using the Dummies 101 CD-ROM

The *Dummies 101* CD-ROM at the back of this book contains all the files you need in order to do the lessons and exercises in this book. By including the files on the CD-ROM, we avoid asking you to do a great deal of tedious typing; we've created sample databases, tables, and records for you to use. You learn how to open the databases on the CD in Unit 1.

Check out Appendix B for all the details about the CD-ROM. Remember that the files are meant to accompany the book's lessons, so try to resist the urge to fool around with them before we tell you to.

The *Dummies 101* CD-ROM does *not* include the Microsoft Access program itself. Microsoft would be justifiably mad if we gave the program away illegally. Instead, you have to buy the program from a software store or get it from the computer department at your office. Our CD-ROM contains database files, not programs.

To use the CD-ROM, you need a computer with a CD-ROM drive, Microsoft Access 97 and Microsoft Windows 95 installed on your computer, at least 8MB of RAM on your computer, and at least 3MB of free hard-disk space available if you want to install just the exercise files.

Here's how to install the files from the *Dummies 101* CD-ROM onto your hard disk. Remember to store the CD-ROM where it will be free from harm so that you can reinstall a file in case the one that's installed on your computer gets messed up.

install exercise files from CD-ROM before starting lessons

on the CD

With Windows 95 running, follow these steps:

1 **Insert the Dummies 101 CD (label side up) into your computer's CD drive and wait about 30 seconds to see whether Windows 95 starts the CD for you.**

Be careful to touch only the edges of the CD. The CD drive is the one that pops out with a circular drawer.

If your computer has the Windows 95 AutoPlay feature, the installation program begins automatically and you see the a window telling you that the program is about to start the installation. If the program does not start after 30 seconds, go to Step 2. If it does, go to Step 4.

2 **If the installation program doesn't start automatically, click the Start button on the Windows 95 Taskbar and choose Run from the menu that appears.**

3 **In the dialog box that appears, type** d:\setup.exe **(if your CD drive is not drive D, substitute the appropriate letter for** d**) and click OK.**

You see a window telling you that the installation program is about to install some icons you can use to finish the installation.

4 **Click OK.**

You see a window asking if you'd like to use the CD now.

Notes:

5 Click Yes to make the End-User License Agreement window appear.

6 Read the license agreement and click Agree to make the Dummies 101: Access 97 For Windows installation window appear.

7 Click Install Exercise Files.

Another message appears, asking whether you want to copy the exercise files to your hard disk.

8 Click OK to continue with the installation, or click Cancel if you want to stop.

You see a window asking where to install the exercise files on your computer. To make the installation and the exercises in this book as simple as possible, let the installer place the exercise files in the recommended location. Unless you change the location, the exercise files are installed in the C:\My Documents\Dummies 101 Access 97 folder.

9 Click OK to install the files in the folder shown.

The installation program copies the exercise files to your computer. You see a little window telling you that the installation is done and referring you to the book for how to use the exercise files.

10 Click OK to make the Dummies 101: Access 97 For Windows installation window reappear.

11 Click the Exit button. The program asks is you really, really want to exit.

12 Click Yes.

If you have problems with the installation process, you can call the IDG Books Worldwide, Inc., Customer Support number: 800-762-2974 (outside the U.S.: 317-596-5261).

Send Us E-Mail

We love to hear from our readers. If you have questions or comments about the book, send us e-mail at 101access97@dummies.com. We can't answer all your questions about Access — after all, we are authors, not consultants — but we'd love to hear how the course worked for you. We've got information about our other books at this Web site: http://net.dummies.com.

If you want to know about other ...*For Dummies* books, call 800-762-2974, e-mail info@idgbooks.com, or look at this page on the World Wide Web: http://www.dummies.com.

If you can't send e-mail, you can always send plain, old paper mail by using the Reader Response Card at the back of this book. You receive an IDG Books Worldwide, Inc., catalog in return, and we authors will see your comments, too.

Database Basics

Part 1

In this part . . .

Starting a new program can be hard, and database programs are more complicated than word-processing or spreadsheet programs. Luckily, Microsoft Access makes it easy to get started slowly, and this book doesn't tell you anything you don't need to know.

In this part of the book, you take a tour of Access and see what a database looks like. You use a database we created for you — the database is stored on the *Dummies 101* CD. If you haven't installed the files from the *Dummies 101* CD yet, skip to the Introduction and follow the instructions in the section "Using the *Dummies 101* CD-ROM."

So get a tall cool glass of juice, a double half-caf cappuccino, or a flat can of Dr. Pepper (your choice), and go on to Unit 1!

Starting Out in Access

Objectives for This Unit

✓ Getting into Access and taking a look around

✓ Using the database window to see what's in the database

✓ Taking a look at a table

✓ Using Access commands and toolbar buttons

✓ Getting out of Access

Prerequisites

▶ Windows 95 installed on your computer (see your manual)

▶ Microsoft Access Version 8.0 installed on your computer (you may receive it as part of Microsoft Office 97)

▶ The *Dummies 101* CD-ROM files installed (see "About the CD-ROM" in the Introduction or Appendix B)

▶ A basic understanding of how to use Windows 95 (check out *Dummies 101: Windows 95* or *Windows 95 For Dummies;* both books are written by Andy Rathbone and published by IDG Books Worldwide, Inc.)

on the CD

▶ Middlebury Tours database (Middlebury Tours.mdb)

This unit starts with the basics. Unlike other programs, such as word processors or e-mail programs, you need to have a little background in database terminology and concepts before you can do serious work in Microsoft Access 97 (we'll just call it Access). In this unit, you take some time to meet some important Access tools and features using a database that already exists. Don't get us wrong; you're not going to blow up the computer if you don't know every Access feature. But you can save yourself time in the long run if you take a look around Access before you try any serious work.

In this unit, you learn how to start up Access and how to look at data in a table. You'll poke around in a few corners and peek behind the scenes at the design for a table.

You may already know that Access is a database program, so what's a database? A *database* is a collection of data, but so is almost anything — a to-do list, an address list, a checkbook, a budget, or a letter. What makes a database special is that the information is arranged according to a fixed structure that makes the information easy to select, sort, display, and print in a variety of formats. A database is made up of a series of *records*, which are like the index cards that make up an address list. Each record contains information in the same format.

table = bunch of records, like stack of file cards

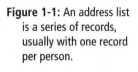

Figure 1-1: An address list is a series of records, usually with one record per person.

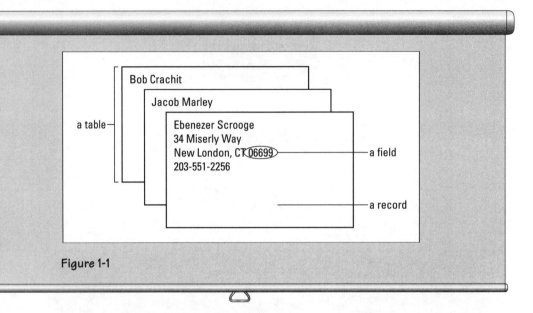

Figure 1-1

In an address list, each record contains information about one person: name, address, and other facts. Each individual piece of information — such as the first name, the last name, or the street address — is called a *field* (see Figure 1-1). A bunch of records together is called a *table*.

An Access database can contain one table or more. For example, a database used for a bookstore may contain a books table, with one record for each book; a publishers table, with one record for each publisher; and a customers table, with one record for each customer. With the information in these tables, a bookstore owner can easily find out which customers buy the most books, which books sell the best, which publishers are the most popular, which authors sell the least, and a host of other useful facts, depending on the types of information included in each table.

After you create an Access database that contains at least one table, you can enter records in the table, make changes to (edit) the records in the table, delete records you don't want anymore, sort the records in various ways, and print your data in a variety of formats, including columnar reports, forms, summaries, mailing labels, and form letters. Reports are what make a database program such as Access worth using to keep track of your address list or other information. You learn how to create and print reports in Unit 7.

A *database management program* such as Access is a general-purpose program, designed for working with almost any type of information in many different ways. For example, you can set up an address database to replace your card file, a wine cellar database with information about each bottle in your cellar, or a bookstore inventory database with information about each title that your store sells. You may be familiar with your library's database of circulating items, which you use to identify, locate, and borrow books.

Many people use *spreadsheet programs*, such as Lotus 1-2-3 or Microsoft Excel, to store lists of records. Some spreadsheet programs have database capabilities, but they aren't designed to do as much as a database program. For example, you can use 1-2-3 to store an address list, and you can enter, edit, delete, and sort the records, but printing mailing labels or form letters is difficult and

---

Handwritten margin notes:

each individual piece of information = field

database can contain one or more tables

Access = database management program

tedious. Spreadsheet programs do not think in terms of tables, records, and fields but rather in terms of *cells* (the basic unit of a spreadsheet), and those programs don't have built-in commands to work with a table record by record. Spreadsheet programs are particularly lousy at producing different reports from the same information and making reports that include information from more than one table. You'll be glad you're using Access for your database!

To see databases, tables, records, and fields for yourself, run Access and take a look around a database that comes on the *Dummies 101* CD-ROM. In this unit, you will open a database that contains a list of the tours that Middlebury Tours, a sightseeing tour company, plans to introduce. Stay tuned for specific instructions in Lesson 1-1!

Running Access

Lesson 1-1

You can start up Access in several different ways:

on the test

> ▶ Use the Windows 95 Start button. (It's on the *Taskbar,* the gray bar that's usually at the bottom of the screen.) Later in this lesson, we give you step-by-step instructions for running Access by using the Start button.

> ▶ Click the Access icon on your Desktop, if you see one. (It looks like a gold key lying on a report.)

> ▶ If you are using Microsoft Office and its Shortcut bar appears along the right edge of your screen, click the bar's gold-key Access icon.

No matter which way you start Access, you get the same program! When you get Access running (as you will later in this lesson), you see the Access window, which is pictured in Figure 1-2. Table 1-1 lists the parts of the Access window and what they do.

Before you get Access up and running, make sure that you see the Windows 95 Desktop on-screen (that's what you usually see when you first run Windows 95).

Starting Access

Follow these steps to start Access:

1 **Fire up your computer, along with the screen, printer, and anything else that you usually turn on.**

The computer needs a few minutes to start up and, especially for Windows 95, to come to life. Relax while you contemplate the clouds on the Windows 95 start-up screen.

2 **Click the Start button on the Windows 95 Taskbar.**

A menu appears above the Start button.

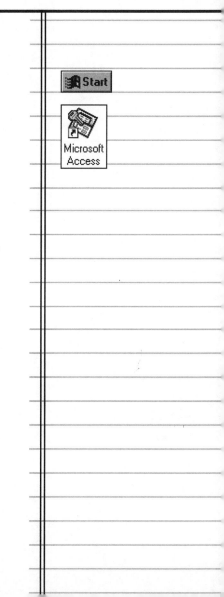

Figure 1-2: A typical Access window.

Notes:

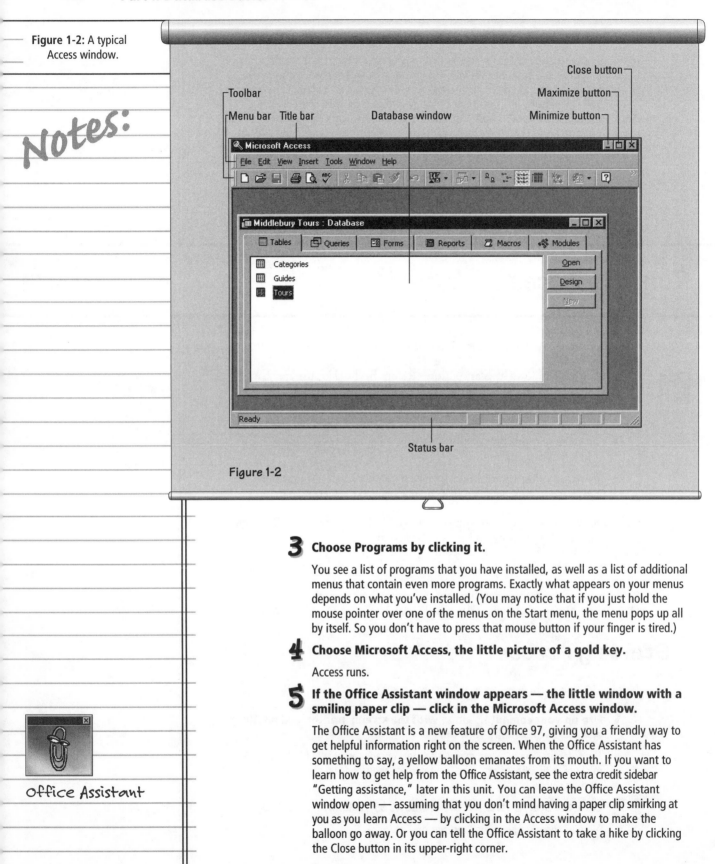

Close button

Maximize button

Minimize button

Toolbar

Menu bar Title bar   Database window

Figure 1-2

Office Assistant

3 Choose Programs by clicking it.

You see a list of programs that you have installed, as well as a list of additional menus that contain even more programs. Exactly what appears on your menus depends on what you've installed. (You may notice that if you just hold the mouse pointer over one of the menus on the Start menu, the menu pops up all by itself. So you don't have to press that mouse button if your finger is tired.)

4 Choose Microsoft Access, the little picture of a gold key.

Access runs.

5 If the Office Assistant window appears — the little window with a smiling paper clip — click in the Microsoft Access window.

The Office Assistant is a new feature of Office 97, giving you a friendly way to get helpful information right on the screen. When the Office Assistant has something to say, a yellow balloon emanates from its mouth. If you want to learn how to get help from the Office Assistant, see the extra credit sidebar "Getting assistance," later in this unit. You can leave the Office Assistant window open — assuming that you don't mind having a paper clip smirking at you as you learn Access — by clicking in the Access window to make the balloon go away. Or you can tell the Office Assistant to take a hike by clicking the Close button in its upper-right corner.

Table 1-1	Parts of the Access Window
Gizmo	*What You Can Do with It*
Title bar	The title bar reveals the astounding news that you're running Microsoft Access. Good to know.
Minimize button	Click it to minimize (iconize) the Access window.
Maximize button	Click it to expand the Access window to take up the entire screen.
Restore button	After you maximize the Access window, click the Restore button to return Access to its usual window. The Restore button — with two overlapping boxes on it — replaces the Maximize button when a window is maximized.
Close button	Click it to exit Access.
Menu bar	Click the words on the menu bar to choose the commands that you use to control Access. You'll find out more about commands in Lesson 1-4.
Toolbar	Click the buttons on this bar for quick shortcuts to frequently used commands.
Database window	This window shows information about the database that's open — see Lesson 1-2.
Status bar	Look at it for information about what you're doing. When nothing is happening, you see the message `Ready`.

Minimize button

Maximize button

Restore button

Close button

After you tell the Office Assistant to clam up (by closing its window or clicking in the Access window), you see a dialog box asking whether you want to create a new database or open an existing database (see Figure 1-3). The Open an Existing Database option is already selected (a little black dot appears in its button). A box at the bottom of the window lists the databases you've used recently, if any. (If this is the first time you have run Access, no box appears.)

recently used databases are listed at bottom of window

Don't worry; you've got a database to open. You installed a bunch of sample databases when you installed the *Dummies 101* CD-ROM that came with this book.

6 **If you see a list of databases at the bottom of the window, click More Files.**

If this is the first time you've used Access, no databases are listed, so skip this step.

7 **Click the OK button.**

You see the Open dialog box, shown in Figure 1-4. This dialog box looks just like the Open dialog box used by every other Windows 95 program, so if you've used other programs, it should look familiar. Access looks in the My Documents folder on your hard disk (unless you've told Access to look elsewhere).

When you installed the files from the *Dummies 101* CD-ROM, they were copied to the *Dummies 101* Access 97 folder, which is in the My Documents folder on your hard disk. If you chose to install the files in a different folder, skip Step 8 and switch to the folder that contains the files.

Notes:

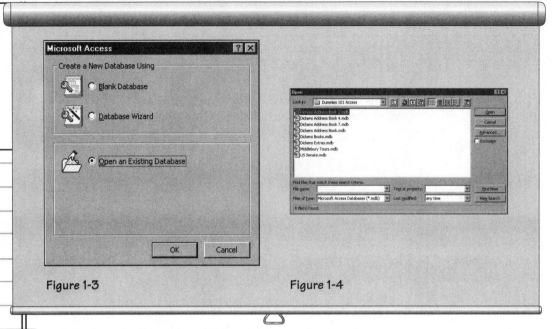

Figure 1-3   Figure 1-4

8   Double-click the Dummies 101 Access 97 folder.

Access looks in the folder and lists the database files it sees. The Office Assistant paper clip may do a little file-opening dance — just ignore it.

on the CD

9   Select the Middlebury Tours database and click OK.

The Middlebury Tours database opens, and you see its database window, as shown back in Figure 1-2.

Now Access is running, and a database is loaded, ready for you to use it. Wow! You're ready to take a look around.

While Access is running — or any other program, for that matter — don't turn off your computer. No, your computer won't collapse into a pile of shrapnel, but Windows 95 and your programs can get confused if you turn off the computer while they're running, and your programs can leave garbage lying around on your hard disk. Exiting Windows 95 before turning off the computer is important. See Lesson 1-5 for how to exit Access and Windows 95.

heads up

extra credit

Yikes! What is Access doing?

If someone has customized your version of Access, a database may automatically open and display a form when you start up Access. If your copy of Access opens a database without your telling it to, talk to someone in charge of the computers at your organization. Ask him or her to create an Access icon on your Windows 95 desktop that starts Access without doing anything else.

extra credit

Getting assistance

A new feature of Microsoft Office 97 is the Office Assistant — a friendly character who helps you get help with Microsoft Office programs. If Office Assistant is installed on your computer, when you start Access, you see an extra little window with a face, usually a paper clip-shaped face. When you have a question about Access, click in the window. A balloon appears, like the ones in comic books, asking what you want to know. You can type a question in English, and the Office Assistant guesses what you mean. When it knows what your question is, the Office Assistant displays the help screen that answers your question. Read the help screen and click its Close button after you are done, or click in the Access window to get back to work.

You can leave the Office Assistant window open in a corner of your screen, just waiting for you to click in it and ask a question. Or you can close its window by clicking its Close button. To get it back, click the Office Assistant button on the toolbar (the button with the question mark in a yellow balloon).

If you don't see the Office Assistant window, click the Office Assistant button on the toolbar. If you still don't see it, you may need to install the Office Assistant program from your Access 97 or Microsoft Office 97 diskettes or CD-ROM. To change settings that control the way that the Office Assistant works, right-click in the Office Assistant window and choose Options from the menu that appears.

Office Assistant window

Office Assistant button

Recess

This first lesson has been long, but we wanted you to see Access appear on your screen in all its glory. If you need a quick break, get up and shake out your arms and legs. If you plan to be away from your computer for long, skip to Lesson 1-5 and follow the instructions to exit Access first.

When you are ready to continue with Lesson 1-2, follow the instructions in Lesson 1-1 to start Access and open the database again. If you are running Access with another database open, close that database and open the Middlebury Tours database by choosing File⇨Open from the menu bar.

☑ **Progress Check**

If you can do the following, you've mastered this lesson:

❑ Run Access.

❑ Open a database.

❑ Recognize the parts of the Access window.

Seeing What's in the Database

Lesson 1-2

on the test

The *database window* shows you what's in your database. Because you can open only one database at a time, you see just one database window, entitled Middlebury Tours : Database. Along the top of the database window are six (count 'em) tabs, with the six kinds of things that live in an Access database.

database window displays six kinds of database items

  ♦ *Tables* are where you put your data. Tables are lists of records, as described at the beginning of this unit. A database can contain lots of tables. For example, a database for a tour operator may contain a table of tours that the company organizes and a table of tour guides.

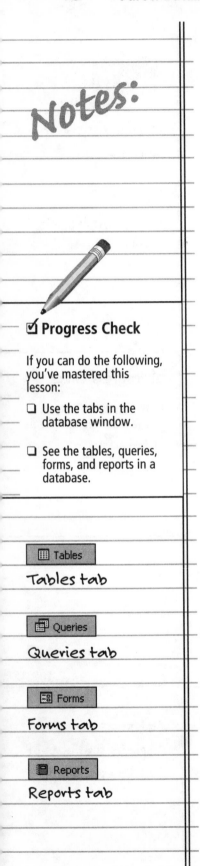

Notes:

☑ **Progress Check**

If you can do the following, you've mastered this lesson:

❑ Use the tabs in the database window.

❑ See the tables, queries, forms, and reports in a database.

⊞ Tables

Tables tab

▦ Queries

Queries tab

▤ Forms

Forms tab

▤ Reports

Reports tab

◆ *Queries* are a means to slice and dice your data. You use queries to select which records you want to include in something like a report. For example, you can create a query that shows you all the tours that cost less than $500 or those that are led by Rodney Lowe.

◆ *Forms* are how you get the data into the tables. You use forms to enter records, edit them, and delete them.

◆ *Reports* are arrangements of information intended for printing. You can make lots of different reports showing data from the same tables. For example, you can make one report that lists all your tours alphabetically, another that lists them by starting date, and a third that lists only tours that are designed for families. Access can create reports in lots of nifty formats, including columnar reports, reports with totals, and mailing labels.

◆ *Macros* are simple keystrokes that take the place of lengthy commands to automate some common tasks, such as printing a report. They use the Access macro programming language.

◆ *Modules* are programs written in the Access Basic programming language. By writing macros and modules, a programmer can make Access do everything but wash the dishes — such as create special commands and buttons just for use in a particular database.

Dummies 101: Access 97 For Windows doesn't teach you about creating macros and modules; these features are used primarily by programmers. If you absolutely *must* learn about them, finish the lessons in this book and then run out and buy *Access Programming For Dummies*, by Rob Krumm (IDG Books Worldwide, Inc.).

Here's how to see what's in the Middlebury Tours database. (If the Middlebury Tours database isn't open, start Access and open the database first.)

on the CD

1   Click the Tables tab in the database window, if it's not already selected.

When the Tables tab is selected, the database window lists the tables in the Middlebury Tours database. This database contains three tables: Tours (the list of tours they offer), Categories (the list of categories the tours fall into), and Guides (the list of tour guides who lead the tours).

2   Click the Queries tab in the database window.

The database window lists the queries in this database, including an alphabetical listing of tours and a listing of tours for less than $500.

3   Click the Forms tab in the database window.

You see a list of the forms in this database. The Middlebury Tours database contains just one form, named Tours, which is used for editing and viewing the records in the Tours table. (You'll use it in Lesson 1-3.)

4   Click the Reports tab in the database window.

The database window lists the reports in this database.

5 **If you want the Access window to be a little bigger, you can adjust the size of the window or make it fill the whole screen.**

To adjust the size of the window, use the mouse to drag the edges of the Access window around the screen. To make the Access window fill the whole screen, click the Maximize button near the upper-right corner of the Access window (the button with the big box on it; refer to Figure 1-2).

You can change the size of the Access window anytime. If you've maximized it and you want to shrink it again, click the Restore button (with two overlapping boxes on it), which replaces the Maximize button when a window is maximized.

Now you know how to look around a database to see what's inside. In the next lesson, you see what a table looks like and use a form to see its records.

If you need to stop, skip ahead to Lesson 1-5 to find out how to exit Access. But come back soon!

> *click Maximize to make the Access window fill the screen*

Looking at the Records in a Table   Lesson 1-3

All these tables, queries, forms, and reports are well and good, we hear you saying. But where's the *data?* It's about time to see what's inside a table.

Access has two ways to show you the records in a table: datasheets and forms. In a *datasheet,* each record appears in a row, and each field appears in its own column. In a *form,* the records and fields are arranged in whatever way the form designer set up the form. You learn how to use forms in Lesson 2-2.

If you look at a table as a datasheet, you're in *Datasheet view.* If you open a form to see the information in a table, you're using *Forms view.* (Logical enough!) Here's how to see the records in Datasheet view. (If the Middlebury Tours database isn't open, start Access and open the database first.)

> *datasheet shows records from table in rows and columns*

1 **Click the Tables tab in the database window.**

You see the tables in this database: Tours, Guides, and Categories.

2 **Click the Tours table in the list of tables to select it and then click the Open button.**

Alternatively, you can double-click the table name. Either way, Access displays the records in the Tours : Table window, shown in Figure 1-5.

You can tell which record you are working on because a right-pointing triangle appears in the left-most column of the row. You start at record 1.

3 **Close the Tours : Table window by clicking its Close button.**

That is, click the Close button (the one with an X) in the upper-right corner of the Tours window. *Don't* click the Close button in the upper-right corner of the Access window — clicking it closes the whole Access program! Clicking the Close button on the Tours window closes only the Tours window.

Figure 1-5: The Tours : Table window displays the records from — what else? — the Tours table.

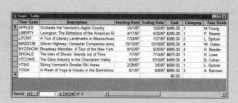

Figure 1-5

You see the database window again. Actually, the window has been open all this time, waiting for you to come back. Several windows can be open at the same time within the Access window.

4 **Click the Forms tab in the database window; then click the Open button.**

Access opens the Tours form, which displays just one record of the Tours table, as shown in Figure 1-6.

At the bottom of the Tours form are the buttons and boxes that tell you what record you're looking at and let you move from record to record. These buttons look like the controls on a VCR, so just pretend that you're fast-forwarding through a tape of last night's reruns.

5 **Click the Next Record button, the little right-pointing arrow button (with no bar or asterisk beside it) along the bottom edge of the Tours window.**

You move to the next record in the Tours table. If you feel like it, click the Next Record button over and over until you've seen all the records in this table. You can tell which record you are on by the record number at the bottom of the Tours window. Also, when you get to the last record in the table, the Next Record button stops working (and turns gray, to tell you that it's no longer available).

☑ **Progress Check**

If you can do the following, you've mastered this lesson:

❏ Choose a table to work with.

❏ View records in a datasheet.

❏ Move from record to record.

❏ Close a window.

extra credit

Using your Microsoft IntelliMouse with Access

If you've got Access 97, you may also have gotten a new mouse to use with it, the Microsoft IntelliMouse. The IntelliMouse has a little wheel between the two mouse buttons. If you've installed the Intellipoint software (by running the Setup.exe program on the diskette that comes with the mouse), you can use this wheel to zoom around your Access database.

Whenever you see a scroll bar down the side or along the bottom of the current window, you can use the IntelliMouse wheel to scroll around the window. Turning the wheel downward scrolls the window down-

ward — ditto for using the wheel to scroll up. The wheel works just like the scroll bars, except that your mouse pointer can be anywhere in the window when you use it.

Alternatively, you can use the wheel like a button. When you press and hold down the IntelliMouse wheel, the mouse pointer turns into a dot with arrows pointing up, down, left, and right. While you hold the wheel down, the window scrolls in the same direction that you move the mouse — up, down, left, or right. When you stop holding the mouse wheel down, the mouse stops scrolling.

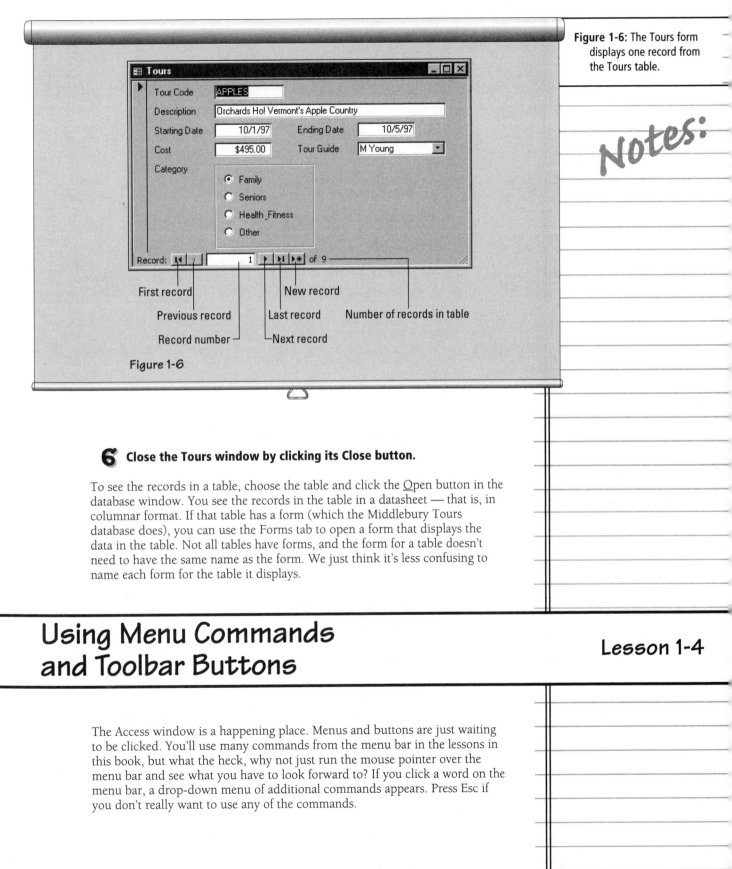

Figure 1-6

6 **Close the Tours window by clicking its Close button.**

To see the records in a table, choose the table and click the Open button in the database window. You see the records in the table in a datasheet — that is, in columnar format. If that table has a form (which the Middlebury Tours database does), you can use the Forms tab to open a form that displays the data in the table. Not all tables have forms, and the form for a table doesn't need to have the same name as the form. We just think it's less confusing to name each form for the table it displays.

Using Menu Commands and Toolbar Buttons

Lesson 1-4

The Access window is a happening place. Menus and buttons are just waiting to be clicked. You'll use many commands from the menu bar in the lessons in this book, but what the heck, why not just run the mouse pointer over the menu bar and see what you have to look forward to? If you click a word on the menu bar, a drop-down menu of additional commands appears. Press Esc if you don't really want to use any of the commands.

Just below the menu bar is the toolbar. Each button is a shortcut to a command that the folks at Microsoft thought you'd be using frequently. If the picture (icon) on the button doesn't make any sense, position the mouse pointer on that button, and a small label, called a *ToolTip,* appears to help you.

In many cases, Access provides three ways to do one task. For example, to print something, you can

- Click File on the menu bar and then click Print.
- Click the Print button on the toolbar.
- Press Ctrl+P on the keyboard.

Click the buttons on the toolbar to use them. For most buttons, no further instructions are required. Some buttons have a downward-pointing triangle button to their right. This little button is called a *list button;* when you click the list button, a tiny list appears from which you can choose a command.

Now that you know how to use menu bar commands and toolbar buttons, you can see the information in the Tours table in another format and print out a report. If the Middlebury Tours database isn't open, start Access and open the database first.

Follow these steps:

1 **Click the Reports tab in the database window, if it's not already selected.**

You see the list of defined reports in this database.

2 **Click the Complete List of Tours report and then click the Preview button.**

Access opens the report in its own window. However, the report is too big to fit into the report window, so you see only the upper-left corner of the report.

3 **To expand the window, click its Maximize button.**

That is, click the Maximize button in the title bar of the report window (*not* the one on the Access title bar). The report window expands to take up the entire inside of the Access window (see Figure 1-7).

4 **Turn on your printer and make sure that paper is in it.**

If you don't have a printer or don't feel like waking up the person in the next cubicle, skip this step and the next one.

5 **Print the report by clicking the Print button on the toolbar.**

The Print button is the second button from the left, featuring a little picture of a printer with paper sticking out the top. Access prints the report.

6 **Close the report by choosing File➪Close from the menu bar.**

(That is, click the word File on the menu bar and then click Close from the menu that appears.)

---

toolbar buttons are shortcuts for commands

to find out what toolbar button does, hover mouse pointer over it

list button = downward-pointing triangle button at right edge of a box or button

☑ Progress Check

If you can do the following, you've mastered this lesson:

❑ Give commands by clicking words on the Access menu bar and then clicking commands on the menus that appear.

❑ Click buttons on the toolbar.

❑ Look at a report.

❑ Print the report (or know how, even if you skipped this step).

❑ Maximize a window so that it takes up the whole Access window.

❑ Restore a window to its usual size.

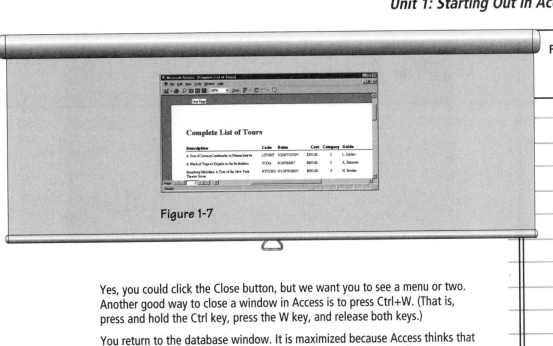

Figure 1-7

Figure 1-7: Here's a report based on information from the Tours table.

Notes:

Yes, you could click the Close button, but we want you to see a menu or two. Another good way to close a window in Access is to press Ctrl+W. (That is, press and hold the Ctrl key, press the W key, and release both keys.)

You return to the database window. It is maximized because Access thinks that you still want windows to expand to take up the whole Access window.

7 **Click the Restore button at the right end of the menu bar.**

Two overlapping squares label the Restore button. In the upper-right corner of the Access window, you now see *six* buttons. The top three (which are at the right end of the title bar) control how big the entire Access window is — leave those three buttons alone. The bottom three (which are at the right end of the menu bar) control how big the report window is within the Access window. Click the two-squares button in the lower set of buttons, the ones on the same row as the menu bar. (To check whether it's the Restore button, hover the mouse pointer over the button until the name of the button appears.)

The database window shrinks back to its normal size.

You can use toolbar buttons and menu commands to display items from the database, such as a report, and do things with them, such as printing.

extra credit

Opening another database

What if you are running Access and have one database open and then you decide to open a different database? No problem! You don't have to exit Access to switch databases. Instead, make sure that you're looking at the database window, choose File➪Open Database from the menu bar, click the Open Database button on the toolbar (it's the second button from the left when you are looking at the database window), or press Ctrl+O. You see the Open dialog box, shown in Figure 1-4. Choose the database you'd like to use and click the Open button. When Access opens the new database, it closes the database you were using before.

Open Database button

Lesson 1-5

Exiting Access

As usual, you've got a choice of ways to get out of Access. The most important thing is to exit Access and Windows 95 before you turn off your computer. You can exit Access by using any of these methods:

- ◗ Click the Close button in the upper-right corner of the Access window.
- ◗ Choose File➪Exit from the menu bar.
- ◗ Double-click the little gold key in the upper-left corner of the Access window.

on the CD

Here are steps for exiting Access and, if you're done working, Windows 95 so that you can turn off your computer. If the Middlebury Tours database isn't open, start Access and open the database first. When you exit Access, Access automatically saves and closes the open database.

1 Exit Access by clicking the Close button.

It's the right-most button on the title bar, the very top-most and right-most button in the Access window, the button with an X on it. Access goes away, and you return to the Windows 95 Desktop or to whatever other programs are running.

2 If you want to do something else with your computer, skip the rest of these steps.

Go right ahead! Just come back soon to take the quiz at the end of this unit.

3 If you want to turn off your computer, click the Start button at the left end of the Windows 95 taskbar and choose Shutdown from the menu.

Windows 95 asks exactly what you want it to do when it shuts down. It suggests the Shut down the computer option, although you also have the option of restarting Windows 95, restarting in DOS, or restarting and logging in as a different user (if you're on a network).

4 Click Yes.

Windows 95 tells you when you can power-off the computer.

Congratulations! You've learned how to run Access, open a database, look around in it, see the records contained in a table, and print information from a table. While you were at it, you learned how to use the Access menu bar, toolbar, and the database window. Nice work! Now you're ready for — yes, you guessed it — the Unit 1 Quiz!

Close button exits Access

☑ **Progress Check**

If you can do the following, you've mastered this lesson:

❑ Remember to exit Access and Windows 95 before turning off the computer.

❑ Use your favorite method to exit Access.

Unit 1 Quiz

For each of the following questions, circle the letter of the correct answer or answers. Remember, more than one answer may be correct for each question.

1. **An Access database is . . .**

   A. Some really basic data.

   B. Something you use Access to manage.

   C. A collection of information.

   D. A set of records, like a stack of index cards or other paper forms.

   E. A file that contains one or more tables, queries, forms, reports, macros, and modules.

2. **Spreadsheet programs aren't as effective at storing databases because . . .**

   A. Spreadsheet programs are designed to work with spreadsheets, not databases.

   B. Spreadsheet programs aren't designed to work with tables, records, and fields.

   C. Spreadsheet programs don't make it easy to create lots of different reports from the same data.

   D. Spreadsheet programs are obsolete, and you should never use them.

   E. Spreadsheet programs don't make it easy to print mailing labels and form letters.

3. **The database window contains tabs for the six types of items that you can store in an Access database:**

   A. Numbers, text, dates, currency, bits, and bytes.

   B. Tables, queries, forms, reports, macros, and modules.

   C. Tables, chairs, stools, sofas, bookcases, and rugs.

   D. Data, information, facts, opinions, opinions about facts, and facts about opinions.

   E. Lists of records, selections of records, on-screen forms for displaying and editing records, report formats, and two types of programs.

4. **To see the records in a table, in the database window, click. . .**

   A. The Tables tab, then the table name, and then <u>O</u>pen.

   B. The Tables tab and then double-click the table name.

   C. The Forms tab, then the name of a form that displays data from the table, and then <u>O</u>pen.

   D. The Forms tab and then double-click the name of a form that displays data from the table.

   E. The Reports tab and then double-click the name of a report that includes data from the table.

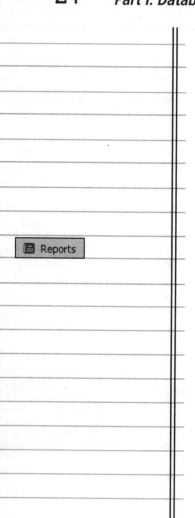

5. **What does this button do?**

   A. Creates a report about the contents of the current database.

   B. Creates a report containing the records from one table in the database.

   C. Ejects a blank page from your printer.

   D. Binds the current report in a nice-looking green cover.

   E. Displays a list of reports in the current database.

6. **In the movie *Star Wars*, what is Chewbacca?**

   A. A very tall guy who needs a shave.

   B. Han Solo's best friend.

   C. The Good Witch of the North.

   D. A wookiee.

   E. Hard to understand.

Unit 1 Exercise

on the CD

1. Run Access.

2. Open the Middlebury Tours database.

3. Open the Guides table.

4. Look around.

5. Close the table.

6. Exit Access.

Creating Your Own Database

Prerequisites

▶ Running Access
(Lesson 1-1)

▶ Using the database
window to see what's
in your database
(Lesson 1-2)

Objectives for This Unit

✓ Letting a wizard do all the hard work of creating a
database

✓ Entering data into your newly created database

✓ Using reports to get information out of your database

✓ Looking at the design of a database

on the CD

▶ Dickens Address
Book 2 database
(Dickens Address
Book 2.mdb)

We made the database that you saw in Unit 1, the Middlebury Tours database. But what if, by some quirk of chance, you don't run a tour business and want some other kind of database? How do you make a new database?

In the Dark Ages of Computing (that is, before Access), learning how to create a database was an arduous task that required years of training in systems analysis. But now, Microsoft has given us the Database Wizard, a program that helps you create new databases, using special screens that walk you through the process step by step. It's a feature that helps make Access better than most other database programs.

on the test

You've probably taught your kids (if any) that wizards are just pretend. In this story, however, wizards are real! Microsoft comes in for a great deal of bad press, much of it richly deserved, but the Database Wizard is one example of Microsoft doing something right. With a few clicks of your mouse, you can create your own databases with tables to hold your data, forms to enter the data, and reports to get your data back out in a more useful format. The Database Wizard uses *templates* — standard popular database designs — which are useful for lots of projects, and it even lets you tailor your new database when no template quite fits your needs.

Microsoft has a whole crowd of templates for the Database Wizard to start with, one template for each commonly used type of database — including address books, membership lists, order entry systems, and students and classes, to name just 4 of the more than 20 templates available. Eventually, you may want to create your own database, but using the Database Wizard to create the first draft of your database is easier than starting from scratch. Who wouldn't prefer doing a little bit of work rather than a great deal, as long as the end result is the same or better? You can make refinements to the database design later (in Unit 10).

In this unit, you create an address book database by using the Database Wizard and then take a whirlwind tour, with *Dummies 101* as your tour guide. In-depth exploration of your database will come later, we promise, but remember those things that pique your interest so you can pay special attention to them when they come up later in the book. You may want to make notes in the margin as you see interesting things go by.

You'll also learn how to enter data into your database. Isn't this great? Here you are, only in Unit 2, and you're already entering data into your very own database!

After typing a few entries into the database, you'll learn how to print that information, using one of the reports that the Database Wizard creates. You've created a database, entered records, and printed a report — it sounds like this could be the end of the book, doesn't it? It's not. You still have plenty of secrets to learn, but at the end of this unit, you'll understand where an Access database comes from. The rest of this book explains more about each of the features you see here, and you'll learn about creating other forms and reports, changing the design of a database, and moving data from other programs into your new database.

Database Wizard creates a new database based on 20+ templates

Notes:

Lesson 2-1   Creating an Address Book

A database can be something as simple as an address book — or even a grocery list. (The idea makes you think twice about what those techno-nerds at the office really mean when they talk about databases, doesn't it?) Because everyone uses an address book, this lesson explains how to build your own address book database, using the Database Wizard with its Address Book template. Other templates are available for other commonly used databases, such as a household inventory, contact management, donations, membership lists, inventory control, and the students and classes in a school.

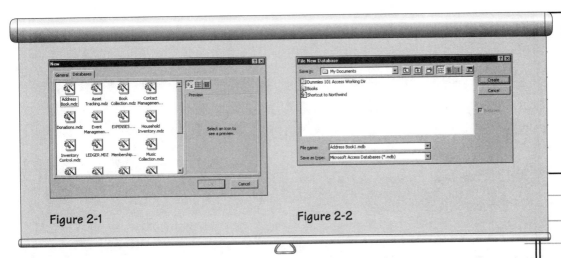

Figure 2-1   Figure 2-2

Figure 2-1: The Database Wizard can create a new database for you based on any of these templates.

Figure 2-2: Where do you want to save your new database, and what do you want to call it?

To make your new database, follow these steps. You'll make a database named Dickens Address Book, in which you can store the addresses of your close personal friends, including those from the fictional works of Charles Dickens.

1 Run Access (review Lesson 1-1 if you've forgotten how).

(If you are already running Access, click the New Database button on the toolbar or choose File⇨New Database from the menu bar. Then skip to Step 3.)

Your machine rumbles a little as your mighty computer reads the Access program from the hard disk into memory.

You see a window asking whether you want to use a Blank Database (that means starting from scratch), summon up a Database Wizard, or open an Existing Database (you'll soon have an existing database to open).

on the test

2 Choose the Database Wizard by clicking the little button to its left. Then click OK.

You see the New window, resembling a couple of file folders with two tabs named General and Databases. For some reason, Microsoft gives you yet another chance to start from scratch with a blank database. That's not what you want to do.

3 Click the Databases tab.

Up pops a list of templates that the Database Wizard can use (see Figure 2-1). The very first icon in the top left-hand corner is the Address Book template.

4 Click the Address Book icon and click OK. (Or double-click the Address Book icon; you get the same result.)

The File New Database window appears so that you can tell Access where to store this new database and what to call it. (See Figure 2-2.)

Access needs to know three things, and it guesses about them all unless you tell it something else:

on the test

- **What to call the new database that you're about to create.** In the File name box, Access suggests Address Book 1.mdb. (*mdb* stands for *Microsoft Database;* all Access databases use this filename extension.) If you type a different name, you don't have to add the MDB filename extension — Access automatically adds this extension to the filename that you type.

Insert New
Database button

Address Book
template for
Database Wizard

Figure 2-3: The Database Wizard is ready to create your address book database.

Figure 2-4: The Main Switchboard window for the Dickens Address Book database.

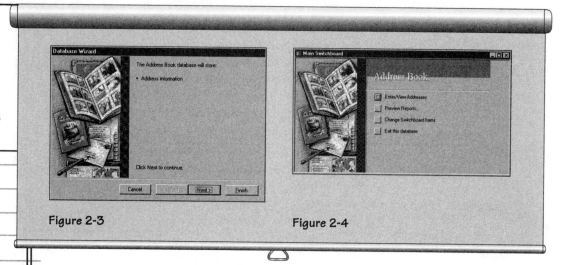

Figure 2-3   Figure 2-4

Access database filenames use the MDB extension

Notes:

wizards let you control some aspects of the database design

- **What type of document you are creating.** Access guessed right, so leave the information in the Save as type box as it is — Microsoft Access Databases.

- **Where to save this new database.** This one is up to you. We recommend that for this tutorial, you stick with the *Dummies 101* Access 97 folder in your My Documents folder.

5 **If you want to store the database in a place other than where Access has suggested, change to the folder in which you want to store the database.**

Access usually suggests putting your new database in the My Documents folder. To move to the *Dummies 101* Access 97 folder, double-click it on the list of folders.

6 **Click in the File name box, edit the filename until it says Dickens Address Book, and click the Create button.**

Windows flash, and your computer whirs as the Database Wizard swings into action. Two windows appear: The first is the database window that you saw in Lesson 1-2; the second (which overlays the first) is the Database Wizard window, which gives you a chance to intervene in the process of creating your new database (see Figure 2-3).

- If your palms are sweating and you need to go outside for a breath of fresh air, you can click the Cancel button at this point.

- If you have total faith in your friends at Microsoft (even though many of them seem never to make it outside at all), click Finish. Clicking Finish tells the Database Wizard to go ahead and make the database any ol' way it wants to, and your chance to intervene is gone.

- The third option, Next, tells the wizard to take you step by step through the setup process and allows some tailoring along the way.

Trust Microsoft just this once and let the wizard create the database without your help.

7 **Click Finish.**

You hear yet more rumbling as Access does its job. The wizard even gives a progress report as it proceeds. The top "thermometer" reading indicates how much of the whole task has been done. The lower reading reports on each individual piece of the database: tables, forms, reports, and so on. After the Database Wizard finishes, you see the Main Switchboard for an Address Book, shown in Figure 2-4.

Recess

How about hopping up and getting a drink of water? We keep hearing that everyone should drink eight glasses of water a day. (We sure don't!) You've just finished creating your first Access database. As you sip contentedly, congratulate yourself. After you get back, you'll work with your first database a little.

Tip: You don't have to tell Access to save the database after the Database Wizard has created it. Access saves your work as it goes along.

If you need to take a long break and want to exit Access, go right ahead, following the instructions in Lesson 1-5. After you come back, start Access and open the Dickens Address Book database that you just created.

☑ **Progress Check**

If you can do the following, you've mastered this lesson:

❑ Summon the Database Wizard.

❑ Choose a template from the menu that the wizard offers.

❑ Create a database using a template.

Access saves
information
automatically

Entering Records Using a Form   Lesson 2-2

A database is like a Mazda Miata: It looks very nice in the driveway, but unless you know how to drive, it just takes up valuable space and makes playing basketball difficult. The aim of this lesson is for you to enter data into your new address book so you can get your driver's license in Access.

When you use the database, you'll find out whether or not the database was well designed. You'll learn how to design databases from scratch in Unit 8 — until then, keep your fingers crossed in the hope that the Database Wizard did a good job.

on the test

The Dickens Address Book database contains a table called Addresses to hold names, addresses, and other information about people. Whenever you (or a Database Wizard) create a table, Access always suggests that the table have a *primary key*. A primary key is a field or a group of fields that have a different value for each record in the table. For example, in a table that lists people, a Social Security Number field would contain a different number for each person (as long as each person has a social security number, anyway).

primary key =
field that
uniquely identifies
each record

on the test

The Social Security Number field would make a good primary key field. The Last Name field would make a lousy primary key field because you can have two people with the same last name.

Some tables don't lend themselves to a good primary key field — for example, you probably don't know your friends' social security numbers, so a Social Security Number field wouldn't work for your address book database. But don't panic! Access is ready to make up a unique number for each record in your table, using an *AutoNumber* field. An AutoNumber field contains a number that Access assigns, starting with 1 for the first record, moving on to 2 for the second record, and so on. The Addresses table in the Dickens Address Book database contains an AutoNumber field called Address ID, as you'll see when you start typing addresses into the table. An AutoNumber field is almost always the primary key field for the table it is in.

Before you get started, take a look at Table 2-1 for a list of what some keys do when you're typing information into a table by using a form, which you'll do in this lesson. You'll learn more data-entry tricks in Unit 3.

Table 2-1   What Keys Do When You're Typing Records

Key	What It Does
Enter	Moves to the next box (field)
Tab	Same as Enter — moves to the next field
Shift+Tab	Moves backward to the preceding field
Arrow key	Moves to another field in more or less the direction indicated by the arrow
Home	Moves to the first editable field on the form
End	Moves to the last editable field on the form
Esc	Undoes the changes you made to the record
Backspace	Deletes the character to the *left* of the cursor; if text is selected, deletes the text
Delete	Deletes the character to the *right* of the cursor; if text is selected, deletes the text

When the Database Wizard created the Dickens Address Book database, it made a form called Main Switchboard, shown back in Figure 2-4. The Main Switchboard has buttons for the tasks that you'll most likely want to do (in the Database Wizard's opinion, anyway).

Typing records

Here's how to enter information about someone into your address book.

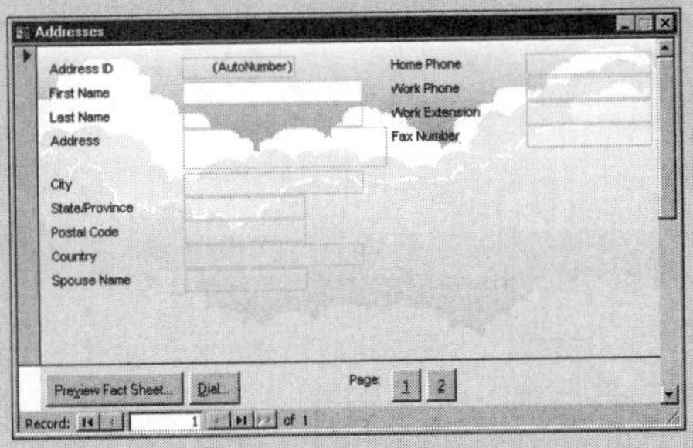

Figure 2-5

Figure 2-5: The Database Wizard created this form to let you display, enter, or edit addresses.

1 **If the Dickens Address Book database isn't already open, open it: Choose File⇨Open Database from the menu bar and choose the Dickens Address Book database.**

If you aren't even in Access, run Access. When Access asks whether you want to create a database or use an existing database, choose the Dickens Address Book database from the list that appears.

You see the Main Switchboard of the Dickens Address Book database (Figure 2-4).

2 **Click the Enter/View Addresses button on the Main Switchboard form.**

You see the Addresses form (shown in Figure 2-5) that *you* created with a little help from your Database Wizard.

When you created this database, we told you to skip the part where you could have tailored the database. Instead of the clouds in the background, you could have gone for a globe, stone, or even a family photograph (if you happen to have such a picture in an appropriate electronic format). You could have changed the fonts used. You could have changed the appearance of the boxes. If you're interested in making some of these changes, see the extra credit sidebar in this unit entitled "Tailoring your database."

The cursor is blinking in a box labeled First Name. Notice that the first field on the form is labeled Address ID and contains `(AutoNumber)`. This field is the primary key to the database, although you can't tell that by looking at the form. When you type information into this record, Access numbers the record. You can't change the number in the Address ID field even if you try.

(AutoNumber) will be replaced by a number

3 **Type** David **in the First Name box and press the Tab or Enter key to move to the next box, Last Name.**

As you type, notice that Access automagically enters a number in the Address ID.

Tab or Enter moves to the next field

4 **Type** Copperfield **in the Last Name field and press Tab or Enter.**

Your cursor moves down into the Address box, which has room for two address lines.

Ctrl+Enter moves to next line of same box

5 **Type** 12 Suffolk St. **Press Ctrl+Enter to move to the second line of the Address box; type** Apt. 2B **on the second line. Then press Tab or Enter.**

Ctrl+Enter tells Access that you want to stay in the same box but move to the next line in the box.

6 **Type** Blunderstone **in the City field and press Tab or Enter.**

You can use the Backspace key to back up if you make a mistake. If your typing gets completely out of control, press Esc to start over.

7 **Type** CT **in the State/Province field and press Tab or Enter.**

Now your cursor is in the box for the Postal Code field.

8 **Type** 05699 **and press Tab or Enter.**

9 **Type** United States of America **in the Country field and press Tab or Enter.**

Shift+Tab backs up to preceding field

10 **Press Shift+Tab to move back up to the Country field.**

The entire country name you typed is selected.

11 **Type** USA.

USA replaces the long country name you typed. This short abbreviation is going to be much easier to type in the other records you enter.

12 **Type** Dora **in the Spouse Name field and press Tab or Enter.**

No other fields are below Spouse Name, so the cursor jumps up into the next column of fields, into the box for the Home Phone field.

Access can format phone numbers automatically

13 **Type** 2035566997 **into the Home Phone field.**

Notice how Access formats the number automatically as you type. You don't have to worry about parentheses, dashes, or even spaces. When the Database Wizard used the Address Book to create this field, it set up this automatic formatting, which is designed to work with U.S.-style phone numbers. (You can remove this automatic formatting if you type non-U.S. numbers, which are formatted differently; see Unit 10.)

This particular family doesn't have any other phone numbers, so you've filled in all the information on this page of the form. But wait! More fields await you in another part of the form!

forms can have multiple pages

14 **In the lower-right corner of the form, where the form says Page, click the <u>2</u> button to go to page 2 of this form.**

Surprise, surprise! You, with help from the Database Wizard, created a form that allows for a second page of information, shown in Figure 2-6. The first box on this second page of the form is Contact Name, which contains the same first and last name that you typed on the first page of the form.

heads up

You can't edit what's in the Contact Name box. If the name is wrong, click the Page <u>1</u> button in the bottom-right corner of the form and fix the name on page 1.

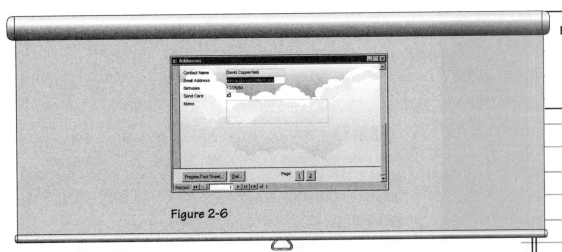

Figure 2-6

Figure 2-6: Forms can contain more than one page, so room is available for lots of fields.

Your cursor is in the first editable field on page 2 of the form, the box for the Email Address field.

15 **Type** davidc@expectations.org **in the Email Address field and press Enter or Tab.**

16 **Type** 122550 **in the Birthday field and then press Tab or Enter.**

As soon as you start typing, slashes appear in the box to separate the month, day, and year parts of the date. After you type **12**, the cursor jumps over the first slash into the day part of the date. After you type **25**, it jumps into the year section. You don't have to type the slashes, but they appear anyway. Pretty cute!

For non-U.S. readers, your copy of Access may be set up to show dates in day/month/year format, so type **251250** instead.

After you press Tab or Enter, a little dotted box appears around Send Card, telling you that your cursor is now in this box. The Send Card field can contain either Yes or No, indicated by a check mark (Yes) or no check mark (No). You can use it to indicate who is on your list to receive holiday greeting cards.

17 **Press the spacebar so the Send Card field contains a check mark.**

Pressing the spacebar switches the Send Card field on or off.

You're done entering information about David Copperfield, the first person in the Dickens Address Book!

18 **Click the Close button in the upper-right corner of the Addresses form to close the form.**

Access stores the information that you just typed. You see the Main Switchboard again.

Your Addresses table now contains one record. You don't have to give any Save command; Access saves the record as soon as you move to the next record or close the form.

don't type slashes or dashes when typing dates

⊠

Insert Close button

Typing more records

While you still have the Dickens Address Book database open, follow these steps to add another three people:

1 **Click the Enter/View Addresses button on the Main Switchboard.**

You see the Addresses form again. Actually, you now know that this is just page 1 of a two-page form. You see record number 1; take a look at the record number in the bottom-left corner of the form. If you are on page 2, click the 1 button.

2 **Click the New Record button to see a blank form.**

This button has a triangle and an asterisk on it and is in the middle of the bottom of the Addresses form, with the VCR-like controls.

If you don't feel like clicking a button (or you can't find it!), you can choose Insert➪New Record from the menu bar instead.

3 **Enter the following information into this new record:**

- First Name: **Wilkins**
- Last Name: **Micawber**
- Address: **23 Windsor Terrace**
- City: **New London**
- State/Province: **CT**
- Postal Code: **06699**
- Country: **USA**
- Home Phone: **2035547985**

Leave the other fields blank; just press Tab or Enter to move to the next field. Use Shift+Tab or the ← key to move back to make corrections, if necessary. You don't have to make any entries on the second page of the form (although if you're feeling creative, go right ahead!).

4 **Click the New Record button again to add another record.**

You see a new, blank record, record number 3. Your cursor is in the same field it was in when you were typing record 2.

5 **Press the Home key to move to the first editable field on the form, the First Name field.**

6 **Type the next record, as follows:**

- First Name: **Ebenezer**
- Last Name: **Scrooge**
- Address: **34 Miserly Way**
- City: **New London**
- State/Province: **CT**

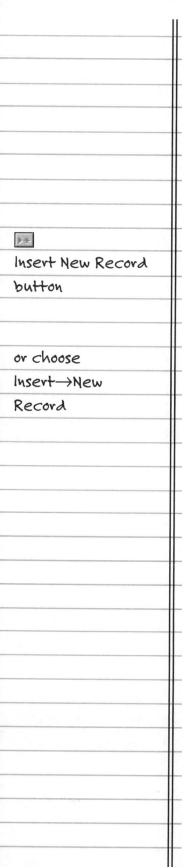

Insert New Record button

or choose Insert→New Record

- Postal Code: **06699**
- Country: **USA**
- Home Phone: **2035512256**
- Email Address: **scrooge@london.freenet.org**

You'll have to switch to the second page to enter his e-mail address. Then switch back to page 1.

7 Click the Next Record button, the one with the right-pointing triangle.

It's just to the right of the record number at the bottom of the Addresses form. No next record exists, so Access figures that you want to make one. Again, you see a blank record, record number 4.

8 Press Home to move to the First Name field; then type the last record (whew!):

- First Name: **Jacob**
- Last Name: **Marley**
- Address: **67 Chains Court**
- City: **Eternity**
- State/Province: **UT**
- Postal Code: **78966**
- Country: **USA**
- Home Phone: **8015549034**
- Email Address: **jmarley@london.freenet.org**

9 Click the Close button in the upper-right corner of the Addresses form to close the form.

You see the Main Switchboard again.

Cruising with the navigation bar

At the bottom of the Addresses form (and most other forms, too) is the *navigation bar,* shown in Figure 2-7. Stop thinking about sailors and alcohol; the navigation bar lets you move around in your table so that you can see the records you want.

The number in the box at the bottom of the window is the sequence number of the record you see. The Addresses form displays records alphabetically by last name, so record number 1 is David Copperfield, the first record in alphabetical order. If you see this record in another form that sorts the records in another order, this record may have a different sequence number. If you've just entered some records, Access may not have had a chance to sort them into alphabetical order yet.

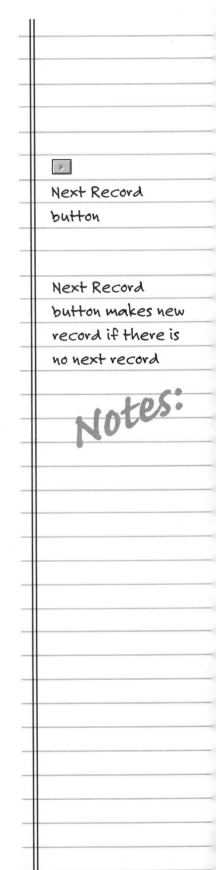

Next Record button

Next Record button makes new record if there is no next record

Notes:

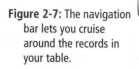

Figure 2-7: The navigation bar lets you cruise around the records in your table.

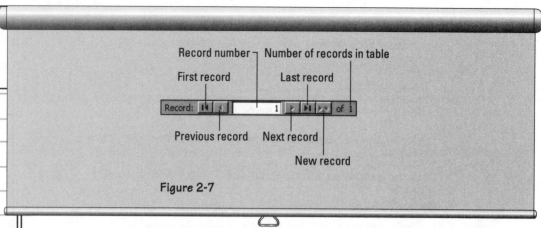

Record number — Number of records in table

First record — Last record

Record: | First | Previous | 1 | Next | Last | New | of 1

Previous record — Next record

New record

Figure 2-7

use buttons on navigation bar to move among records

type number in record number box to jump to that record

Last Record button

Notes:

On either side of the record number are buttons with arrows (well, triangles, actually). These buttons move you forward or backward through your alphabetized table, one record at a time. Figure 2-7 shows which button does what. Sometimes a button appears in gray because you can't use it right now. For example, if you're looking at the first record, the Previous Record button is gray because no previous record exists.

If you know roughly where the record that you're looking for is, you can type your guess into the record number box and press Enter to take you directly to that record.

1 **Click the Enter/View Addresses button on the Main Switchboard.**

You see the Addresses form again.

2 **Click the Last Record button, the one with a right-pointing triangle and a vertical bar, near the lower-left corner of the Addresses window.**

You zip to the last record in alphabetical order, for Ebenezer Scrooge. He happens to have an Address ID of 3, which means that you typed his record third. The Address ID never changes, no matter what order you see the records in.

3 **Click the record number box, press Delete to delete the number there, type 2, and press Enter.**

You fly to the second record in alphabetical order, for Jacob Marley, Scrooge's business partner.

4 **Click the Close button to close the Addresses form.**

Access stores all four of the records that you have so painstakingly typed. You see the Main Switchboard, which has been open all this time but was covered up by the Addresses form.

Recess

Not only have you created a database, but it even has data in it! Imagine how curious the folks at the office will be when they see your address book and the folks you hang around with. Give yourself a pat on the back, if you can reach.

extra credit

Tailoring your database

You have just created a very nice address book. Sadly, the names of characters from the works of Charles Dickens are unlikely to be of much use to you. What you'd like is a database that you could use yourself. One major advantage to using this Dickens Address Book database as an example is that you know what you want to have in an address book without thinking too much about it, and you can easily identify any shortcomings in the one created by the Database Wizard.

If you want an address book to track your own friends, use the Database Wizard to create your own address book, but this time, when you see the Database Wizard window, click Next instead of just letting the wizard take over and Finish for you. Clicking Next shows you a series of additional windows that let you make the following changes to the design:

▶ Add Mobile Phone to the Address Information. (Everyone seems to have one except us.)

▶ Add Children's Names to the Address Information. Kids are important, too!

▶ Choose a different background for your screen displays. Be bold.

▶ Choose a different style of lettering — but remember, you'll be looking at it every day.

▶ Personalize the title of the address book — maybe "The Most Important People in the World."

▶ Finish up by entering your own address list. You don't need to type the names of everyone you know to get the extra credit. Just type enough people to see how the database looks.

☑ **Progress Check**

If you can do the following, you've mastered this lesson:

❏ Use the Main Switchboard to open the Addresses form.

❏ Type records into both pages of the form.

❏ Type two address lines into a field by pressing Ctrl+Enter between lines.

❏ Go to an empty form to type a new record.

❏ Move to the first or last record in a table.

Another Way into Your Database   Lesson 2-3

The entryway provided by the Main Switchboard is like the front door of a house. It looks very welcoming, but you don't have to use it all the time — other doors are available that you may prefer, depending on the situation.

You'll find the Main Switchboard very handy for entering records, looking at them, and printing the standard reports that the Database Wizard makes. But it's not the only way to look at your database; in this lesson, you'll learn to use the side door, the database window.

Figure 2-8: The database
window shows what's
behind the scenes in
the database.

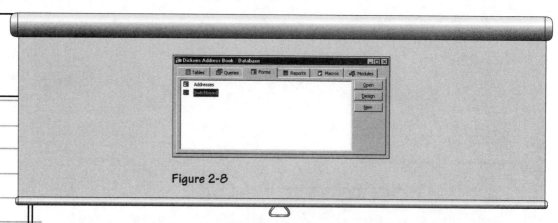

Figure 2-8

database window
lists all the
components of the
database

on the test

The *database window,* shown in Figure 2-8, is like Mission Control for your
database. Every database has one automatically — neither you nor the Database Wizard has to create it. The database window lets you see all the components of the database, with a tab for each type:

▶ Tables

▶ Queries

▶ Forms

▶ Reports

▶ Macros

▶ Modules

After you click a tab, you see a list of all the items in the database of that type.
In Figure 2-8, the Forms tab is selected, and you see a list of the forms in the
database.

The Main Switchboard contains the forms and reports that the Database
Wizard thought you'd like. But the advantage of using the database window is
that you can see *every* table, query, form, and report in the database, not just
those listed on the Main Switchboard.

Insert Minimize
button

Windows→Database
name : Database
displays the
database window

The database window is always open when you're using a database. When you
close the database window, Access closes the database. If you want to get the
database window out of the way while you use other windows (like the Main
Switchboard, for example), you can *minimize it* by clicking its Minimize
button. When the Database Wizard creates a database, it minimizes the
database window automatically so that the Main Switchboard is the first
window you see. You don't see the database window when you open the
Dickens Address Book database because it gets minimized when the Main
Switchboard is displayed.

To see the database window, choose Window from the menu and choose the
database window from the list of open windows that appears. For example, the
database window for the Dickens Address Book database is listed as *Dickens
Address Book : Database* on the Window menu. The database window pops
into view.

heads up

If your Access window is wide enough, a Database Window button appears on the toolbar. It's got three overlapping boxes on it. Because it's the twenty-first button from the left, the button doesn't appear if your Access window isn't either maximized or rather large.

In this lesson, you tour the database window and learn how to use it. You already saw the database window in Lesson 1-2. (Flip back to Lesson 1-2 if you want to read short descriptions of each of the types of elements in the database, if you like, but don't worry — we'll explain what you see as you go along in this lesson.)

In this lesson, you use the database window to see exactly what the Database Wizard gave you when it created the Dickens Address Book database using the Address Book template.

What forms are in this database?

Here's how to use the database window to see what you've got:

on the CD

1 **If the Dickens Address Book database isn't already open, open it. Choose File⇨Open Database from the menu bar and choose the Dickens Address Book database.**

If you didn't get around to typing the records in Lesson 2-2, you can cheat and open the Dickens Address Book 2 database that came on the *Dummies 101* CD-ROM. The Dickens Address Book 2 database is in the *Dummies 101* Access 97 folder in the My Documents folder, unless you installed the files somewhere else.

2 **Close the Main Switchboard by clicking its Close button.**

Poof! It goes away. We tell you how to get it back in a minute. Your Access window looks pretty empty, except for the tiny little Dickens Address Book database window in the lower-left corner of the Access window. The Dickens Address Book database window is small because the Database Wizard minimized it to keep the database window out of the way. In fact, the window is so small that the title is lopped off halfway through the word *Address*.

3 **Open the Dickens Address Book database window by double-clicking it.**

Or click its Restore button, the button with the two little squares on it. You can also click the title of the window once and choose <u>R</u>estore from the menu that appears. You see the database window, shown in Figure 2-8.

4 **Click the Forms tab, if it's not already selected.**

heads up

You see the two forms that you and the Database Wizard created. The first is the Addresses form, the same one you used to enter data in Lesson 2-2. The second is the Main Switchboard form. Yes, the Main Switchboard is a special type of form, using information from the Switchboard table. The Switchboard table and Main Switchboard form are special and use some special wizardry that you shouldn't try to make any changes to.

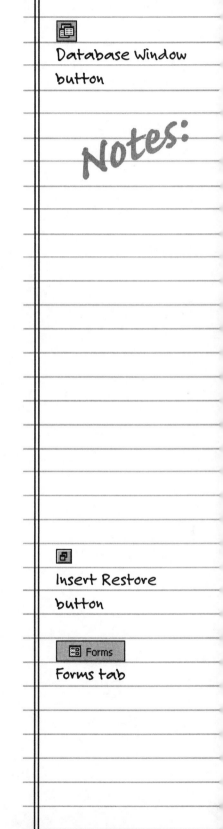

Database Window button

Notes:

Insert Restore button

Forms tab

On the Forms tab of the database window are buttons to <u>O</u>pen a form, change the <u>D</u>esign of a form, or create a <u>N</u>ew form. (You'll learn about changing and creating forms in Unit 10.)

5 Select the Switchboard form and click the Open button.

Unless you blink, you see Access minimize the database window and slide it back down into the bottom-left corner of the Access window. Do you recognize the window that appears? Yes, it's the same Main Switchboard window that you saw when you first created the database.

6 Close the Main Switchboard by clicking its Close button.

7 Open the database window again by double-clicking its title bar or clicking its Restore button.

8 Double-click the Addresses form to open the form.

Or click the Addresses form once to select it and then click the <u>O</u>pen button. It's faster to double-click, but some people prefer the slow, steady route.

The Addresses form is the same form that you used to enter records in Lesson 2-2.

9 Click the Close button on the Addresses form.

The Addresses form disappears.

You can open the Addresses form from the database window or from the Main Switchboard; the result is the same.

What tables are in this database?

You can use the database window to take a look at the tables in your database, too. You can see a table in Datasheet view (displaying the records in the table in a spreadsheet-like grid) or in Design view (displaying the definition of each field in the table). See Unit 3 for more details on your different viewing options. For now, here's how to see a table in one of these views:

1 Click the Tables tab in the database window.

You see the two tables that you and the Database Wizard created. The first is the Addresses table, which contains the address records you typed in Lesson 2-2. The second is the Switchboard table, which contains information about what buttons appear on the Main Switchboard. As on the Forms tab, you see <u>O</u>pen, <u>D</u>esign, and <u>N</u>ew buttons for opening a table in Datasheet view, changing the design of a table, and creating a new table, respectively. You try the last two tasks in Unit 8.

Note: Don't fool with the Switchboard table. Changing what's on the Main Switchboard is not for the faint of heart!

2 Double-click the Addresses table to open it, or click it once and click the <u>O</u>pen button, or click it once and press Enter.

Margin notes:

<u>O</u>pen button opens a form

Switchboard form = Main Switchboard for database

or double-click form name to open it

🔲 Tables

Tables tab

double-click table to open it in Datasheet view

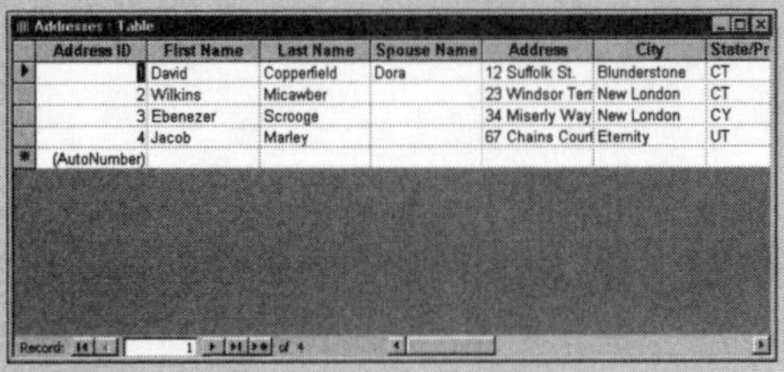

Figure 2-9: In Datasheet view, your table looks kind of like a spreadsheet.

Figure 2-9

Recognize anything? Good! You're looking at the Addresses table in Datasheet view (as shown in Figure 2-9), with the four records that you entered using the Addresses form. You saw the Datasheet view in Lesson 1-3, and here it is again.) If you want to see more columns in the datasheet, you can make the Addresses: Table window wider by dragging its edges with the mouse.

The Addresses table that you're looking at is where all the information you entered in the Addresses form is stored. If you want to impress your less knowledgeable friends, you can open a table in Datasheet view and tell them that you're looking at the "raw data." (Ooh, sounds technical!)

3 **Click the last (blank) line of the table, in the First Name column.**

You can type records in Datasheet view, too, not just in forms.

4 **Type a new address on the last line of the datasheet, pressing Tab or Enter to move from one column to the next.**

- First Name: **Bob**
- Last Name: **Cratchit**
- Address: **27 Clerk Street**
- City: **Christmas**
- State/Province: **NJ**
- Postal Code: **08542**
- Country: **USA**
- Email Address: **tinytimsdad@aol.com**
- Home Phone: **6095579097**

As you move from field to field, Access scrolls the datasheet to the left to bring the rest of the fields into view. Don't worry if an entry is too wide to fit in a column: Access scrolls the information leftward within the column as you type. Notice that as soon as you have entered information in the record, the Address ID entry changes from *(AutoNumber)* to *5*, the next record number.

5 **Click the Close button to close the Addresses table datasheet.**

Access automatically saves the new record that you entered. The Addresses table is still highlighted in the database window.

type records into the Datasheet view by clicking in a blank row

Notes:

Figure 2-10: In Design view, you see the name and definition of each field the table includes.

Notes:

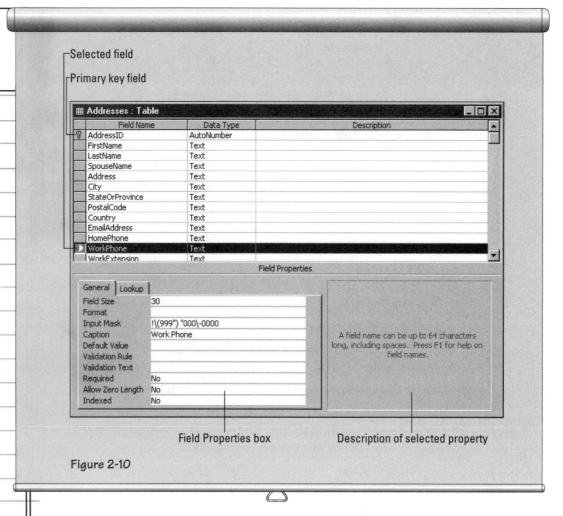

Selected field

Primary key field

Field Properties box

Description of selected property

Figure 2-10

Design button shows table in Design view

data type = type of information the field holds, like text, numbers, or dates

6 **Click the Design button to open the Addresses table in Design view.**

Figure 2-10 shows the Addresses table in Design view, showing all the fields in the Addresses table. Design view lets you see what *fields* the table contains, rather than what records. Each field in the table has one row in Design view, with the field name, data type, and description of each field. If the table has too many fields to fit in the window, you can scroll down the window to see the rest of the fields: Click the lower part of the scroll bar along the right side of the window.

Take a look at the Data Type column of the Addresses window. Most of the fields (rows) are *text fields,* in which you can type alphabetical, numerical, and special characters such as %$#@*(). Text fields are good for holding text up to 255 characters long (usually much shorter), like names, ID codes, addresses, and descriptions.

A few of the fields are not text fields. The Birthdate field is a Date/Time field, so Access lets you type only valid dates when you enter records. The Send Card field is a Yes/No field, which is why it appeared as a check box when you entered the information for David Copperfield in Lesson 2-2. The Notes field is defined as a memo field, which is intended to hold a whole paragraph or more.

Memos are good for long descriptions, but you can't sort records based on the information in a memo field.

The other data type shown here is AutoNumber. The first field, Address ID, is an AutoNumber; you may remember that records were numbered automagically when you entered records in Lesson 2-2. Now that you know about field types, the Address ID field may seem a little more automatic than automagic.

See that tiny little key in the left-most column of the Address ID row? That key tells you that the Address ID field is the primary key field for this table. (Primary key fields are described in Lesson 2-2.) In a table with an AutoNumber field, that field is usually the primary key field because uniquely identifying records is the purpose for AutoNumber fields.

7 **Click the WorkPhone field (row) of the Design view.**

After you select a field by clicking its row, more information about the field appears in the lower part of the window, which is called the *Field Properties box*. This information is called the *field properties*. In Figure 2-10, the WorkPhone field is selected, so the Field Properties box shows the properties of the WorkPhone field.

Depending on the type of the field, you see a different list of properties. For example, a text field has a field size, format, and other properties. A Date/Time field doesn't have a Field Size property; all dates and times are the same length.

You'll find out more about how to change the design of a table in Unit 10.

Note: If you enter non-U.S. phone numbers into the WorkPhone field, you can stop Access from formatting them as U.S. phone numbers by erasing the contents of the Input Mask setting in the field properties for the WorkPhone field.

8 **Click the row for the Address ID field and then press the ↓ key to select each field in turn. As you go, take a look at how the field properties change.**

Notice that each text field has a Field Size property. The field size for the EmailAddress field is set to 50, which is why you could enter an address too long to fit in the datasheet column.

After you select the HomePhone or WorkPhone field, you see an Input Mask property, a gobbledygook of characters that tells Access how you want your phone numbers automatically formatted when you enter them. Don't worry — I don't understand input masks without looking them up, either. Input masks help with fields that have a structure (a predefined method of grouping or dividing) to them, like telephone numbers, zip codes, and social security numbers.

None of the field names has a blank space in it, but this is only because the Database Wizard's spacebar must be broken (that's the only reason I can think of for the Database Wizard running allitswordstogether). You can use spaces in your field names if you get the urge, after you get around to creating your own field names in Unit 8.

9 **Click the Close button to close the Addresses window.**

If you get a message asking whether you want to save changes, *CLICK NO!* Sorry, but I had to shout that. If you followed the steps in this book exactly, you don't see any message about saving changes. However, while taking this tour of Design view, you may have accidentally changed something. If you have

heads up

---

text field = field that holds up to 255 characters of text

key icon indicates primary key field

click field to see its properties

Input mask = predefined formatting for selected field

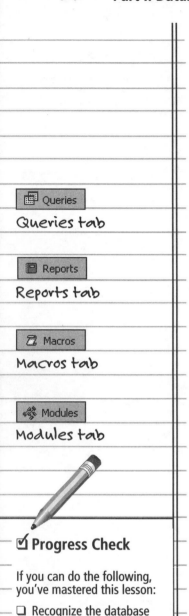

Queries tab

Reports tab

Macros tab

Modules tab

☑ Progress Check

If you can do the following, you've mastered this lesson:

❑ Recognize the database window, and minimize and restore it.

❑ View all the contents of a database using the tabs on the database window.

❑ Open a table in Datasheet view.

❑ Open a table in Design view to see field properties.

changed anything in Design view, Access asks you what you want to do with the changes when you close the window. Access gives you a chance to save the changes you have made or leave the table the way it was. Because you weren't supposed to change anything in this exercise, if Access thinks you have changed something, whatever you do, don't save it.

You see the database window again.

Reading every message that the computer displays is good practice. It's especially important to think about those messages that mention saving changes. Think: Did you plan on making changes? Do you want the ones that you made to be saved and therefore take effect? If you made changes accidentally or have changed your mind, the message is your opportunity to wipe the slate clean and start again. Just click No.

What else is in this database?

What about all those other tabs in the database window, like Queries, Reports, Macros, and Modules?

1 Click the Queries tab.

Hmm . . . nothing there. The Database Wizard didn't make any queries for this database. (But you'll learn what queries are and how to make them in Unit 4, when you learn to work with selected records from a table.)

Once again, you see Open, Design, and New buttons for opening a query, modifying it, and making a new one.

2 Click the Reports tab.

Ooh, look! You see four reports! You'll open reports (using the Open button) and print them in Lesson 2-4. You'll use the New button to create new reports in Unit 7, and you'll make changes to existing reports (with the Design button) in Unit 10.

3 Click the Macros tab.

Nope, nothing. Macros (programs written in the Access macro programming language) aren't necessary for the tasks that this database of addresses is designed to do.

4 Click the Modules tab.

No modules, either. (Modules are programs written in the Access Basic programming language, and the Database Wizard didn't create any.) You've seen all the objects (tables, forms, and reports) in this database.

Take another stroll around your office (or wherever you are working) and move on to the next lesson. You're making great progress!

Printing Reports   Lesson 2-4

At our request, you have just expended a great deal of typing effort putting data into the Dickens Address Book. So before the keyboard even has time to cool down, you're going to print your data — no point typing stuff in if you can't get it out!

When the Database Wizard created the Dickens Address Book database, four reports were part of the brew. In this lesson, you look at one of the reports on-screen and print it out on paper. If you haven't already done so, start up Access and open the Dickens Address Book database (or the Dickens Address Book 2 database, if you want to use the database we created for you).

1 If you don't see the Main Switchboard, open the database window, click the Forms tab, and double-click the Switchboard form.

The Main Switchboard appears.

2 Click the Preview Reports button.

The three periods (ellipsis) at the end of the name of the button tell you that you will have more choices after you click this button. In this case, you see a window labeled Reports Switchboard. The window looks just like the Main Switchboard, but it lists the reports that the Database Wizard created.

3 Click the button for Preview the Addresses by Last Name Report.

You see the report requested in a new window. You can move around on this page by using the scroll bars. If you had typed the addresses of every character in every Dickens novel, your report would be many pages long. You can move from page to page in this window in the same way that you moved from record to record in the Addresses table during Lesson 2-2.

4 Make sure that your printer is turned on and contains paper.

5 Click the Print button on the Access toolbar.

When Access displays a report on-screen, the Print button is the second button from the left on the toolbar, with a little picture of a printer. If your printer is working, you get a nice report of the people in your Dickens Address Book. If your printer isn't working, you won't get a nice report — or any kind of report at all. Oh, well.

6 Close the report window and the Reports Switchboard.

Your Access window is now empty except for the minimized Dickens Address Book database window.

This lesson was an important one because it completed a circle — data in, data out. You can now create a database, make it useful by putting data into it, and finally make it useable by getting data out of it. Go outside and see if the mail or newspaper have arrived and then come back for the Unit 2 Quiz.

Notes:

Insert Print button

☑ **Progress Check**

If you can do the following, you've mastered this lesson:

❑ See the Reports switchboard.

❑ Preview a report listed on the Reports Switchboard.

❑ Print that report.

extra credit

Making an icon for your database

Wouldn't it be nice if you had a special icon on your Windows 95 desktop just for your favorite Access database? You can! In My Computer or Windows Explorer, find your database. Use your mouse to right-click the filename and then choose Create Short-cut from the menu that appears. Use the mouse to drag the shortcut out of the My Computer or Explorer window onto your Windows 95 desktop. Windows 95 creates an icon for the database. Double-clicking the icon starts up Access and opens your database — convenient!

Unit 2 Quiz

For each of the following questions, circle the letter of the correct answer or answers. Remember, each question may have more than one right answer.

1. **What is the Database Wizard?**

    A. A database full of technical information about Access.

    B. A program that you can buy to teach you Access.

    C. A program that analyzes your database for correctness.

    D. A program that creates Access databases for you.

    E. A program that makes Access databases go up in smoke.

2. **MDB, a filename extension, stands for . . .**

    A. Microsoft *database*.

    B. *My database*.

    C. Microsoft *does* data*b*ases.

    D. *M*ix *data* and ta*b*les.

    E. No one knows.

3. **A primary key is . . .**

    A. The largest thing on your key ring after the shrunken head.

    B. What the janitor uses at the local elementary school.

    C. What you need in order to win a presidential nomination.

    D. A field or group of fields that have different values for each record in the database.

    E. The most important field in your database.

4. **AutoNumber fields are good for . . .**

   A. Filling your table with numbers so that it looks like you've got some real data when you actually don't.

   B. Numbering each record sequentially.

   C. Providing a value that uniquely identifies each record in a table.

   D. Entering license plate numbers of cars.

   E. Using as primary key fields.

5. **Which of the following is *not* a button on the navigation bar?**

   A. Next Record.

   B. Previous Record.

   C. Last Record.

   D. New Record.

   E. Break Record.

6. **You can use the database window to . . .:**

   A. See a list of tables in the database.

   B. See a list of reports in the database.

   C. See a list of forms in the database.

   D. Open a form.

   E. Open a table in Datasheet view.

Unit 2 Exercise

1. Close the Dickens Address Book database (by closing its database window) if it is open. If Access isn't running, run it.

2. Choose File⇨New Database to create a new database.

3. Click the Databases tab to see the wide variety of templates that the Database Wizard can use.

4. Choose to create a database using the Book Collection, Household Inventory, Music Collection, Wine List, or Video Collection template. Or create another Address Book database for people you actually know.

5. Save the database in your *Dummies 101* Access 97 folder, unless you have another place you'd rather put it.

6. After you see the Database Wizard window, click Finish to create the database using the standard options of the Database Wizard. (**Extra Credit:** Click Next to review the options for creating the database and make your own choices. Keep clicking Next until the database is done.)

7. Enter data into your database by using the forms that the Database Wizard created.

8. Print one report from the database.

Part I Review

Unit 1 Summary

- **Opening an Access database:** Double-click any database icon or run Access from the Windows 95 Start button.

- **Database contents:** Access databases contain six types of elements: tables, queries, forms, reports, macros, and modules.

- **Tables:** Lists of records. Your data is stored here.

- **Queries:** Use to select information from one or more tables, to modify or create tables, or to combine information from related tables.

- **Forms:** On-screen windows that help you get data into your database and edit it on the way in.

- **Reports:** Provide a neat way of printing your data, in myriad different ways.

- **Macros:** Automate common tasks, using the Access macro programming language.

- **Modules:** Programs written in Visual Basic to handle those things that even Access can't do without programming help.

- **Looking at data in a table:** Click the Tables tab in the database window to get a list of tables. Then double-click the selected table or select the table and choose Open.

- **Closing a window in Access:** Choose File⇨Close from the menu or click the Close button in the top-right corner of the window.

- **Exiting Access:** Choose File⇨Exit from the menu bar, click the Close button in the top-right corner of the Access window, or double-click the Access icon in the top-left corner of the Access window.

Unit 2 Summary

- **Creating databases:** Use the Database Wizard to create a database based on one of the templates supplied with Access. Or start with a blank database and build your own database from scratch. Choose File⇨New Database from the menu bar or click the New Database button (the left-most button on the toolbar).

- **Primary key:** A field that uniquely identifies each record in a table. AutoNumber fields are a good choice for primary key fields.

- **Entering information on a form:** Pressing Enter or Tab moves you to the next field. Shift+Tab moves backward. Arrow keys move left, right, up, or down. Home moves to the first editable field. End moves to the last editable field. Ctrl+Z undoes the changes to this record. Esc undoes changes to this record. F2 moves to the beginning of the field and lets you edit its contents. Backspace deletes the character (or selected text) to the left. Delete deletes the character (or selected text) to the right.

- **Inserting new records in a form:** Choose Insert⇨New Record from the menu bar or click the New Record button on the navigation bar.

- **Moving from record to record in forms:** The navigation bar lets you move to the first record, to the preceding record, to a specific record number, to the next record, to the last record, or to a blank form to enter a new record. This bar also keeps you informed of the number of records in this view of the data.

- **Viewing tables:** You can see a table in Design view to inspect or change the definition of a table, or you can look in Datasheet view to display the actual data, record by record, in a spreadsheetlike grid. Switch between the two modes by clicking the Table View button (the left-most button on the toolbar).

- **Types of fields:** Text, Date/Time, Yes/No, AutoNumber, Memo, Number, and Currency.

- **Printing:** Click the Print Preview button on the toolbar to review the appearance of your printout before sending it to the printer.

Part I Test

The questions on this test cover all the material presented in Part I, Units 1 and 2.

True False

T   F   1. A datasheet is the data from a table placed in rows and columns.

T   F   2. If you aren't a programmer, you can't use Access.

T   F   3. The primary key for a table must be the Social Security Number.

T   F   4. The Database Wizard is not a medieval magician but is, in fact, a great tool that you can use to create an Access database.

T   F   5. The only kind of database the Database Wizard can create is an address book database.

T   F   6. Records in a database are stored in tables.

T   F   7. An Access database must have tables, queries, forms, reports, macros, and modules.

T   F   8. The only way to print information from a database is to export it to a word processor.

T   F   9. The navigation bar on a form lets you move to any record in the table or query that the form displays.

T   F   10. You can type records into a table using either a form or Datasheet view.

Multiple Choice

For each of the following questions, circle the correct answer or answers. Remember, each question may have more than one right answer.

11. **Why is AutoNumber a good choice for the field type of a primary key?**

   A. Access gives each record a unique number, so you don't have to assign numbers.

   B. Access won't allow you to use any other type of field.

   C. You are absolutely guaranteed that the value of this field is unique for all the records in the table.

   D. Anything that is automatic is good.

   E. No AutoDate field type exists.

12. **A switchboard is . . .**

   A. Something with a pretty picture in the background that the Database Wizard builds for you.

   B. A form.

   C. A special type of datasheet.

   D. A medieval instrument of torture.

   E. A modern instrument of torture.

Part I Test

13. What happens after you close the database window?

  A. Windows 95 shuts down.

  B. Access exits.

  C. The database window disappears.

  D. Access closes the database.

  E. Access deletes your database from your hard disk permanently.

14. A datasheet . . .

  A. Is a list of records in a table.

  B. Is a list of records that result from a query.

  C. Looks like a spreadsheet.

  D. Can be used to enter data into a table.

  E. Is what you see when you double-click a table in the database window.

15. Match the Toolbar or navigation bar button with its name.

  A.   1. Print button

  B.   2. New Database button

  C.   3. First Record button

  D.   4. New Record button

  E.   5. Database Window button

16. Match each of the following navigation bar buttons with what it does after you click it.

  A.   1. Moves to the last record

  B.   2. Moves to the preceding record

  C.   3. Enters a new record

  D.   4. Moves to the first record

  E.   5. Moves to the next record

Part I Lab Assignment

The following lab problems are the first of several that appear at the end of each part throughout this book. These lab problems are designed to let you apply the skills that you gained while studying the lessons in realistic situations. (Well, almost realistic, anyway; your real-life database chores probably won't be as much fun as these.)

In this lab, you pretend that books are taking over your living space and you've got to get rid of some of them. The first thing you want to do is take an inventory of all your books. (Remember, we did say "almost-realistic situations.")

Part I Lab Assignment

Step 1: Create a database with the Database Wizard, using the Book Collection template

Let the Database Wizard do all the work if you want, but if you're feeling confident, why not tailor a few things along the way? Refer to Lesson 2-1 if you want to review how to use the Database Wizard.

Call the database whatever you want; this personal inventory is yours, after all!

Step 2: Enter data into the database, using the Books Inventory form

Enter every single book that you own — just kidding. Enter information about books lying around on your desk, or books you particularly like, or books you wished you owned.

Step 3: Enter data into the Books table, using a datasheet

Enter another book or two. Did you remember to enter this one?

Step 4: Preview each of the reports and print them out

Use the Preview button on the Reports Switchboard.

Getting Data into Your Database

Part II

In this part . . .

Now that you know how to run Access and create a database, the time has come to learn how to get some data into it. You may want to type new records into your Access database (you learn how to do that in Unit 3) or use information that is already stored in another file (which you'll learn more about in Unit 5).

After you fill your database with information, you'll also want to sift through your records to find specific records. There's no point in creating a database if you can't slice and dice the information, selecting and sorting at will. That's what you'll learn in Unit 4 — using Access queries to select and sort records.

Editing, Finding, and Deleting Records

Objectives for This Unit

✓ Tips and tricks for typing new records into a table

✓ Changing information in existing records in a table

✓ Deleting records you no longer want

✓ Using handy shortcuts when entering data

✓ Finding the particular record you want

Prerequisites

▶ Running Access (Lesson 1-1)

▶ Viewing a table (Lesson 1-3)

▶ Typing records in a form (Lesson 2-2)

on the CD

▶ Middlebury Tours database (Middlebury Tours.mdb)

Your address book database looks terrific, and you've got all your friends, business contacts, and favorite take-out pizza places all typed in. Then it happens! Some thoughtless friend goes and moves. Or you make a new friend. Rats! Your data just won't stay still!

The world is a cruel place: Data changes almost as fast as you can type it (although the characters in Dickens' novels haven't changed in quite a while). Eventually, you'll need to know how to edit and delete records, too.

In Unit 2, you typed some records into a table. In this unit, you type records into a table in different ways, delete unwanted records, edit records that are no longer correct, and find particular records. You'll use the Middlebury Tours database that you saw in Unit 1. (If you skipped Unit 1, don't panic. The Middlebury Tours database contains a list of the tours offered by a fictitious travel agency.)

use datasheets
or forms to edit
records

You can look at the records in a table in two ways:

- In a datasheet, with one row for each record and one column for each field
- In a form

Forms can be set up in many different ways, depending on the whim of the person who makes the form. Usually, you see one record at a time, with one box per field. But forms can also be designed to look like datasheets, in a columnar format. For tables with many fields, forms can have multiple pages for each record. For example, in the Dickens Address Book database (which you created in Unit 2), the Addresses table has so many fields for each record that the Addresses form has one page for the basic information about each person and another page for the stuff that didn't fit on the first page. Some forms don't include all the fields in the table, and some include fields from several tables. In Unit 10, when you change the design of a table, you'll learn how to design forms, too.

Whether you use datasheets or forms to edit the records in a table, you can use most of the same keystrokes and mouse clicks you've already used — check out the list in Table 3-1. In Unit 2, you learned to move the cursor from field to field in a form or datasheet. Now you'll find out how to edit what's in a field, as well as how to avoid typing the same stuff over and over. You'll also run into other ways that a form may ask you for information — *combo boxes* and *radio boxes*. (Those terms may sound highly technical, but you're gonna love 'em.)

Table 3-1	Keys for Editing Records
Key	*What It Does*
Tab or Enter	Moves to the next field in the current record. If you're in the last field, moves to the first field in the next record. In the last field of the last record, moves to the first field in the current record.
F2	Moves the cursor to the end of the field so that you can edit the contents of the field.
Ctrl+Z or Esc	Undoes what you typed in the current record. If you've pressed F2 to edit the contents of a field, undoes changes to the current field.
Ctrl+;	Enters the current date in the current field.
Ctrl+'	Enters in the current field the same thing that appears in the same field of the preceding record.
Esc	Cancels editing the record. If you have pressed F2 to edit the contents of a field, cancels changes to the field.
Home	Moves to the first field for this record. If you have pressed F2 to edit a field, moves to the beginning of the field.

Ctrl+Z undoes last
change

Key	What It Does
End	Moves to the last field for this record. If you have pressed F2 to edit a field, moves to the end of the field.
PgDn	Moves to the next record. For multipage forms, moves to the next page of the form. In a datasheet, moves down one screenful of records.
PgUp	Moves to the preceding record. For multipage forms, moves to the preceding page of the form. In a datasheet, moves up one screenful of records.
Ctrl+↓	Moves to the current field in the last record in the table.
Ctrl+↑	Moves to the current field in the first record in the table.
Ctrl+Home	Moves to the first field in the first record. If you have pressed F2 to edit a field, moves to the beginning of the field.
Ctrl+End	Moves to the last field in the last record. If you have pressed F2 to edit a field, moves to the end of the field.
Ctrl+Enter	Enters a *newline character* (carriage return) in a text field. (You typed one in Lesson 2-2.)

extra credit

How many ways can you open a database?

In a word — oodles. Here are three ways to run Access and open a database:

- Click the Windows 95 Start button, choose <u>D</u>ocuments, and choose the database filename from the menu that appears. This method doesn't work if you haven't opened the database recently; the Documents menu lists only recently used files.

- Click the Windows 95 Start button, choose <u>P</u>rograms, and choose Microsoft Access from the menus. (You may have to choose Microsoft Office and then Microsoft Access, depending on how your Windows 95 menus are arranged.) When Access asks what database you want to use, choose <u>O</u>pen an Existing Database and select the

file from the list at the bottom of the window. If you haven't opened the database recently, choose More Files. When you see the Open dialog box, double-click the name of the database you want. (You may have to change folders first.)

- Run My Computer or Windows Explorer. Find the database by clicking or double-clicking folders. For example, to find the databases you use with this book, click the folder for your hard disk, click the My Documents folder, and then click *Dummies 101* Access 97. You see the files in that folder, which include the databases used in this book. Double-click the database you want to open. Access runs and opens the database.

(continued)

Notes:

(continued)

If Access is already running and you want to open a database, choose File⇔Open Database from the menu bar, click the Open Database button on the Toolbar (the little yellow folder) if it appears, or press Ctrl+O. When you see the Open dialog box, select the filename of the database you want and click OK. Access closes the current database and opens the new one. You can have only one database open at one time.

Lesson 3-1

Editing and Copying Entries

In Unit 2, you typed information into a form and a datasheet. In this lesson, you learn new ways to move around in a datasheet and to save time when typing records into the Tours table in the Middlebury Tours database.

When you're looking at a record, Access shows what's going on with the current record by displaying little icons in the left margin of the form or datasheet. The gray box in the left margin for each record is called the *record selector*. Table 3-2 lists the icons that you may see in the record selector.

record selector =
gray box to left of
record

If you want to change the contents of a field, you have two choices:

▶ Replace the existing value with something new.

▶ Edit the existing value, adjusting it until it's right.

To replace the existing value, move your cursor to the field, select the value, if it's not already selected, and type a new value. What you type replaces what was selected.

record selector
tells you status of
current record

Table 3-2	What's Happening to the Current Record
Icon	*What It Means in the Record Selector*
▶	You have selected this record.
✎	You're editing this record, and Access hasn't saved your changes yet.
⊘	You can't edit this record, because someone else is using it. (Appears only when you're using a shared database on a multiuser or networked system.)
✳	New, blank record.

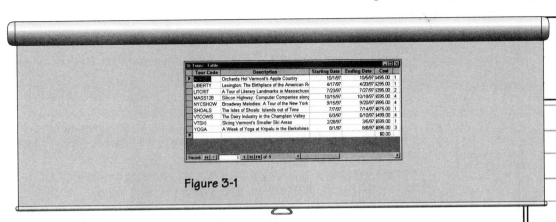

Figure 3-1

Figure 3-1: The Tours datasheet lists the records in the Tours table.

on the test

To edit the value of a field, move your cursor to the field (by clicking there or by using the Tab, Enter, or arrow keys to get there). Then press the F2 key or click in the box for the field. The entry for the field is no longer highlighted, and you can move your cursor around within the box for the field. Use the Delete and Backspace keys to remove offending characters; then type new characters. When you're done, press Tab or Enter to move to the next field.

heads up

After the entire field is highlighted, watch out for the Delete and Backspace keys! They delete the entire entry. You must press F2 or click again in the field box before you can use Backspace or Delete to delete individual characters.

F2 edits field

If the entry doesn't look right, you can edit it by pressing F2 or clicking in the field box. Here's how:

1 **Your computer's on, right?**

on the CD

2 **Run Access by clicking the Windows 95 Start button and choosing Documents⇨Middlebury Tours.mdb.**

Because you opened the Middlebury Tours database in Unit 1, Windows 95 remembers that you've used this database recently and lists it on your Documents menu. When you give this command, Windows 95 runs Access, and Access opens the Middlebury Tours database. Slick!

If you're already running Access and using another database, open the Middlebury Tours database by choosing File⇨Open Database from the menu bar, choosing Middlebury Tours.mdb from the menu, and clicking OK.

You see the Middlebury Tours database window. Because we created this database ourselves, without the magical help of the Database Wizard, it doesn't have a Main Switchboard window. Instead, you see the Middlebury Tours database window.

3 **Click the Tables tab, if it's not already selected, select the Tours table, and click the Open button.**

You see the Tours table in Datasheet view, as shown in Figure 3-1, with all the records in the table. If you had more records than could fit in the window, you would see the first screenful of records, and a scroll bar would appear along the right edge of the window to help you scroll down to see the rest of the records. (The scroll bar is the gray strip that runs down the right edge of the window: Click the arrow buttons at the top and bottom ends of the scroll bar to move up and down the window.)

New Record button

Ctrl+' duplicates
value of field

F2 edits field

4 **Add a new record by clicking the New Record button on the navigation bar.**

You saw the navigation bar in Lesson 2-2: It shows buttons that look like VCR controls for moving from record to record. To add a new record, you can also click in the new, blank row at the bottom of the datasheet. The asterisk in the last row of the table turns into a triangle, showing that you just made this new row the current record.

5 **Start typing a new record, entering** YOGA2 **in the Product Code column; press Tab or Enter to move to the next column.**

This tour is a second offering of the popular yoga tour in the preceding record. How boring to have to type the same tour description again! There must be a better way.

on the test

6 **In the column for the Description field, press Ctrl+' (that is, hold down the Ctrl key and type an apostrophe). Then press Tab.**

The Ctrl+' key combination copies the entry in the same field in the preceding record and sticks it into the current record.

7 **For the Starting Date, type** 8/8/97, **and for the Ending Date, type** 8/15/97.

The YOGA2 tour is the week after the YOGA tour.

8 **For the Cost, Category, and Tour Guide columns, press Ctrl+' to duplicate the entry from the preceding record. Don't press Tab after your entry in the Tour Guide column.**

Wait! Alison Barrows isn't available to lead this tour (she'll be exhausted from the previous week), so her mother Sheila is taking over.

on the test

9 **Press F2 to tell Access that you want to edit this field.**

The field is no longer highlighted, and the cursor appears at the end of the field.

10 **Press Home to move to the beginning of the field, press Del to delete the A, and press S (for Sheila).**

Now the Tour Guide field says *S. Barrows.*

Note: If your Num Lock key is on, the keys on the numeric keypad on your keyboard — the group of number keys way off to the right — type numbers. If Num Lock is on, the Del or Delete key on the numeric keypad types a period, which isn't what you want. Use the other Delete key, the one nearer the letter keys.

11 **Press the Tab or Enter key.**

Your cursor zips to the next row, in the Tour Code column. Access saves the record you just entered.

12 **Close the Tours window.**

As usual, just click the Close button in the window's upper-right corner.

If you're entering records in which the value of a field is the same for all of them, you can avoid typing the same value over and over — just press Ctrl+' to repeat the value. To edit the value of a field, press F2.

Stupid Data-Entry Tricks   Lesson 3-2

on the test

Like other Windows programs, Access uses the Windows Cut and Paste commands to store information on the invisible Windows Clipboard. The information can be a few characters, an entire six-page essay, a record from a table — almost anything.

To copy something to the Clipboard, you select the thing that you want to copy and then press Ctrl+C. (That's easy to remember: *C* is for Copy.) Alternatively, you can choose Edit⇨Copy from the menu bar, but why bother when pressing Ctrl+C is so quick? If you like clicking buttons, you can also click the Copy button on the toolbar. Whichever method you choose, the information that you selected gets stored on the Windows Clipboard, replacing whatever was on the Clipboard before.

After you have stored something on the Clipboard, you can copy it back into your Access database as many times as you like. For that matter, you can copy it into almost any other Windows-based program, too. Just put your cursor where you want the information to appear, and press Ctrl+V. (Hmm . . . *V* doesn't stand for *insert* or *paste*. We remember *V* because it's right next to the *C* on the keyboard.) When you "paste" the information from the Clipboard into your Access database, the information remains on the Clipboard, so you can paste it again and again, as often as you want — until you store something new on the Clipboard. If you prefer to use the menu, choose Edit⇨Paste.

So far, you have used *text boxes* to enter information into fields. That is, you've typed stuff into a little white box on the form. But text boxes aren't the only way to enter a value into a field. Access provides other types of *controls* — that is, other kinds of things that appear on forms — for entering information. Two cool ones are *combo boxes* and *radio buttons*. You use them in this lesson.

on the test

A *combo box* lets you select a value of a field from a list. For example, the Tour Guide field can contain only the names of guides who work for Middlebury Tours. Rather than type the name of the guide, you can select it from a list of tour guides. In Figure 3-2, which shows the Tours form for editing records in the Tours table, the Tour Guide field doesn't appear in a regular text box. Do you see that little button at the right end of the box for the Tour Guide field, with the downward-pointing triangle on it? That button is the telltale sign of a combo box. Combo boxes can appear on both datasheets and forms. In Figure 3-2, you see a combo box on a form.

To select a tour guide from the list, click the little button at the right end of the combo box (the *list button*) or press F4. A little menu of guides' names appears right below the combo box, as if a window shade had rolled down from the box. Click one of the names or use the cursor keys to move down to the one you want and press Enter.

Windows Clipboard = invisible holding area for information

Copy button or Ctrl+C copies info to Clipboard

Paste button or Ctrl+V pastes info from Clipboard

M. Young
combo box

select value from combo box by clicking its button or pressing F4

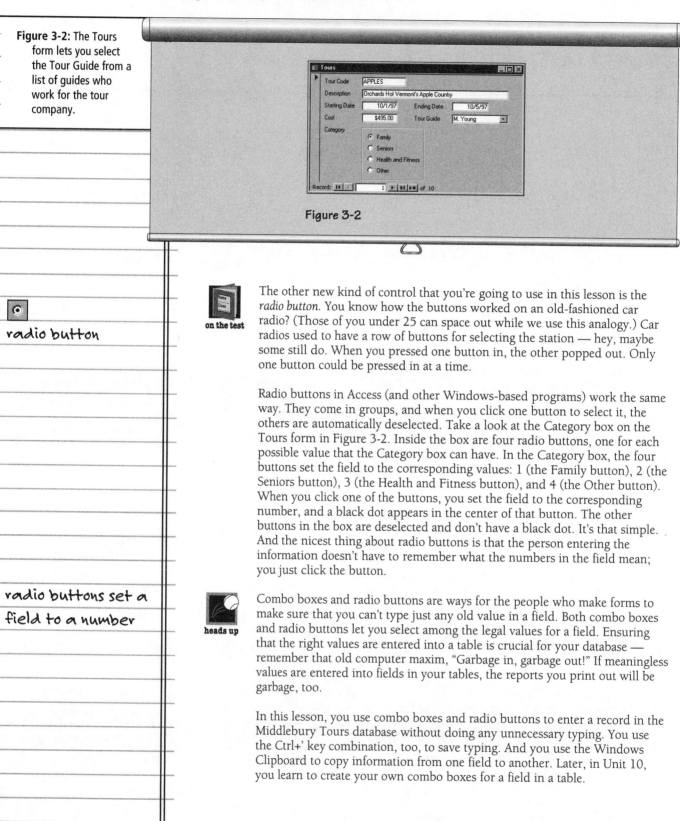

Figure 3-2: The Tours form lets you select the Tour Guide from a list of guides who work for the tour company.

Figure 3-2

on the test

The other new kind of control that you're going to use in this lesson is the *radio button*. You know how the buttons worked on an old-fashioned car radio? (Those of you under 25 can space out while we use this analogy.) Car radios used to have a row of buttons for selecting the station — hey, maybe some still do. When you pressed one button in, the other popped out. Only one button could be pressed in at a time.

Radio buttons in Access (and other Windows-based programs) work the same way. They come in groups, and when you click one button to select it, the others are automatically deselected. Take a look at the Category box on the Tours form in Figure 3-2. Inside the box are four radio buttons, one for each possible value that the Category box can have. In the Category box, the four buttons set the field to the corresponding values: 1 (the Family button), 2 (the Seniors button), 3 (the Health and Fitness button), and 4 (the Other button). When you click one of the buttons, you set the field to the corresponding number, and a black dot appears in the center of that button. The other buttons in the box are deselected and don't have a black dot. It's that simple. And the nicest thing about radio buttons is that the person entering the information doesn't have to remember what the numbers in the field mean; you just click the button.

heads up

Combo boxes and radio buttons are ways for the people who make forms to make sure that you can't type just any old value in a field. Both combo boxes and radio buttons let you select among the legal values for a field. Ensuring that the right values are entered into a table is crucial for your database — remember that old computer maxim, "Garbage in, garbage out!" If meaningless values are entered into fields in your tables, the reports you print out will be garbage, too.

In this lesson, you use combo boxes and radio buttons to enter a record in the Middlebury Tours database without doing any unnecessary typing. You use the Ctrl+' key combination, too, to save typing. And you use the Windows Clipboard to copy information from one field to another. Later, in Unit 10, you learn to create your own combo boxes for a field in a table.

radio button

radio buttons set a field to a number

Copying values from one field to another

First, use the Windows Cut and Paste commands to copy information from an existing record in the Tours table to a new record.

on the CD

1 **If you aren't running Access with the Middlebury Tours database open, run Access and open the Middlebury Tours database.**

See the first two steps in Lesson 3-1 if you need a reminder of what to do. You see the database window.

2 **Click the Forms tab to see the list of forms.**

You see only one form — does that count as a list? The form, Tours, is already selected.

3 **Click the Open button.**

You see the Tours form, which looks like Figure 3-2, displaying the "Orchards Ho! Vermont's Apple Country" tour, tour code APPLES. You're about to enter another Vermont tour: another orchard-related tour. Some information for the new tour will be the same as the information for this tour. Instead of typing this information in the new record, you can just paste it from the Clipboard.

4 **With your mouse, select the text Orchards Ho! from the Description field.**

Click at the beginning of the field, hold down the mouse button, and drag to the exclamation point. Alternatively, you can click at the beginning of the field, hold down the Shift key, and click after the exclamation point. Either way, Access highlights the selected text in black.

5 **Press Ctrl+C to copy this text to the Windows Clipboard.**

When you press Ctrl+C, absolutely nothing appears to happen. What went wrong? Nothing! The Clipboard just doesn't make much noise about what's on it.

6 **Click the New Record button on the navigation bar to start entering a brand-spanking-new record.**

You see a new, blank record, and your cursor is in the Description field.

7 **In the Description field, press Ctrl+V and then type a space and the words** Apple-Picking in Vermont.

You see Orchards Ho! Apple-Picking in Vermont in the Tours box. You didn't have to type the whole entry — instead, you pasted some of it from the Windows Clipboard.

8 **Back up to the Tour Code field (by pressing Shift+Tab) and type** APPLE2.

9 **Press Tab twice to move down to the Starting Date field.**

Here's another trick; this tour starts today.

10 **Press Ctrl+;.**

That is, hold down the Ctrl key and type a semicolon. Today's date appears.

on the test

(Notes:)

select text by dragging mouse or shift+clicking

Shift+Tab to move backward one field

Ctrl+; enters today's date

Notes:

11 **For the Ending Date, type a date three days from now and then type** 295 **for the Cost (pressing Tab to move from field to field). Press Tab to move to the Tour Guide field.**

You're ready to try the combo box for the Tour Guide field in the next part of the lesson.

You can press Ctrl+C to copy selected text to the Windows Clipboard and Ctrl+V to paste the information from the Clipboard to wherever the cursor is. You can paste the same value as many times as you want. The Clipboard never runs dry, as long as you don't put anything new on the Clipboard.

Using combo boxes and radio buttons

When you continue entering the record for the apple-picking tour, you run into two new types of controls: combo boxes and radio buttons. You enter a value in the next field, Tour Guide, differently than you do for the other fields you've seen. The list button at the right end of the box for this field indicates that this is a combo box, where you can select a value from a list. If you want to type an entry, as if this were a text box, you've got that option, but why do extra work?

Have fun! And enjoy this alternative to typing.

1 **Click the list button (at the right end of the Tour Guide combo box) or press the F4 key.**

The list of guides appears below the combo box.

2 **Choose L. Spitzer from the combo box list, either by clicking that name with the mouse or by pressing the ↓ key until L. Spitzer is highlighted and then pressing Enter.**

Either way, Ms. Spitzer's name now appears in the Tour Guide box. If the list of guides were really long, you could press the first letter of the name that you wanted to select, and Access would move the highlight to the first entry that starts with the letter you typed.

The next field, Category, appears on the Tours form as a group of radio buttons. The radio buttons are inside a box labeled *Category*, just to give you a hint. If you click the Family button, Access enters *1* in the Category field, the code for family-oriented tours. If you click the Seniors button, Access enters *2*. If you click the Health and Fitness button, Access enters *3*. And if you click the Other button, Access enters *4*. Currently, the Family button is selected; you can tell because it contains a black dot.

3 **Click the Health and Fitness button.**

The black dot vanishes from the Family button and appears in the Health and Fitness button. Only one button can be selected at a time in a group of radio buttons. (This tour features aerobic exercises combined with apple-picking and is too strenuous for small children.)

4 **Close the Tours form.**

click radio button to set value of field

only one radio button can be selected at a time

You used several tricks when you typed this record — nice work! When you avoid retyping values, you do more than save time: Entries made by using combo boxes or radio buttons are also more accurate because you can't make a typo.

extra credit

Cutting and pasting information from other programs

The Windows Clipboard works with other Windows-based programs, too. After information is on the Clipboard, you can paste it into almost any program. For example, if you've typed a name into a WordPerfect or Word document, you can select it and press Ctrl+C to copy it to the Clipboard. Then switch to Access, put the cursor into the field where you want to enter the name, and press Ctrl+V. Access "types" the information from the Clipboard into the field. You don't have to close your word-processing program to switch to Access: Just click anywhere in the Access window if it is visible or press Alt+Tab until Access appears.

☑ **Progress Check**

If you can do the following, you've mastered this lesson:

❑ Use the Windows Clipboard when you want to copy information from one record to another.

❑ Press Ctrl+' to duplicate the entire value of one field from one record to the next.

❑ Press Ctrl+; to type today's date.

❑ Choose a value from a combo box list.

❑ Click one radio button in a group to set the value for a field.

Fixing Mistakes

Lesson 3-3

When typing is involved, all kinds of things can go wrong. Spelling something wrong, typing the right information in the wrong field or record — the possibilities are endless. Luckily, Access provides several ways to fix your mistakes:

- ◆ Press the Backspace key to delete the character you just typed. If some text is selected (highlighted), Backspace deletes the text.

- ◆ Press the Delete (or Del, depending on your keyboard) key to delete the character to the right of the cursor. If text is selected, Delete blows all that text away.

- ◆ When you're editing a field, press Ctrl+Z or Esc to undo the changes you've made to the current field.

- ◆ When you're not editing a field, press Ctrl+Z or Esc to undo all the changes you've made to the current record.

Ctrl+Z or Esc undoes changes you've made

Datasheet view
shows the fields
from the form as
columns on
datasheet

Design view lets
you change the
layout of form

View button
switches among
Form view,
Datasheet view,
and Design view

Access also lets you use a form to see your records in three different *views* —
that is, three different appearances on-screen:

- *Form view* shows you the form in the regular way. You used the Tours form in Form view in Lesson 3-2.

- *Datasheet view* shows you a datasheet with the fields in the same order in which they appear on the form. Forms don't have to include all the records in a table, so if a field doesn't appear on the form, it doesn't appear in Datasheet view, either. Fields that appear as combo boxes on the form have combo boxes in Datasheet view, too.

- *Design view* shows you the programmer's-eye view of the form. You use Design view to create a form or change the way it works. You'll use Design view in Lesson 10-4.

"Datasheet view?" you may ask. "Didn't I use a datasheet in Lesson 3-1?"
Yes, you did. In Access, you can open a *table* in Datasheet view, as you did
in Lesson 3-1, and you can open a *form* in Datasheet view. Here are the
differences:

- The Datasheet view of a *table* includes all the fields in the table.

- The Datasheet view of a *form* includes only the fields that appear on the form. A form doesn't have to show all the fields in a table.

When you're looking at a form, the left-most button on the toolbar is the View
button. This button is tricky; depending on which view you're using, the
button shows an icon for one of the other two views. If you're in Form or
Datasheet view, the button shows the icon for Design view (a picture of a
triangle, ruler, and pencil). In Design view, it shows an icon for Form view (a
tiny form with tiny text boxes). If you don't see the icon for the view you want,
the button works like a tiny combo box: Click the list button at the right side
of the button, and Access displays a little menu of the three views so you can
pick the one you want. Or find a view the old-fashioned way: Choose
View⇨Design View, View⇨Form View, or View⇨Datasheet View from the
Access menu bar. (Some forms are designed to be seen only in Form view or
Datasheet view; if you open a form like this, the View⇨Form View or
View⇨Datasheet View command may not appear on the menu.)

Oops! Fixing a mistake in a field

In this lesson, you make a bunch of mistakes and fix them. You make a few
changes to the Tours table in the Middlebury Tours database. If you don't see
the Middlebury Tours database window on-screen, go back to Lesson 3-1 and
follow the first two steps there.

1   **Click the Forms tab, if it's not already selected.**

2   **Double-click the Tours form.**

Double-clicking the name of a form opens the form in Form view. You see the
Tours form shown back in Figure 3-2, but now it shows the APPLE2 tour,
Orchards Ho! Apple-Picking in Vermont, rather than the APPLES tour you saw

Notes:

the last time. Your APPLES tour is still there, but because APPLE2 comes first in alphabetical order (the way computers alphabetize, anyway), the APPLE2 tour is the one you see first.

Your legal department has reported that another company has trademarked the name Orchards Ho! You decide to change the names of your two orchard tours to Country Orchards and the two tour codes to ORCH1 and ORCH2.

The Tour Code is highlighted, showing that the text is selected. If you type something, that something replaces the current value.

3 **Type** ORCH2 **and press Tab or Enter.**

typing replaces highlighted text

The new tour code replaces the old one because the old tour code was selected when you started typing. When you move to the Description field, the name of the tour is selected.

4 **Press** C.

The *C* replaces the previous entry in this field. Rats! You didn't want to replace it — you wanted to edit it!

5 **Press Ctrl+Z or Esc.**

when editing field, Ctrl+Z or Esc undoes changes

The *C* disappears, and the original value of the field reappears. Whew!

6 **Press F2 to edit the field.**

The field is no longer selected, and the cursor appears at the end of the field.

7 **Press the Home key to move to the beginning of the box for the field. Then press Delete repeatedly to delete the first two words, including the exclamation point. Type** Country Orchards: **into the box.**

when editing, Home moves cursor to beginning of field

The name of the tour is now Country Orchards: Apple-Picking in Vermont.

If you notice that you've made a mistake, press Esc or Ctrl+Z to undo it. You have fixed two mistakes — the tour code and the description — by replacing one value and by editing the other. Nice work!

heads up

Warning: As soon as you move to another record, Access saves the changes that you made. When that happens, Ctrl+Z and Esc don't work — you have to fix the broken record by hand.

Using a form in Datasheet view

You need to fix the APPLES tour, too — the other orchard-related tour. Use the form in Datasheet view so you can see both orchard records at the same time.

1 **Switch to Datasheet view of this form, either by choosing View⇨Datasheet View from the menu bar or by clicking the list button at the right end of the toolbar's View button and choosing Datasheet View.**

View button

The View button is the left-most button on the toolbar when you're looking at a form. It disappears when you close the form because it's only usable from a form.

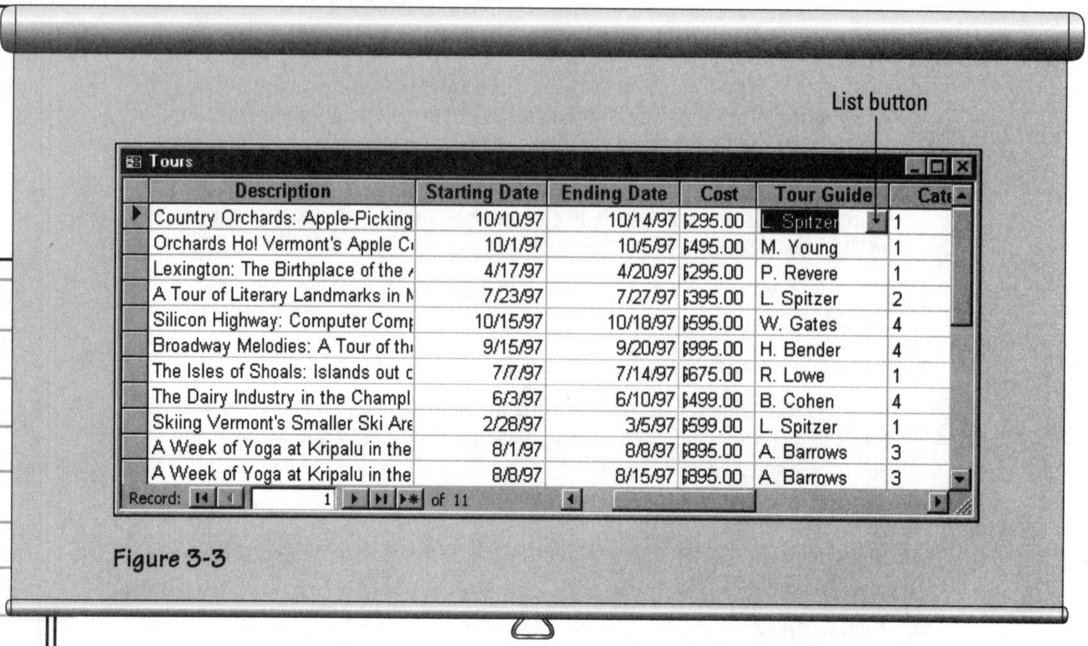
List button
Tours
Description | Starting Date | Ending Date | Cost | Tour Guide | Cat
Country Orchards: Apple-Picking | 10/10/97 | 10/14/97 | $295.00 | L. Spitzer | 1
Orchards Ho! Vermont's Apple C | 10/1/97 | 10/5/97 | $495.00 | M. Young | 1
Lexington: The Birthplace of the | 4/17/97 | 4/20/97 | $295.00 | P. Revere | 1
A Tour of Literary Landmarks in | 7/23/97 | 7/27/97 | $395.00 | L. Spitzer | 2
Silicon Highway: Computer Com | 10/15/97 | 10/18/97 | $595.00 | W. Gates | 4
Broadway Melodies: A Tour of th | 9/15/97 | 9/20/97 | $995.00 | H. Bender | 4
The Isles of Shoals: Islands out c | 7/7/97 | 7/14/97 | $675.00 | R. Lowe | 1
The Dairy Industry in the Champl | 6/3/97 | 6/10/97 | $499.00 | B. Cohen | 4
Skiing Vermont's Smaller Ski Are | 2/28/97 | 3/5/97 | $599.00 | L. Spitzer | 1
A Week of Yoga at Kripalu in the | 8/1/97 | 8/8/97 | $895.00 | A. Barrows | 3
A Week of Yoga at Kripalu in the | 8/8/97 | 8/15/97 | $895.00 | A. Barrows | 3
Record: 1 of 11
Figure 3-3

Figure 3-3: When you view the Tours form in Datasheet view, the Tour Guide column works like a combo box, so you can select a value from a list.

combo boxes work in Datasheet view, too

Notes:

2 The Datasheet view window is the same size as the Form view window for the form — small. Make it wider by dragging the right edge of the window to the right.

You can see more columns (fields) if the window is wider.

When you see the form in Datasheet view, it looks just like when you open a table. Well, not quite. If you tab over to the Tour Guide column, a list button appears at the right edge of the column, showing that this is a combo box. You can click the button to select a guide's name from a list. Because the form displays the field as a combo box, Datasheet view of the form shows a combo box for the field, too. Similarly, the Category column lets you enter only 1, 2, 3, or 4 because those are the only values that the radio buttons let you enter on the form. Figure 3-3 shows the Tour Guide column with a combo-box button in it.

3 Press the Home key to move your cursor to the first column (Tour Code), if it's not already there.

When you're moving your cursor around in a form (in Form view or Datasheet view), press Home to get to the first field and End to get to the last. When you've pressed F2 to edit a field, Home and End move to the beginning and the end (respectively) of the field you're editing.

4 Move the cursor down a row to the APPLES tour.

This tour needs to be edited, too. The new tour code for this tour is *ORCH1*.

5 Press Ctrl+' to enter the same value as in the preceding record: ORCH2.

The old code, APPLES, is replaced by ORCH2. Right now, it looks as if you've got two tours with the same tour code, ORCH2. What happens if you forget that you need to edit this field to read ORCH1*?* You'll find out in a minute!

6 **Press the down-arrow key to move to the next record.**

When you're done making changes to a record, Access checks to see whether the record violates any of the Access data-checking rules. Yes, indeed, it does! You see a message explaining that the changes you requested were not successful, because they violate one of the rules, in this case, the rule against two records having the same value for the primary key field (Tour Code).

7 **Click OK.**

Your cursor returns to the record that has the problem. In this table, Tour Code is the *primary key field,* which means that every record must have a different code. You learned about primary key fields, which uniquely identify each record in a table, in Lesson 2-2. You must fix the Tour Code for the second record so it is different from all other tour codes in the table.

8 **Press F2 to edit the Product Code and change the 2 to a 1. Press Tab to move to the Description column.**

The *Orchards Ho!* part has to go.

9 **Press Ctrl+' to duplicate the tour name from the previous record. Then press F2 to change the name to Country Orchards and Vermont Farms.**

Now this record looks right.

10 **Press ↓ to move to the next record.**

No error message — each record has a unique Tour Code now.

11 **Close the Tours form.**

You see the database window again.

You can use a form in Datasheet view and see the same fields that appear on the form. Access stops you from making certain kinds of mistakes, like entering duplicate values in a primary key field.

Recess

You're probably ready for a walk in a Vermont orchard right now! If one isn't immediately available, get up and stretch your legs anyway. If you take a break, follow the first two steps in Lesson 3-1 to get ready for Lesson 3-4.

Deleting Stuff

Lesson 3-4

Deleting records is easy, whether you're looking at a form or a table, whatever the view. To select a record to delete, click the record selector for the record — the gray box at the left edge of the record (the box where the triangle and pencil icons appear, telling you which record you have selected or are editing). Access highlights the entire record. Press the Delete key or choose Edit⇨Delete or Edit⇨Delete Record from the menu bar. Access (or the Office

☑ **Progress Check**

If you can do the following, you've mastered this lesson:

❑ Fix typing errors by using the Backspace and Delete keys.

❑ Leave the current field the way it was before you began editing, by pressing Ctrl+Z or Esc.

❑ Avoid panicking when Access flashes you an error message about duplicate primary keys.

to delete record, select it and press Delete

Figure 3-4: The Guides table contains a list of available tour guides.

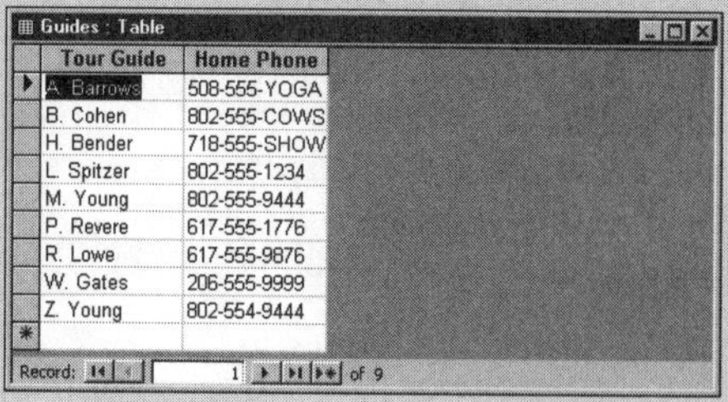

Tour Guide	Home Phone
A. Barrows	508-555-YOGA
B. Cohen	802-555-COWS
H. Bender	718-555-SHOW
L. Spitzer	802-555-1234
M. Young	802-555-9444
P. Revere	617-555-1776
R. Lowe	617-555-9876
W. Gates	206-555-9999
Z. Young	802-554-9444

Figure 3-4

Notes:

to select several records in row, click first record and then Shift + click last record

or select a group of records by dragging with mouse

warning message appears before Access deletes record

Access may refuse to delete record required for related table

Assistant, if it is running) asks whether you really, *really* want to delete the record forever and ever. Double-check that the right record disappeared, and if it did, click Yes.

When you're using Datasheet view and can see lots of records at once, you can delete a bunch of records at once, if you like. The records have to appear together in the datasheet. Click the record selector of the first record to delete, and then drag the mouse down to the last record to delete. Or select the first record to delete and then hold down the Shift key while you click the last record to delete. Access highlights all the records that you selected. Then delete them as we just described.

In this lesson, you decide to delete a few tour guides from the Guides table.

on the CD

If you don't see the Middlebury Tours database window on-screen, go back to Lesson 3-1 and follow the first two steps there.

1 **Click the Tables tab in the database window and then double-click the Guides table.**

You see a list of the tour guides in the Guides table (see Figure 3-4). When we created this database, we created a relationship between the records in the Tours table and the Guides table, so that names in the Tour Guide field in the Tours table must correspond with names in the Guides table. In fact, the Guides table provides the names that appear in the Tour Guides combo box you saw in Lesson 3-2.

2 **Click the record selector for the Z. Young record — the gray box in the left margin of the form, where a right-pointing triangle appears.**

The whole left margin of the form turns dark gray. You need to delete Zac Young from the list of guides, because he is graduating from college and moving away.

3 **Press the Delete key.**

You see a message warning you that you're about to delete a record. (Big news, right?)

heads up

4 **Click Yes.**

Access deletes the record. It's gone; Ctrl+Z and Esc don't work to undo deleting a record.

5 **Click the record selector for the W. Gates record.**

The whole row for the record turns black. This guy is never available; he's always too busy with his software business. Time to delete him, too.

6 **Press Delete.**

You see a message telling you that Access can't delete the record because the Tours table contains related records. That is, the Tours table contains records that have W. Gates as the entry in the Tour Guide field. Because the Tour Guide field must contain entries that exist in the Guides table, you can't delete the W. Gates entry. You learn more about this in Unit 8. You've just had an introduction to multitable databases!

7 **Click OK when Access tells you that it can't delete the record.**

No record is deleted.

8 **Close the Tours window.**

W. Gates has survived for another day.

There is no looking back now. You already know how to enter and delete records. Before long, you're going to be creating reports, forms, and whole databases! But first you'd better take a long stretch.

☑ Progress Check

If you can do the following, you've mastered this lesson:

❑ Delete a record by selecting it and pressing the Delete key.

❑ Delete a bunch of records from a datasheet by selecting them and pressing Delete.

Finding Records

Lesson 3-5

When you've got only ten records in your table, finding the record that you want to look at, edit, or delete isn't hard. But what if you have a table with hundreds or thousands of records? You need help from Access.

You can ask Access to search the contents of one field in all the records in a table, looking for a particular value. For example, you could search for records with *ORCH* in the Tour Code field. You can also tell Access to look for records that include some text in a particular field — for example, records with the word *Vermont* in the Description field. You can even ask Access to look in all the fields in the table, in case you're not sure which field the information is in.

To search for information in a table, you use the Find button on the Toolbar, or you press Ctrl+F or choose Edit⇨Find from the menu. Whichever way you chose, you see the Find in field dialog box, shown in Figure 3-5.

Searching for codes

on the CD

In this lesson, you search for records in the Middlebury Tours database. If Access isn't running or the Middlebury Tours database isn't open, skip back to Lesson 3-1 and follow the first two steps.

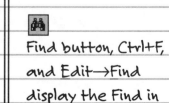
Find button, Ctrl+F, and Edit→Find display the Find in field dialog box

Figure 3-5: The Find in field dialog box lets you type information to search for.

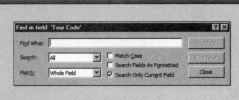

Figure 3-5

Find button

Find First starts at beginning of table

move Find in field dialog box by dragging its title bar

Find Next starts at the current record

To begin searching for a record:

1 Open the Tours form.

Before starting to search, open the form or datasheet that includes the field to search for and move to the field. For example, you may be looking up information about the SHOALS tour, so your cursor should be in the Tour Code field.

2 Click the Find button on the Toolbar or press Ctrl+F.

The Find button has a little picture of binoculars. If you prefer to use a command, choose Edit⇨Find from the menu bar. You see the Find in field dialog box, shown in Figure 3-5. The title bar of the dialog box includes the name of the field Access will search in.

3 In the Find What box, type the information that you're looking for, that is, SHOALS.

You can capitalize the letters or type them as small letters: Access doesn't pay any attention to capitalization when searching unless you click the Match Case box.

4 Click the Find First button to find the first record in the table that contains that tour code.

The record appears. The Find in field window stays open, in case you didn't find the record you wanted.

5 If the Find in field window covers up the part of the Tours form that you want to see, move the Find in field window by dragging its title bar (the heading that says Find in field: 'Tour Code') with the mouse.

If you want to search for another record, you can type something different into the Find What box and search again.

6 To look for another record that contains the same information, click the Find Next button.

No other record with *SHOALS* in the Tour Code exists, and you see a message telling you so.

7 Click OK.

8 After you're done searching, click the Close button in the Find in field dialog box.

If Access can't find any records that match your request, you see a message telling you that Access gives up. Click the OK button to make the message go away. The Find in field window is waiting for you to try another search.

Tips for searching

If you can't find the record you're looking for and you're *sure* it's in there somewhere, try these tricks:

- Check that you typed the information you're looking for correctly. Remember that computers have absolutely no imagination whatsoever, so if you didn't type the information exactly right, Access has no idea what you're talking about.

- Check that you're searching in the right field. To search in another field, close the Find in field window, move to the field that contains the information you're looking for, and click the Find button or press Ctrl+F to see the Find in field window again.

- If a database contains several tables, make sure that you're looking in the table that contains the record you're looking for. For example, the Middlebury Tours database contains three tables: Tours, Guides, and Categories. If you're looking for a record about a tour, you won't find it in the Guides table.

Here are other searching tips:

- You can tell Access to search in all the fields in the table at once. If your table is large, this type of search can take a while. In the Find in field window, click the Search Only Current Field box so that it doesn't contain a check mark. Then click Find First or Find Next to begin searching.

- If you think that the record you want comes after the current record in the form or datasheet, click the list button at the right end of the Search box. From the little menu that appears, choose Down to tell Access to search downward through the table. Then click Find Next to start looking from the current record. If you think that the record you're looking for comes before the current record, you can choose Up from the Search box menu.

- To search for a record that contains nothing at all in the current field, you can't just leave the Find What box blank. Instead, type "" (two double quotes) in the Find What box and click the Find First button.

  Then try typing **Is Null** into the Find What box and click the Find First button. Typing double quotes finds one type of blank entries, and Is Null finds another type. You don't have to understand what this Is Null stuff is about; just remember that it's the same thing as an empty field. You'll run into Is Null again in Lesson 4-3.

- What if you don't know the entire exact entry in the field but you know part of it? Type the part you know. Then click the downward-pointing triangle button at the right end of the Match box and choose Any Part of Field from the menu that appears. If you're sure that the part you remember is at the beginning of the entry for the field, choose Start of Field to speed up the search.

- Even after you close the Find in field window, you can press Shift+F4 to find the next record that matches the last search you did.

Notes:

to search all fields in table, clear Search Only Current Field box

to look for blank field, type "" or Is Null in Find What box

Shift +F4 to find next match of last search

Searching for a word or phrase

Search for tours that contain a specific word anywhere in the tour description.

1 **Click the First Record button on the navigation bar in the Tours form (or press Ctrl+↑) to return to the first record. Move to the Description field.**

How about finding all the tours with the word Vermont in the description?

2 **Press Ctrl+F, click the Find icon on the toolbar, or choose Edit⇨Find from the menu bar.**

Some people are toolbar people, and others are Ctrl key people. Hey, it takes all kinds! You see the Find in field window, shown back in Figure 3-5. The title of the window you see now is actually Find in field: 'Description.' The window title reminds you which field you're searching.

3 **In the Find What box, type the word** Vermont.

4 **Click the Search Only Current Field box so that its check mark disappears.**

Now Access will search all the fields in the table. The title of the window changes to Find (from Find in field) — a subtle confirmation that Access understands what you want.

5 **Click Find First.**

Drat! Access displays a message saying that it searched all the records and didn't find a thing? What happened? Oh, yeah — Access is looking for fields that contain only the word *Vermont* and nothing else.

6 **Click OK to make the message go away.**

7 **Click the list button at the right end of the Match field and choose Any Part of Field from the list that appears.**

Now Access looks for any record in which any field contains the word Vermont in any part of the field. That sounds right!

8 **Click the Find First button again.**

This time, Access finds the ORCH1 tour, Country Orchards, and Vermont Farms.

9 **Click Find Next.**

Access displays another record about a Vermont tour.

10 **Click Find Next again.**

You see the VTSKI tour, Skiing Vermont's Smaller Ski Areas. Good enough!

11 **Click Find First.**

Access starts over from the top of the table and shows you the first record with *Vermont* in it again.

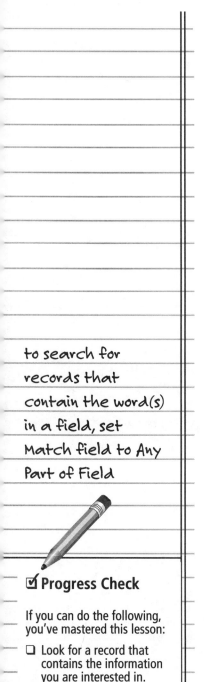

to search for records that contain the word(s) in a field, set Match field to Any Part of Field

☑ **Progress Check**

If you can do the following, you've mastered this lesson:

❑ Look for a record that contains the information you are interested in.

❑ Search in a particular field or in all the fields of a table.

❑ Search for records when you know only a word or two, not the whole contents of the field.

12 **Click the Close button (either one) on the Find dialog box and again on the Tours window.**

You're done finding records in the Tours table.

You've used the Find and Find in field windows to find just the records you wanted in the Tours table. Nice work!

Recess

You're done with this unit, It's time to whiz through the quiz!

Unit 3 Quiz

For each of the following questions, circle the letter of the correct answer or answers. Remember, each question may have more than one right answer.

1. **To edit the value of a field in a form or datasheet, you . . .**

   A. Press the F2 key.

   B. Click in the box that displays the field.

   C. Choose Edit⇨This Record from the menu.

   D. Click the Edit button on the toolbar, the button that looks like the tiny face of a copy editor.

   E. Delete the value by pressing the Delete key and then type the new value.

2. **When you press Ctrl+', Access . . .**

   A. Puts the text in the current field in quotes.

   B. Enters the same text that the preceding record contains.

   C. Enters a pithy quotation, like "Consistency is the hobgoblin of little minds and database programs."

   D. Fills the current field with quote marks.

   E. Duplicates the value of the current field in the preceding record.

3. **To enter the current date, you . . .**

   A. Press Ctrl+;.

   B. Press Ctrl+D.

   C. Choose Edit⇨Current Date from the menu.

   D. Click the Date button on the toolbar.

   E. Type it yourself, after double-checking the date on a calendar.

4. **The Windows Clipboard is . . .**

    A. A program you can buy directly from Microsoft that adds conferencing capabilities to Windows 95.

    B. An invisible storage space for information that you want to move or duplicate.

    C. Where the selected information is copied to when you press Ctrl+C.

    D. A buffer.

    E. Where the information comes from when you press Ctrl+V.

5. **Who was the only U.S. President from Vermont?**

    A. Chester A. Arthur.

    B. Ben Franklin.

    C. Trick question: There has never been a President from Vermont.

    D. Daniel Webster.

    E. Calvin Coolidge.

6. **Combo boxes and radio buttons are useful when . . .**

    A. The field can have only one of a short list of values.

    B. You can't remember how to spell the entry for the field.

    C. You want to make sure that you don't enter garbage (wrong information) into the field.

    D. You want to change the radio station.

    E. You want to order a taco combination plate.

Unit 3 Exercise

on the CD

1. Open the Middlebury Tours database.

2. Open the Tours form.

3. Switch to Datasheet view.

4. Enter a new record for another skiing tour, duplicating or copying information from the VTSKI tour.

5. Close the Tours form.

6. Exit Access.

Slicing and Dicing Your Data

Prerequisites

▶ Running Access
  (Lesson 1-1)

▶ Viewing a table
  (Lesson 1-3)

Objectives for This Unit

✓ Creating queries to select records from a table

✓ Using queries to select which fields to display

✓ Sorting the records in a table by using a query

on the CD

▶ Dickens Address
  Book 4 database
  (Dickens Address
  Book 4.mdb)

With a little sample database like the ones you've used so far, you can see all the records easily and find the ones you want quickly. But when you're working with dozens, hundreds, or even thousands of records, you frequently want to zero in on a group of records that interests you. For example, if your address book contains 2,645 people, you might want to look at subgroups of your friends and acquaintances, like those in a particular state or those with e-mail addresses.

In this unit, you find out how to tell Access which records you want to look at, which fields interest you, and what order you want to see the records in. You'll use a new type of database component, called a *query*. Queries are vital to taking advantage of the power of Access; you can use queries to find the valuable needles in your haystacks of data.

Getting Answers with Queries

query = way to ask Access about information in database

on the test

select queries = queries that select records from one or more tables

make a query using New Object button, Insert→Query command, or New button on Queries tab of database window

New Object button

So far, you have used three of the six kinds of things stored in an Access database: tables, forms, and (briefly) reports. In this lesson, you learn how to create and use a fourth: queries.

A *query* is a way to ask Access a question about your database. Queries find information from one or more tables in the database, and they present the records and fields you specify. A query can also ask Access to summarize the information in a table — for example, you could ask for a count of the records in an address table by state.

To see what queries your database contains, you click the Queries tab in the database window. The Dickens Address Book database doesn't have any queries yet (unless you've leaped ahead and made some yourself).

You can actually create a bunch of different kinds of queries, as listed in Table 4-1. Queries can combine information from two or more tables, and you'll learn how to use multitable queries in Unit 9. In this unit, you learn about *select queries,* which are by far the most commonly used type of query — select queries let you look at selected information from one table.

Table 4-1	Types of Queries
Type	*What It Does*
Select	Shows you the records and fields you selected
Crosstab	Summarizes the information in a table
Make table	Makes a new table containing the records and fields you selected
Update	Makes changes to one or more fields in the records you selected
Append	Adds the records and fields you selected to an existing table
Delete	Deletes the records you selected

Before you start to make a query, ask yourself these questions:

◆ Which records do you want to see? How can you identify these records to Access? For example, do they all have the same value in a certain field, like *NY* in the State field?

◆ Which fields in those records contain the information that you want to know? Or do you want to see all the fields in each record?

on the test

When you've got the answers to those two questions, you're ready to create an Access query. To make a query, you choose Insert⇨Query from the menu bar or click the Queries tab in the database window and then click the New button. Or you can use the New Object button on the toolbar: Click the list button at the right edge of the New Object button, and you see a menu of the objects that you can create; choose New Query from the little menu.

The New Object button keeps changing!

The New Object button works two ways: You can click the button itself to make the same kind of object that you created the last time you clicked it. Or you can click the downward-pointing triangle button at the right end of the New Object button and choose the type of object that you want to create from the menu that appears.

The New Object button remembers what you created the last time you clicked it, and it displays the appropriate icon on the face of the button. If you don't remember which icon means what, look at the six tabs on the database window to remind yourself. If the New Object button contains an icon for the kind of object that you feel like making, you can just click the button. If the button shows the icon for a different kind of object, or if you're not sure, the surefire way to use the New Object button is to click the list button (the downward-pointing triangle) at its right end and choose the type of object you want from the menu that appears.

If the New Object button shows two overlapping squares with a gold sparkle, the button makes a new query when you click it.

Whether you use the menu bar or the toolbar, you see the New Query dialog box, shown in Figure 4-1. You can create a query with your bare hands in Design view, or you can ask a Query Wizard to make one for you. To make a new query from scratch without the help of a wizard, choose Design View from the list. Otherwise, choose the wizard that sounds the most helpful. The Query Wizards are

- ▶ Simple Query Wizard: Selects records and fields from a table (that's the kind of query you make in this lesson)
- ▶ Crosstab Query Wizard: Counts or sums up the number of records by category, using information from the fields you specify
- ▶ Find Duplicates Query Wizard: Finds duplicate records in a table
- ▶ Find Unmatched Query Wizard: In a database with related tables, finds records in one table that have no matching record in another table

After you create a query, you can look at it in one of two views:

- ▶ Design view, for looking at and changing the design of the query
- ▶ Datasheet view, for looking at the results of the query (Another Datasheet view! You can look at tables, forms, or queries as datasheets.)

You can switch back and forth between these two views, changing the design and looking at the results, until the query displays the information you want.

When you're done fooling with a query and close it, Access asks whether you want to save the query. If you plan to use it again, go ahead and save it. If you don't think that you'll want to look at the results of this query again later, you can close the query window without saving the query.

Notes:

Simple Query Wizard creates a select query

Figure 4-1: Do you want a wizard to help you to create your query?

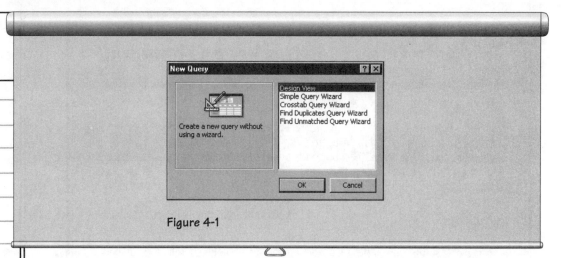

Figure 4-1

Access runs the
query each time it
opens the query

heads up

When you save a query, you save the design of the query — the description of the question you are asking. You don't save the results of the query: The next time you open the query, Access *runs* the query again and displays an updated set of results based on the current information in the tables in your database.

In Access, you use queries to see a selection of records from a table or to choose the records that will appear in a form or report. In this unit, you'll see the results of queries in a datasheet, but in later units, the results of queries will appear in reports, too.

queries can
combine data
from several
tables

A query can use one table as its source of information, or it can use several tables. A query can even use the results of another query as its data source. You learn more about these advanced types of queries in Unit 9.

Enough talk — it's time to try making one of these famous queries for yourself.

Looking at selected fields

We wouldn't take the chance of calling a Wizard "simple," at least not to the Wizard's face, but Simple Query Wizard is the official name of this useful wizard.

1 Run Access.

If Access is already running, click the Open Database button on the toolbar, the yellow folder icon, and skip to Step 3.

2 When Access asks what database you want to open, click More Files and click OK.

You see the Open dialog box, showing the files in the My Documents folder.

on the CD

3 Double-click the Dummies 101 Access 97 folder to open it and then double-click the Dickens Address Book 4 database.

Dickens Address Book 4 is just like the Dickens Address Book database that you created in Unit 2, except that it contains more records. You installed it on your hard disk when you installed the *Dummies 101* CD-ROM. To see how queries work, you need enough records to slice and dice into queries.

You see the Main Switchboard window for the Dickens Address Book 4 database.

4 **Open the database window by clicking the Database Window button on the toolbar and then click the Queries tab.**

If you don't see the Database Windows button, close the Main Switchboard window and click the Restore button on the database window icon.

Nope, no queries in this database yet.

5 **Choose Insert⇨Query from the menu bar. Or click the list button of the New Object button on the toolbar and choose New Query. Or click the New button on the Queries tab of the database window.**

Either way, you see the New Query dialog box, shown in Figure 4-1.

6 **Select Simple Query Wizard from the list and click OK.**

You see the Simple Query Wizard window, shown in Figure 4-2. The Tables/Queries box shows which tables or queries this query is using as the source of its information — in our case, the Addresses table.

The Available Fields list shows the fields in the Addresses table that are available for inclusion in the query. To include information from a field, click it and click the right-pointing arrow button. The field name moves to the Selected Fields list.

7 **Click FirstName and the right-pointing arrow button.**

The FirstName field moves from the Available Fields list to the Selected Fields list. LastName is now selected in the Available Fields list.

8 **Click the right-pointing arrow button.**

The LastName field jumps into the Selected Fields list.

9 **Scroll down the Available Fields list by using its scroll bar. When you see StateOrProvince, click and move it to the Selected Fields list.**

Now you've selected FirstName, LastName, and StateOrProvince.

10 **Click the Next button.**

The Simple Query Wizard displays its last window, shown in Figure 4-3.

11 **In the box at the top of the Simple Query Wizard window, type Names and States as the title of the query.**

Access also wants to know whether you want to see the results of the query in Datasheet view or see and change the design of the query in Design view. The Open the query to view information option is already selected, so you'll see the Datasheet view.

12 **Click Finish.**

The Wizard does your bidding and creates the query in a new window entitled (just as you requested) Names and States : Select Query, shown in Figure 4-4. The Datasheet view contains only the three fields you selected for all the records in the table.

Notes:

tell Simple Query Wizard which fields to include

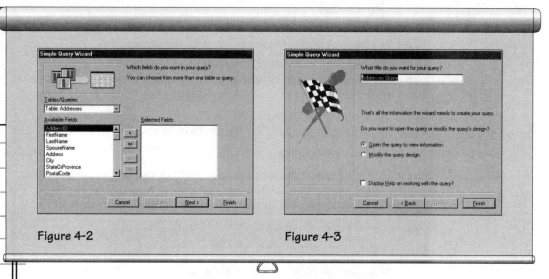

Figure 4-2: You can choose which tables and fields to include in your query.

Figure 4-3: The Simple Query Wizard is ready to make your query!

Figure 4-2   Figure 4-3

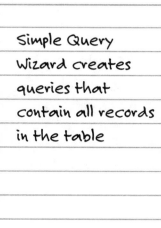

Notes:

Simple Query
Wizard creates
queries that
contain all records
in the table

to display results
of query in
Datasheet view,
click Open

edit results of a
query, just like
tables

13 **Close the query window by clicking the Close button.**

If Access asks whether you want to save changes to the query, click Yes. The query window closes.

You've created a new kind of database object — a query. You can see the queries that your database contains by clicking the Queries tab in the database window.

Looking at the results of a query

After you create a query and save it, you can open the query and take a look at it anytime. If the information in the table has changed in the meantime, Access automatically updates the query. With many queries, you can even change the data that appears in Datasheet view. Here's how:

1 **In the Dickens Address Book 4 database window, click the Queries tab if it's not already selected.**

There it is: the Names and States query!

2 **Double-click the Names and States query. Alternatively, you can click the query and click Open. Or click the query with your right mouse button and choose Open from the menu that appears.**

You see the results of the query again in Datasheet view, as shown in Figure 4-4. Access used to call the results of a select query a *dynaset,* but no one liked this word, so you don't see it much these days, not even in the Access manuals.

3 **Edit the first name for Bob Cratchit, changing it to Robert.**

In most queries, you can edit the information in the results of the query. Access updates the information in the table in which the information is stored. In this example, Access updates Bob's first name in the Addresses table. Cool!

At this point, you could print the datasheet, if you wanted to show the query results to someone else. You would click the Print button on the toolbar — see Unit 6 for more information on printing datasheets.

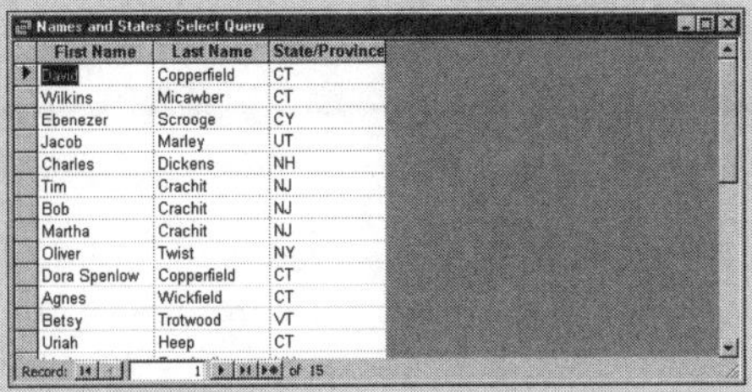

First Name	Last Name	State/Province
David	Copperfield	CT
Wilkins	Micawber	CT
Ebenezer	Scrooge	CY
Jacob	Marley	UT
Charles	Dickens	NH
Tim	Crachit	NJ
Bob	Crachit	NJ
Martha	Crachit	NJ
Oliver	Twist	NY
Dora Spenlow	Copperfield	CT
Agnes	Wickfield	CT
Betsy	Trotwood	VT
Uriah	Heep	CT

Figure 4-4

Figure 4-4: Here's the query you ordered, with the fields you asked for.

4 Close the query.

Access doesn't ask you whether it should save changes to the query, because you didn't make any changes to the query. You changed some data in one of the records in the results of the query, and Access saved that change in the Addresses table, where the information in this query comes from. But you didn't change the query design — the specifications about what tables, records, and fields to select.

Kudos to you! You've created, saved, opened, and closed a query. In the rest of the lessons in this unit, you learn how to change the design of a query, sort the records that appear, and select which records to include.

Recess

Here's a query for you: Do you want to take a break? And here's another: Do you want to keep working? If you take a break, close Access. When you're ready for Lesson 4-2, run Access and open the Dickens Address Book 4 database again.

extra credit

Deleting queries that you don't need anymore

Creating queries is a quick way to look at the data in a table, and you may find that you make a bunch of them. At some point, however, you may find that a query has outlived its usefulness. To delete a query that you don't need anymore, click the Queries tab in the database window, select the query to delete, and press the Delete key. Access asks you to confirm that you want to delete the query — click Yes.

☑ Progress Check

If you can do the following, you've mastered this lesson:

- ❑ Create a new query.
- ❑ View the queries that a database contains.
- ❑ Use the Simple Query Wizard to select records and fields from a table.
- ❑ Edit information in a table while viewing query results.

Lesson 4-2

Looking at Selected Records

QBE = query by
example

View button

Design view shows
design grid and
field lists

The Simple Query Wizard created a very nice query in Lesson 4-1 — thank you very much! — but the query includes *all* the records in the Addresses table. What if you want to look at only the addresses in New Hampshire? Or all the people with last names that start with the letters *M* through *Z*? You had a chance to select which fields to include, but not which records.

This lesson fixes this dreadful situation. You'll learn how to tell Access exactly which records you want to see in your query. In order to specify the records that you want, you use a system called *query by example,* or *QBE.* (Amaze your friends with this geeky acronym!) QBE lets you show Access which fields you want to include by making a sort of mock-up of the datasheet you want. The mock-up, called the *design grid,* contains the same columns that the results of the query will include, with the same widths and in the same order. You use the design grid to tell Access which records to include.

To see a query in Design view so you can change its design, click the query name in the database window and then click the Design button. If the query is already open, choose View⇨Query Design from the menu bar or click the View button on the toolbar. The View button works like the New Object button that you used in Lesson 4-1: You can click the list button at its right end to see a menu of views.

In Design view, the Names and States query that you made in Lesson 4-1 looks like Figure 4-5. The top half of the query window shows lists of fields for each table from which information is to be included. For our query, only one list appears, for the Addresses table. The bottom half of the window shows the design grid that defines the query. The design grid includes a column for each column in the result of the query. The rows of the grid are

  ♦ **Field and Table:** The names of the field and the table from which the information comes. In Figure 4-5, the Field row of the first column says FirstName and the Table row says Addresses, indicating that this column of the query result contains information from the FirstName field of the Addresses table.

  ♦ **Sort:** If you select Ascending or Descending in this row, Access sorts the query results by the contents of this column. To use the Sort column, click in it, click the list button that appears at the right end of the Sort column, and select Ascending or Descending from the list that appears.

  ♦ **Show:** If a check appears in the box in this row, the column appears in the query results. Sometimes you need to include information in the design grid that you don't want to appear in the query results — if so, click the box to remove the check. For example, if you are selecting records for which a field is blank, including the field in the query results is pointless — the field will be blank for all the records in the query results!

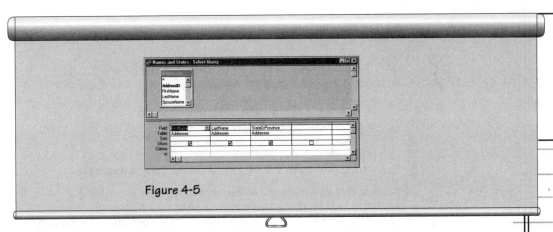

Figure 4-5: The lower part of the Design view window shows the design grid, which specifies which fields and records the query includes.

Figure 4-5

Notes:

on the test

▶ **Criteria:** Access selects only the records that match your entry in this row. For example, if you type Copperfield in the Criteria row of the LastName column, Access includes only records from the Addresses table in which the LastName field is Copperfield. You can also enter formulas; for example, >100 indicates that you want all entries that are greater than 100. You'll learn more about criteria in Lesson 4-3.

▶ **or:** This row lets you enter more than one criterion for a column. For example, if you want records where the last name is either Copperfield or Wickfield, you'd type Copperfield in the Criteria row and Wickfield in the or row.

After you make changes to the design of the query, you can switch back to Datasheet view to see the results. Click the View button on the toolbar or choose View⇨Datasheet from the menu bar. You can switch back and forth between Design view and Datasheet view, changing the design of the query, until you get the results you want.

Instead of starting from scratch or using a wizard to create a query, you can also start with a copy of an existing query. To copy a query, select it in the database window, press Ctrl+C to copy the whole query to the Windows Clipboard, and press Ctrl+V to paste a copy of the query back into your database. Access asks what name you want to use for the new copy. Now you can make changes to the new copy without changing the original query.

use Cut and Paste to copy queries

heads up

Here's one more important piece of information about queries: Suppose you create a query using information from the Addresses table today and store the query. Tomorrow, you update the records in the Addresses table. The next time you open your query, Access updates the query results, using the new information in the Addresses table. In other words, Access updates your query each time you open it, so the information is always up-to-date!

Notes:

Copying a query

In this lesson, you select the folks from the Addresses table of the Dickens Address Book 4 database who should be included in your queries. To start, you'll make a copy of the Names and States query that you created in Lesson 4-1 so you can make changes to the new copy.

on the CD

1 **Run Access and open the Dickens Address Book 4 database.**

If you want to try a different method for running Access and opening a database, double-click the My Computer icon on your Windows 95 desktop (or run the Windows Explorer program). Double-click the disk drive that contains your files, double-click the *Dummies 101* Access 97 folder, and then double-click the file Dickens Address Book 4.mdb. Access runs, and the Dickens Address Book 4 database opens.

2 **Open the database window by clicking its Restore button or the Database Window button on the toolbar.**

The database window is lurking in the lower-left corner of the Access window. The Restore button is the one with two overlapping squares. You see the database window.

3 **Click the Queries tab.**

You see the list of queries in your database — all one of them. You'll see more soon! The Names and States query is highlighted.

4 **Press Ctrl+C to copy the Names and States query to the Windows Clipboard.**

Nothing seems to happen.

5 **Press Ctrl+V to paste a copy of the query back into your database.**

You see the Paste As dialog box asking for the name to give the new query.

6 **Type New Jersey Addresses and click OK.**

You see? The list of queries has gotten longer already! However, right now the New Jersey Addresses query includes everyone in the Addresses table, not just people with *NJ* in the StateOrProvince field.

Ctrl+C copies query to Clipboard

Ctrl+V pastes a copy of a query back into the database

Copying a query — or almost anything in Access — is easy using the Clipboard. Just select the item to copy, press Ctrl+C to copy it to the Clipboard, and press Ctrl+V to copy it back to your database. After you copy a query, you can change the copy.

Changing a query's design

Now you're ready to change the New Jersey Addresses query to include only people who live in New Jersey.

1 **Open the New Jersey Addresses query in Design view by selecting it and clicking the <u>D</u>esign button or by right-clicking the query and choosing <u>D</u>esign from the menu that appears.**

The query looks just like Figure 4-5, except for the name of the query.

2 **Click the design grid in the StateOrProvince column and the Criteria row.**

A blinking cursor appears in the box you clicked.

3 **Type** NJ **and press Tab or Enter.**

The cursor moves to the next column. Access automatically puts quotes around the name you typed, indicating that it knows that the entry is text and not a number or a date.

By entering *NJ* in the Criteria row of the StateOrProvince column, you tell Access to look for records in which the StateOrProvince field is *NJ*. Easy enough!

4 **Switch to Datasheet view to see the query results: Click the View or Run button on the toolbar or choose <u>V</u>iew⇨<u>Data</u>sheet View from the menu bar.**

Access *runs* the query — that is, it sifts through the records in the Addresses table and finds the ones that match what you typed in the design grid. For complex queries using large tables, queries can take several minutes or more to run.

Access finds three people: the Cratchit family of Christmas, New Jersey. The query includes the same fields as in Lesson 4-1: FirstName, LastName, and StateOrProvince.

5 **Close the query window by clicking the Close button.**

You can close the query when you're in either Design view or Datasheet view — it doesn't matter. Access (or the Office Assistant, if it is running) asks whether you want to save changes to the query.

6 **Click <u>Y</u>es.**

The query window closes, and you see the database window.

Looking for all the records in a table that have a particular value (like *NJ*) in a field is easy: Just type the value into the design grid!

---

type value in Criteria row to select records

!

Run button

✓ **Progress Check**

If you can do the following, you've mastered this lesson:

❑ Specify which records you want to see in a query by entering criteria in the QBE design grid.

❑ Create a copy of an existing query to edit instead of starting from scratch.

Designing a Query from Scratch

Lesson 4-3

Instead of calling on a wizard to conjure up a query, you can make your own magic. To do so, you choose Design View when Access asks how you want to make a query. In this lesson, you make a query from scratch to select names that begin with certain letters and a query to find people from certain towns. Table 4-2 lists the kinds of things that you can type in the Criteria row of the design grid of a query.

Notes:

Table 4-2	What You Can Type in the Criteria Row	
Symbol	**Example**	**What It Means**
>	>10	Greater than 10
<=	<=100	Less than or equal to 100
>	>M	Starting with N or later
Between	Between 2 and 5	Between 2 and 5, including both 2 and 5
And	>2 And <5	Between 2 and 5, not including either 2 or 5
Is Null		Does not contain a value
Is Not Null		Does contain a value

Starting fresh

You can look for records that contain a range of values. For example, you can look for people with last names that begin with *P* or that start with *M* through *T*. Here's how:

on the CD

1 **If Access isn't running already, run Access. Open the Dickens Address Book 4 database.**

2 **Open the database window and click the Queries tab.**

3 **Make a new, blank query by clicking the <u>N</u>ew button on the database window (not the New Database button on the toolbar!), choosing Design View, and clicking OK.**

Access creates a new, blank query window named Query1. No field lists appear in the top half of the query window, because you haven't told Access which table (or tables) will provide the source of records for the query. Instead, Access displays the Show Table window shown in Figure 4-6. The Addresses table is highlighted.

4 **Click <u>A</u>dd (the Addresses table is already selected).**

A field list box for the Addresses table appears in the top half of the query window.

5 **Click <u>C</u>lose to get rid of the Show Table window.**

Now you can get a good look at the new query that you've created. The design grid in the lower half of the window is totally empty. Time to fill it in!

First, choose some fields to appear in the query result. An easy way is to enter some field names into the Field row of the design grid, which you do by dragging them from the field list in the upper half of the query window.

6 **Click FirstName in the field list in the top half of the query window. Holding down the mouse button, drag the field name to the Field row, in the first column of the design grid.**

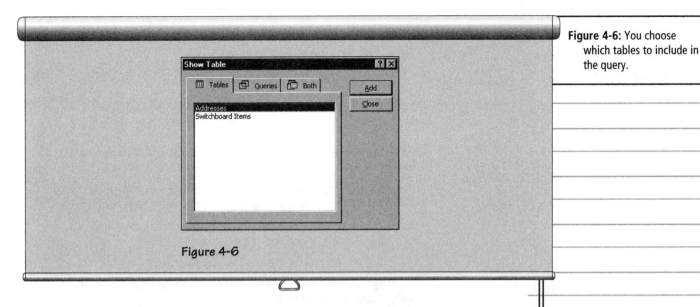

Figure 4-6

Figure 4-6: You choose which tables to include in the query.

FirstName appears in the Field row, and *Addresses* appears in the Table row, telling you exactly where the information for this column comes from. A check appears in the Show box for the column, indicating that the information will appear in the query results. Good enough.

Another way to add a field to the design grid is to double-click it in the field list.

7 **Double-click LastName in the field list.**

It appears in the Field row of the next blank column in the design grid.

8 **Scroll down the field list, using the little scroll bar to its right. Double-click the EmailAddress field and the HomePhone field.**

These two fields appear in the next two columns of the design grid. Your query result will have four columns. Sounds like a good number. Look at the query in Datasheet view to see how it's coming.

9 **Click the View button on the toolbar or choose View➪Datasheet View from the menu bar.**

You see four columns of information, sucked out of the Addresses table and shown on-screen.

10 **Switch back to Design view.**

To tell Access which fields to include in a query, you don't even have to type the field names — you can just click them in the field list in the top half of the query window.

When you use Design View to create a query instead of asking a wizard to do it, the query doesn't have a name until you close it. When you close the query, Access asks whether you want to save the query and, if you do, what name to use.

Tip: If you drag a field that you don't want after all, select the column in the design grid by clicking the gray bar at the top of the column and then press the Delete key to delete the column.

Notes:

Access puts quotes
around text in
Criteria row

Backspace and
Del delete
characters in
design grid

"Between" selects
a range of values

Selecting a range of names

But which records will appear? In Lesson 4-2, you entered a specific value in the Criteria row of the design grid to look for records that contain that value. In this lesson, you learn other ways to use the Criteria row to select records.

on the test

1 **In the Criteria row of the LastName column in the design grid, type >=M. Then press Tab or Enter.**

That is, you want people whose last names start with a letter greater than or equal to *M*. To computers, *greater than* means later in the alphabet.

When the cursor leaves the cell in the grid, Access puts quotes around the *M* to show that it is text information, not a number or a date.

2 **Switch to Datasheet view and look at the result.**

You see everybody from *Marley* to *Wickfield*. In the process of selecting people by their last names, Access alphabetizes the names, so they appear in Datasheet view in alphabetical order.

3 **Switch back to Design view.**

What if you want people whose last names start with letters from *M* to *T*?

4 **Click the LastName column in the Criteria row again and delete its contents.**

You can use the Backspace or Delete key to delete the characters in the cell, or you can select the contents of the cell with your mouse and press the Delete key.

5 **Type between m and t and press Tab or Enter.**

Access turns this entry into *Between "m" And "t"*. Whatever!

6 **Switch to Datasheet view.**

Now you see folks with names from *Marley* to *Scrooge*. (No one's name begins with *T* in this table.)

7 **Close the query window by clicking the window's Close button.**

Access asks whether you want to save changes to the query, which is currently named Query1.

8 **Click Yes.**

Access asks for the name of the query, suggesting Query1.

9 **Type People M Through T in the Query Name box and click OK.**

Access saves the query, and the new query name appears in the database window.

Entering formulas like >=M in the Criteria row of the design grid is easy. (Wow! Doesn't that sound impressive! Go tell someone that you just entered a formula in the Criteria row of a design grid.)

Looking for missing information

Some of the records in the Addresses table don't include phone numbers. How can you see only the records that don't have phone numbers? Read on, and you shall learn!

1 **Create a new query by copying the People M Through T query: Click the query in the database window, press Ctrl+C to copy it to the Windows Clipboard, and press Ctrl+V to paste it back. Name the new query Missing Phone Number.**

2 **Open the Missing Phone Number query in Design view by selecting it and clicking Design.**

This query includes the HomePhone field, which you use to select the records that you want to see.

3 **Delete the entry in the Criteria row of the LastName column.**

That is, take out the entry that tells Access to include only people with last names from *M* to *T*. One easy way is to highlight the entry with your mouse and then press the Delete key.

4 **In the Criteria row of the HomePhone column, type Is Null.**

This entry tells Access to include only records that have nothing in the HomePhone field. Your query should look like Figure 4-7.

5 **Switch to Datasheet view (by clicking the View button, the leftmost one on the toolbar).**

You see the one person who doesn't have a phone number. It's always possible that she doesn't *have* a phone — too bad you can't call her and ask!

6 **Close the query window.**

When Access asks whether you want to save your changes, click <u>Y</u>es.

The *Is Null* operator (that's its technical name) is useful for finding records that are missing information. Just type Is Null in the Criteria row of the design grid.

"Is Null" selects records with blank fields

Sorting the Results of a Query

Lesson 4-4

The results of queries can be very useful. In fact, printing a query in Datasheet view creates a report that doesn't look half bad. Most reports, however, require the records to be in some order, like alphabetical. In this lesson, you learn how to put the records in order by sorting them in the query.

on the test

To sort records, you use the Sort row in the design grid (logically enough). When you click in this row, a list button appears at the right end of the cell. When you click this button, you see a little menu with three choices: Ascending, Descending, and (*not sorted*). *Ascending* sorts text alphabetically from A to Z, numbers from lowest to highest, and dates from first to last. *Descending* sorts in exactly the opposite order of what Ascending uses. Choosing (*not sorted*) cancels sorting on this field.

sort records by setting Sort row to Ascending or Descending

Figure 4-7: The Is Null criterion selects people who don't have an entry in the HomePhone field.

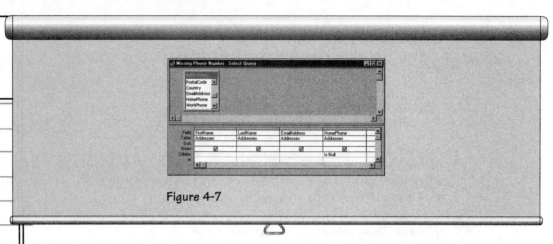

Figure 4-7

You can sort on more than one field if you like. Access sorts the leftmost column first (that is, the leftmost column for which you've chosen Ascending or Descending in the Sort row). For records in which the values of the leftmost column are the same, it sorts by the next column that you've told Access to sort by. For example, if you choose Ascending sorts for both LastName and FirstName and two records have the same last name, Access sorts those two records by first name.

In this lesson, you make a phone list for Dickens Address Book 4, sorting people by last name and first name. If Access isn't running with the Dickens Address Book 4 database open, run Access and open the database now.

Omitting fields from a query

1 **Make a new query by copying the Names and States query. Call the new query Phone List.**

Copy and paste the query by selecting it and pressing Ctrl+C and then Ctrl+V.

2 **Open the new query in Design view by clicking the Design button.**

This query contains columns for the fields FirstName, LastName, and StateOrProvince. Get rid of the StateOrProvince column and add a HomePhone column.

3 **Click the gray bar along the top of the design grid above the StateOrProvince column.**

The entire column turns black, showing that you have selected it.

4 **Press the Delete key.**

Access deletes the unwanted column. Don't worry — you haven't deleted the field from the Addresses table! You've just told Access not to include the field in this query.

5 **Double-click the HomePhone field in the field list in the top part of the query window.**

You have to scroll down the field list to find the HomePhone field. After you double-click the field, the field name and table name appear in the Field and Table rows of the third column of the design grid.

Notes:

6 **Switch to Datasheet view to see how your phone list looks so far: Click the View button.**

The list looks just fine, except that you need to tell Access to alphabetize the names. Also, the HomePhone column looks a little crowded — you'll widen it a bit.

7 **Switch back to Design view by clicking the View button again. Save the query by clicking the Save button on the toolbar (the icon of a diskette).**

The query remains open, but you've saved your work so far. You can save your query when you are in Design view or Datasheet view — it doesn't matter. If you don't like toolbar buttons, you can also choose File⇨Save from the menu bar or press Ctrl+S.

Nice work so far! You've got the beginnings of a very useful query.

Alphabetizing names

Now you can tell Access to sort your phone list into alphabetical order.

on the test

1 **Click the Sort row in the LastName column. Then click the gray triangle list button that appears at the right end of the cell.**

You see three choices: Ascending, Descending, and (not sorted).

2 **Choose Ascending to sort people's names from A to Z.**

3 **Switch to Datasheet view to see how it looks.**

When people have the same last name (like David and Dora Copperfield), it would be a good idea to sort them by first name.

4 **Switch back to Design view.**

5 **Set the Sort row in the FirstName column to Ascending.**

The LastName column therefore must be to the left of the FirstName column so that Access will alphabetize the names correctly — by last name and then (within the same last name) by first name. You can move the FirstName column to the right or the LastName column to the left.

6 **Click the gray bar along the top of the design grid above the FirstName column.**

The entire column turns black, showing that you have selected it.

7 **With your mouse pointer aimed at the gray bar along the top of the FirstName column, drag the whole column to the right, between the LastName and HomePhone columns.**

Release the mouse button when it points to the vertical line between the LastName and HomePhone columns. Now the LastName column comes before the FirstName column.

8 **Switch to Datasheet view to see how it looks now.**

save query by clicking Save button, pressing Ctrl+S, or choosing File→Save

Set Sort row to Ascending to alphabetize

select column by clicking gray bar at top

drag selected column where you want it

change column
width by dragging
column divider

9 **Widen the HomePhone column a bit by dragging the column divider (on the right) a little to the right.**

Move your mouse pointer to the top end of the column divider (the vertical line along the right end of a column). When your mouse pointer is on the top end of the column divider, the mouse pointer changes shape to a vertical line with arrows that point left and right. Hold down the mouse button and drag the column divider to the right.

The list is in the right order, and the HomePhone column is wider. Looks good!

10 **Close the window, saving your changes.**

You've created a great-looking phone list, with just the columns you wanted. Why not get on the phone yourself and tell someone how well you're learning Access!

extra credit

Making a new table with a query

You can store the result of a query in a new table, if you want. Usually, you don't need to create a new table to contain the result of a query, because you can just open the query to see its result. Also, if you store the result of a query today and the information in your tables changes tomorrow, the results you stored aren't automatically updated, the way query results are.

However, sometimes you may want to store the results of a query — for example, so that you can play around with the data in the new table without messing up the information in the original table. Or you may want to export the results of the query — save it in a file that another program can read.

To save the result of a query as a new table, create the query and work on it until it produces the result you want. In Design view, choose Query⇨Make-Table Query from the menu bar. When you see the Make Table dialog box, type the name for the new table and click OK. The query changes from a select query to a make table query. To make the new table, click the Run button on the toolbar (the one with the !) or choose Query⇨Run from the menu bar. Access asks you to confirm that you want to paste the records resulting from the query into a new table. Click Yes. Access makes the new table containing the results of the query.

☑ Progress Check

If you can do the following, you've mastered this lesson:

❑ Delete fields from a query.

❑ Sort a list in ascending or descending order on a particular field.

❑ Sort on more than one field.

❑ Change the sorting order when sorting on more than one field.

❑ Adjust column width.

Recess

Now you know how to use queries to see the information in your tables, selecting which fields and records you'd like to see. Don't stop now! You're ready to answer some queries about queries — the Unit 4 Quiz.

Unit 4 Quiz

For each of the following questions, circle the letter of the correct answer or answers. Remember, there may be more than one right answer for each question.

1. **A query is a way to . . .**

   A. Ask a question about a table (or several tables).

   B. See selected records from a table (or from several tables).

   C. See records sorted alphabetically.

   D. See only a few of the fields from a table.

   E. Drive yourself crazy.

2. **In the modern classic movie The Princess Bride, the unwilling princess' name is:**

   A. Alice

   B. Blondie

   C. Diana

   D. Queenie

   E. Buttercup

3. **To create a query, you can . . .**

   A. Enter information in the design grid in Design view.

   B. Use a Query Wizard.

   C. Type a question in English.

   D. Copy an existing query.

   E. Hire someone who knows how.

4. **You use the Criteria row of the design grid to:**

   A. Select the records to include in the query.

   B. Type the value that you want all records to match.

   C. Tell Access not to include records with a blank in a particular field.

   D. Specify the range of values to include.

   E. Enter critical remarks about the database.

5. **Which of the following are valid entries in the Criteria row of the QBE grid?**

   A. G

   B. Between A and Z

   C. No Kidding

   D. > 1000

   E. Is Nuts

6. **To sort the results of a query by LastName, then FirstName:**

   A. Set the LastName Sort row to Ascending.

   B. Set the FirstName Sort row to Ascending.

   C. Make sure that no other fields have entries in the Sort row.

   D. Make sure that the LastName column appears to the left of the FirstName column.

   E. All of the above.

Unit 4 Exercise

on the CD

1. Run Access and open the Dickens Address Book 4 database.

2. Create a new query by using the Simple Query Wizard. Include the LastName, FirstName, StateOrProvince, and EmailAddress fields.

3. Look at the query in Datasheet view.

4. Hmm. . . . Some people don't have e-mail addresses, so you decide to leave them out. In Design view, specify that you want only records with a value in the EmailAddress field. (Hint: Use the criterion Is Not Null.)

5. Sort the list by LastName and then FirstName.

6. Look at the result in Datasheet view.

7. Close the query, saving it as E-mail Address Directory.

Importing Information into Access

Prerequisites
▶ Running Access (Lesson 1-1)
▶ Creating and running a query (Lesson 4-1)

▶ Dickens Address Book 4 database (Dickens Address Book 4.mdb)
▶ Dickens Address Book 5 database (Dickens Address Book 5.mdb)
▶ Dickens Extras database (Dickens Extras.mdb)
▶ Dickens Extras Web page (Dickens Extras.htm)
▶ More Dickens Extras Web page (More Dickens Extras.htm)
▶ Dickens Extras text document (Dickens Extras.txt)

Objectives for This Unit

✓ Using information from an earlier version of Access

✓ Importing a table from another Access database

✓ Importing data from a Web page

✓ Importing data from a text file

on the test

*C*reating a database using Access is easy and doesn't require a lot of boring typing. But what about getting the information into the tables in the database? A database isn't of too much use without data. What if you need to enter the 1,000 customers that your boss wants you to analyze — think of all that typing! Well, take heart: If that data exists somewhere else on your PC, you can probably load it into your database. Access gives you the ability to *import* (that is, copy) data that's stored in many of the most popular formats:

▶ **Other Access databases.** You can import not only data from tables in other Access databases but any of the design elements as well, such as forms or queries.

▶ **Microsoft Excel spreadsheets.** Spreadsheets are so widely used and so easy to set up that a tremendous amount of information, in the business world at least, ends up in an Excel spreadsheet.

▶ **Lotus 1-2-3 spreadsheets.** If that data doesn't end up in an Excel spreadsheet, it's probably in a 1-2-3 spreadsheet. Access can handle any of the formats going all the way back to the prehistoric .wks formats. (Those were the days when your only choice other than Lotus 1-2-3 was a sharpened pencil.)

importing = copying info from other files

importable spreadsheets: Excel and Lotus 1-2-3

importable databases: Access, dBASE, FoxPro, and Paradox files

tables in Web pages are importable

importing makes a copy, leaving original unaffected

on the test

▶ **Tables in Microsoft Word or just about any other word processor.** If what you're looking at on your monitor is in tabular form, it can probably be put into Access.

▶ **dBASE files.** Access can read files created by dBASE Versions III, IV, and 5.

▶ **FoxPro files.** FoxPro is Microsoft's other database. Why does Microsoft need two? Good question — ask Bill Gates and let us know what his answer is.

▶ **Paradox tables.** Paradox is Corel's database and a competitor to Access and FoxPro. It comes with Corel WordPerfect and Perfect Office.

▶ **Comma-delimited files.** Comma-delimited files or comma-separated variables (or CSV) are a popular way of handling structured information, meaning things like tables, columns, rows, and such, as opposed to sentences and paragraphs. Each field in a file of this type is separated from the next field by a comma. If a field is empty, you see two commas right next to each other.

▶ **Fixed-width text files.** This file format is even more basic than comma-delimited files. To import fixed-width text files, you need to specify where each field is on the record, character by character. Not much fun, and time consuming!

▶ **HTML tables.** World Wide Web pages, or intranet pages, are written in HTML. You usually look at them using a Web browser such as Netscape. Web pages can contain tables of information in the form of lists or columnar tables.

▶ **ODBC.** *Open Database Connectivity* was developed by Microsoft to be a way for Access to communicate with other types of databases, like Sybase and Oracle, on other (usually more powerful) computers. In plain English, that means welcome to techno-nerd land. If you need to get at ODBC data on another machine, ask your local techno-nerd to put it on your PC. Tell her you'll accept it as a flat file in comma-delimited format. She'll be so impressed to hear you talk her language that she'll do it immediately.

If the application that you want data from can't produce a file in one of the formats listed, the hardware being used is probably pencil and paper, or even quill pens and parchment. If your source is an electronic medium, then more likely than not, you will be able to get the data into your Access database — it may just take a couple of steps.

extra credit

Importing versus linking

Although you are about to import data from other sources into Access, you should know that you have another way to use that data in Access. It's called *linking,* and you can link to almost anything you can import. When you import data, you make a copy of the data and bring it into Access. When you link, you connect with the data where it resides, no copy is made, and if the file you are linked to is deleted, your link will be broken. We don't cover linking in this book, so if you have this irresistible urge to link rather than import, we recommend *Access 97 For Windows For Dummies* by John Kaufeld (IDG Books Worldwide, Inc.).

extra credit

Using older versions of Access

Access 97 (also known as Access Version 8.0) stores its database in files with the MDB extension. Older versions of Access, such as Access 7 and Access 2.0, use this extension, too. However, Access 97 uses a new, improved file format that older versions of Access can't read.

Here's how it works: If you have a database created by an older version of Access, Access 97 can read it just fine. When you open an older database, Access 97 eagerly points out that the database is in an older format and asks whether you'd like to convert the database into the new Access 97 format. If you plan to use the database with both Access 97 and an older version of Access (for example, if you and a coworker

both use the database, and the coworker uses Access 7), decline Access 97's offer to convert the database into Access 97 format. You can open and use the database without converting it to the new file format, although you won't be able to make any design changes.

If you plan to use this database only with Access 97, go ahead and do the conversion. Access asks you for a new name to give the converted database. After you convert the database to Access 97 format, older versions of Access will choke if they try to read it. But you'll be able to use Access 97 to open and use the database, including making changes to the database design.

When you import data from another file, whatever its type, you don't change the data in the original file. When you import a rare pre-Columbian artifact from Peru, you deprive Peru of that artifact, but when you import data from another file into an Access database, the information exists unaffected in the original file. Importing makes a *copy* of the data. When you make changes to the information in Access, the original file isn't updated.

heads up

When you (or whoever) installed Access, you may not have installed all the importing options. If you want to import a type of file that your version of Access doesn't include (on the Import dialog box, which you'll see in Lesson 5-1), run the Access or Office 97 setup program again, click Add/Remove, choose Data Access as the type of options to add, and click Change Option. Be sure that the Database Drivers option is checked and then click OK and Continue.

In this unit, you'll import tables that bear a striking resemblance to the Addresses table that you created as part of the Dickens Address Book in Unit 2. You'll take the records you imported and append them to that table. *Append*, by the way, is a posh techno-speak way of saying "add to the end of." Imagine that you and your significant other have both read this tutorial and have decided to merge your address books into one. You append your S.O.'s address table to the end of your address table. If that scenario is too difficult to imagine, then pretend that you have wasted so much time trying to learn about Access before picking up this book that your better half has filed for divorce. Now you need to import all the addresses from your joint address book into your new, private address book.

As well as importing data from another Access database, you will import data from an Excel spreadsheet and a comma-delimited file. To get some extra credit, you can even try pulling a table from a Word document. These are the most common sources of data that you are likely to come across.

Notes:

appending =
adding records to
an existing table

heads up

Importing data isn't too complicated. But just because it's easy doesn't mean you don't need to think about why you're doing it. Remember that you're making a copy of the data. As soon as the import is complete, you'll have two tables in separate files with the same data. The two copies may remain identical for two seconds if you're lucky. One or both of those tables will undoubtedly change at some point, and if you're sharing resources with other people on a network, you may not even be the one making the changes.

Lesson 5-1

Importing Data from Another Access Database

Notes:

Wouldn't you know it? The data you want is in another Access database. You can't touch that database because it took you hours to create, and you couldn't live with yourself if you botched things up and broke it. A cowardly approach to take, we agree, but you had better believe that this, or something very like it, will happen to you. Or the database that contains the data you want will belong to someone else, who will kill you if you fool with it. You know what to do — import the data into your new database.

Here's another scenario: The data you want is in another Access database. You created that database ages ago, but it has fallen into disuse. However, it has one table that you would like to rescue for your current project. Again, you know what to do — import the data.

In general, you should import information into Access when you plan to use Access to maintain the data. In this lesson, you import a table named Addresses from the Dickens Extras database, an Access database, into the Dickens Address Book 4 database.

on the CD

1 **Run Access. Open the Dickens Address Book 4 database, close the Main Switchboard window, and maximize the database window.**

You don't really need to maximize the window, but we want you to try using maximized windows for a while so you can decide whether you like them. (*Hint*: Another way to maximize a window is to double-click in the title bar of the window. Cool!)

2 **Choose File➪Get External Data➪Import.**

You see the Import dialog box. Access starts by looking in the My Documents folder (as shown in the Look in box at the top of the dialog box). (If you are already looking in the *Dummies 101* Access 97 folder, skip to Step 4.)

import from Access
databases with
File→Get External
Data→Import

3 **Double-click the *Dummies 101* Access 97 folder.**

The Import dialog box now looks like Figure 5-1. The Files of type box shows what kind of file contains the information you want — right now, Microsoft Access is selected. You see a list of the Access databases in the *Dummies 101* Access 97 folder.

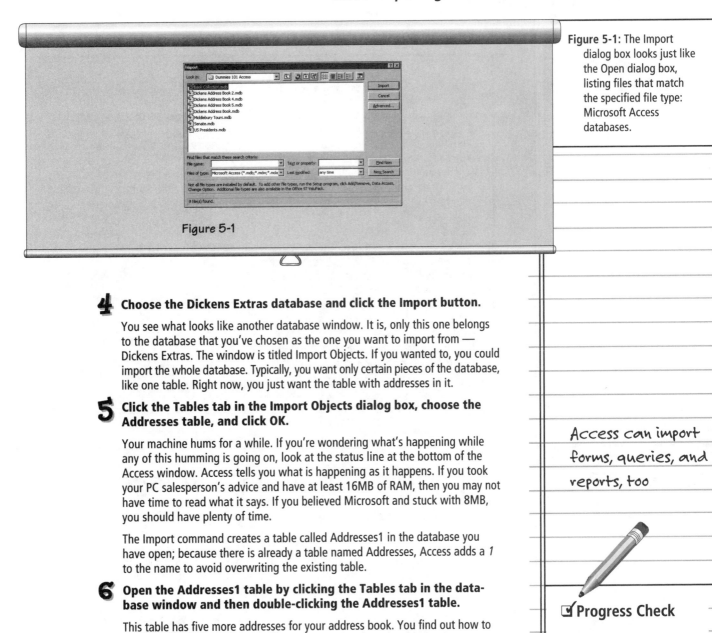

Figure 5-1: The Import
dialog box looks just like
the Open dialog box,
listing files that match
the specified file type:
Microsoft Access
databases.

Figure 5-1

4 Choose the Dickens Extras database and click the Import button.

You see what looks like another database window. It is, only this one belongs
to the database that you've chosen as the one you want to import from —
Dickens Extras. The window is titled Import Objects. If you wanted to, you could
import the whole database. Typically, you want only certain pieces of the database,
like one table. Right now, you just want the table with addresses in it.

**5 Click the Tables tab in the Import Objects dialog box, choose the
Addresses table, and click OK.**

Your machine hums for a while. If you're wondering what's happening while
any of this humming is going on, look at the status line at the bottom of the
Access window. Access tells you what is happening as it happens. If you took
your PC salesperson's advice and have at least 16MB of RAM, then you may not
have time to read what it says. If you believed Microsoft and stuck with 8MB,
you should have plenty of time.

The Import command creates a table called Addresses1 in the database you
have open; because there is already a table named Addresses, Access adds a *1*
to the name to avoid overwriting the existing table.

**6 Open the Addresses1 table by clicking the Tables tab in the data-
base window and then double-clicking the Addresses1 table.**

This table has five more addresses for your address book. You find out how to
combine these addresses with those in the Addresses table in Lesson 5-4.

**7 Close the Addresses1 table by clicking its Close (X) button, which is
just below the Close button for the whole Access window.**

You just moved some data from one Access database to another, and you
learned the principles of importing. It's all downhill from here!

This lesson showed you how to use a very powerful tool. Why retype information that's already in the computer when you can import it?

*Access can import
forms, queries, and
reports, too*

☑ **Progress Check**

If you can do the following,
you've mastered this lesson:

❑ Locate another database
by using the Import
window.

❑ Import a table from
another Access
database.

Notes:

Importing spreadsheet data

Some people like spreadsheet programs (like Lotus 1-2-3 and Excel) so much that everything they touch ends up in a spreadsheet: month-end numbers, a running P&L statement, that memo they sent to you last week, and their Christmas letter to Mom and Dad. Many wonderful spreadsheet products are available, and they can handle all of those things with a little bit of finagling. However, just as you should really use something like Word for writing your Christmas letters, sometimes you should really use Access. For example, spreadsheets are weak at sorting records, not so hot at selecting the records you want to work with, lousy at creating reports, and hopeless at printing mailing labels or form letters from information in a table.

If you want to import data from a spreadsheet, the spreadsheet must be formatted as a database. That is, each record must be on a separate row, with each field in a column. For example, column A contains the FirstName field, column B the LastName field, and so on. The first row of the spreadsheet can contain column headings so that the first record is on row 2. Or the records can start right on row 1.

To import a table from an Excel spreadsheet into Access, choose File⇨Get External Data⇨Import from the menu, set the Files of type setting to Microsoft Excel spreadsheets, and follow the directions on the screen. If Microsoft Excel doesn't appear as a type of file to import, you need to install additional Data Access options (see the introduction to this unit).

Lesson 5-2　Importing Data from Web Pages

Lots of information is now available on the World Wide Web, one of the most popular services on the Internet. If you work for a large organization, it may have its own internal Web, called an *intranet*. Whether a Web page is on the publicly available Internet or a private intranet, you can import data into Access.

Web page can contain tables of data

In order for importing to work, the data to be imported must be in a *table* on the Web page, that is, a section of the Web page formatted in rows and columns. Figure 5-2 shows a Web page with a table containing additional names and addresses for our Dickens Address Book 4 database. The Web page has to be stored on your hard disk, or on a disk that your computer can access. Saving Web pages is easy; in most browsers, you choose File⇨Save As (or Save As File) from the menu, choose where to save the file, and click Save. Be sure to save the Web page in HTML format so that it contains the formatting codes that Access looks for when importing from a Web page. Any Web page that contains a table of information imports very nicely into Access.

on the CD

In this lesson, you import a table from Dickens Extras.htm, a file containing the Web page shown in Figure 5-2, into the Dickens Address Book 4 database.

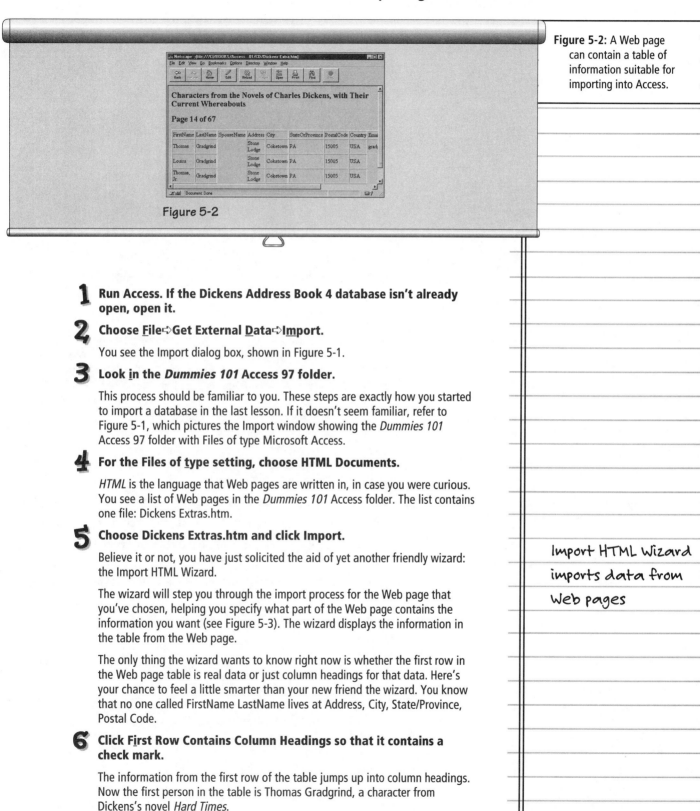

Figure 5-2

1 **Run Access. If the Dickens Address Book 4 database isn't already open, open it.**

2 **Choose File⇨Get External Data⇨Import.**

You see the Import dialog box, shown in Figure 5-1.

3 **Look in the *Dummies 101* Access 97 folder.**

This process should be familiar to you. These steps are exactly how you started to import a database in the last lesson. If it doesn't seem familiar, refer to Figure 5-1, which pictures the Import window showing the *Dummies 101* Access 97 folder with Files of type Microsoft Access.

4 **For the Files of type setting, choose HTML Documents.**

HTML is the language that Web pages are written in, in case you were curious. You see a list of Web pages in the *Dummies 101* Access folder. The list contains one file: Dickens Extras.htm.

5 **Choose Dickens Extras.htm and click Import.**

Believe it or not, you have just solicited the aid of yet another friendly wizard: the Import HTML Wizard.

The wizard will step you through the import process for the Web page that you've chosen, helping you specify what part of the Web page contains the information you want (see Figure 5-3). The wizard displays the information in the table from the Web page.

The only thing the wizard wants to know right now is whether the first row in the Web page table is real data or just column headings for that data. Here's your chance to feel a little smarter than your new friend the wizard. You know that no one called FirstName LastName lives at Address, City, State/Province, Postal Code.

6 **Click First Row Contains Column Headings so that it contains a check mark.**

The information from the first row of the table jumps up into column headings. Now the first person in the table is Thomas Gradgrind, a character from Dickens's novel *Hard Times*.

Import HTML Wizard imports data from Web pages

Figure 5-3: The Import HTML Wizard helps you import data from Web pages.

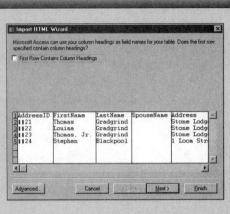

Figure 5-3

Notes:

7 **Click Finish.**

You could have chosen Next if you wanted to selectively include or exclude fields or change some of their attributes if required, including which field is to be used as a primary key. By choosing Finish, you ask the wizard to use all the fields in the spreadsheet just as they are. Because the wizard is not sure which of the fields would work as a primary key, the wizard also creates a new AutoNumber field to be used as primary key for the table.

When finished, the wizard lets you know that it has Finished importing file 'C:\...\DickensExtras.xls' to table 'Table.' Not a particularly creative name: you'd better change the table name so you remember where the information came from.

8 **Read the message to check what you have done, and then click OK.**

Each column in the Web page table has turned into a field in the Table table.

9 **If the Table table isn't selected in the database window, click it once to select it. Then click it again.**

This action tells Access that you want to edit the name of the table. Your cursor appears at the end of the table name, which is highlighted.

10 **Type Addresses From Web Page and press Enter.**

Access changes the name of the table.

11 **Open the new Addresses From Web Pages table, take a look, and close the window.**

Now you know how to grab information from the Internet or your organization's intranet and stick it into Access. Cool!

Tip: You just learned how to rename a table. You can use the same method to rename queries, forms, and reports in Access.

rename table by clicking name twice (slowly), then typing new name

☑ **Progress Check**

If you can do the following, you've mastered this lesson:

❑ Import a table on a Web page into Access.

❑ Rename a table.

Importing Text Files into Access

Lesson 5-3

Text files are everywhere, because almost every program can create them. Text files can contain almost anything, from love letters to memos to laundry lists. Most text files can't and shouldn't be imported into Access, because they don't contain lists of items that will fit nicely into tables. However, if a text file is properly formatted, Access can import the information in it into an Access database. The most convenient format for importing text files is *comma-delimited text*, described at the beginning of this unit.

Importing text is a lot like importing an Access table or a Web page. Because we don't want you to get bored, you will take control of the process yourself in this lesson rather than let the wizard do all the work.

on the CD

In this lesson you import Dickens Extras.txt, the text file shown in Figure 5-4, into the same database you've been using in this unit.

1 **Open the Dickens Address Book 4 database.**

You're going to import the text file shown in Figure 5-4, a comma-delimited file. Each record is on a separate line in the text file. The fields are separated by commas. In some comma-delimited files, each field is enclosed in quotes.

2 **Choose File⇨Get External Data⇨Import.**

You see the Import window, shown in Figure 5-1.

3 **Look in the *Dummies 101* Access 97 folder.**

This process must be getting pretty boring by now. You've done this three times! That means you have no excuse for making a mistake.

4 **Set the Files of type to Text Files. Choose Dickens Extras.txt and click Import.**

Access runs the Import Text Wizard window (shown in Figure 5-5), a good friend of the Import Spreadsheet Wizard that you met in the last lesson. It shows the records from the text file you are importing. This wizard can import two kinds of text files: comma-delimited files (like one you are importing) and fixed-width text files, described at the beginning of this unit.

Your resident magician wants to know which type of text file you're importing. It has guessed correctly that this is a delimited file, with commas delimiting (separating) the fields. Each line in the file contains one record. As you scan the two records, notice that the extra commas indicate empty fields.

5 **Click Next.**

The Import Text Wizard prompts you for more information about the type of delimiter used in the file. Although commas are usually the field delimiters in these sorts of files, you may find other special characters like the ones listed here. The wizard knows about the most common ones but lets you specify just about anything as a delimiter, so this wizard can deal with many different types of files. The lower window shows you how the information from the file would be split into fields if you used the delimiter indicated in the upper window.

---

comma-delimited file = text file with one record per line, fields separated by commas

tell wizard whether your fields are separated by commas

Figure 5-4: You can import comma-delimited files, in which each record is on one line and each field is enclosed in quotes and separated by a comma from the next field.

Figure 5-5: The Import Text Wizard shows the two records you are about to import.

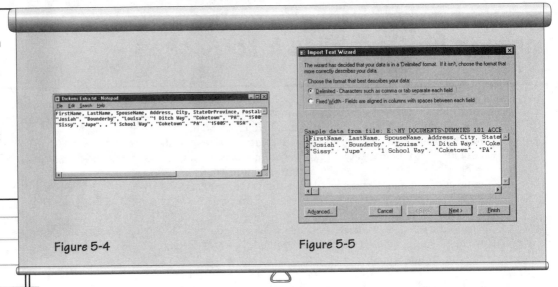

Figure 5-4   Figure 5-5

Notes:

If you happen to be importing a text table that has column headings in the first line of the file (which, in fact, you are), you can recognize them as column headings rather than text, just as you did when importing the spreadsheet.

6 Click First Row Contains Field Names so that its box contains a check mark.

This setting avoids importing a record for FirstName LastName living in City, State. The text in the first row of the text file stops appearing as a record to be imported and now appears as column headings.

The names in the two records appear with quotes around each field. The quotes shouldn't be imported as part of the finished table, should they?

7 Click the gray list button at the right end of the Text Qualifier box and choose " from the menu that appears.

The quotes disappear. Now Access knows that the quotes aren't part of the data you want to import.

8 Click Next.

Access now wants to know whether to add these records to an existing table, if an existing table has exactly the same fields in the same order as the table that you're importing, or whether to put the records in a new table.

9 Click In a New Table if it's not already selected, and then click Next.

The wizard now asks for information about each field (see Figure 5-6). If the first line of the text file didn't contain field names you could type them in now.

As you highlight each column in the lower part of the window, you see the information about that column in the Field Options section. For each column, you can specify the Field Name to use, whether the field should be indexed (so you can tell Access if one of the fields should be the primary key field), and what type of information the field contains. If the column contains unimportant information or is empty, you can click the Do not import field (Skip) box to skip importing the column.

All the fields in this table look worth importing, so don't skip any.

if first row contains field names, tell Access

Text Qualifier = character that surrounds each text field, if any

skip columns you don't want to import

10 **Click Next.**

Access wants to know whether to add a primary key field to the table. Sure, why not?

11 **Click Next.**

Access suggests importing the data into a new table named Dickens Extras. Sounds good to us!

12 **Click Finish.**

You hear more humming from your PC as the wizard does everything you just asked it to do. The wizard tells you `Finished importing file 'C:\...\Dickens Extras.txt' to table 'Dickens Extras.'`

13 **Click OK to make the message go away. Then open the Dickens Extras table and look around.**

Did Access get it right when it divided each line of the text file into fields?

You covered a lot of ground here, so take some time to understand what you just did. If you want to try again, you can go through the same steps again. You'll end up creating another table with a different name, but that's okay.

☑ Progress Check

If you can do the following, you've mastered this lesson:

❏ Identify the type of text file you're importing.

❏ Tell Access whether your text file contains field names.

❏ Choose which fields to import and which to skip.

Combining Data from Two Tables

Lesson 5-4

You're probably thinking to yourself, "All that work, and the data is still in separate tables — none of which is the one I want! Who wants tables named Addresses, Addresses1, Dickens Extras, and Addresses From Web Page?" That's true, but you can now easily take the records from the tables you just created and put them in another table. In this lesson, you copy all the data from the tables you imported into your Addresses table.

on the test

The tool you use to perform this wondrous feat is called a *query*. As you learned in Unit 4, queries are multifaceted tools. One of their uses is to take data from one table and add it to another table. This type of query is known as an *append query*. To create an append query, make a select query (the kind you made in Unit 4) and then use Query⇨Append Query command to change it into an append query. You can make the select query any way you like; in this exercise, you'll get the Simple Query Wizard to help you.

append query copies records from one table to another

on the CD

In this lesson, you'll copy the records from the tables you created in Lessons 5-1, 5-2, and 5-3 into the Addresses table in the Dickens Address Book 4 database. Once you've got all the imported records in the Addresses table, you can delete the tables you imported.

1 **If the Dickens Address Book 4 database isn't already open, open it. Close the Main Switchboard window and open the database window.**

If you didn't do the steps in Lessons 5-1, 5-2, and 5-3, open the Dickens Address Book 5 database, which has the tables that you would have created.

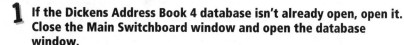

Figure 5-6: The Import Text Wizard lets you enter field names and skip importing fields you don't want.

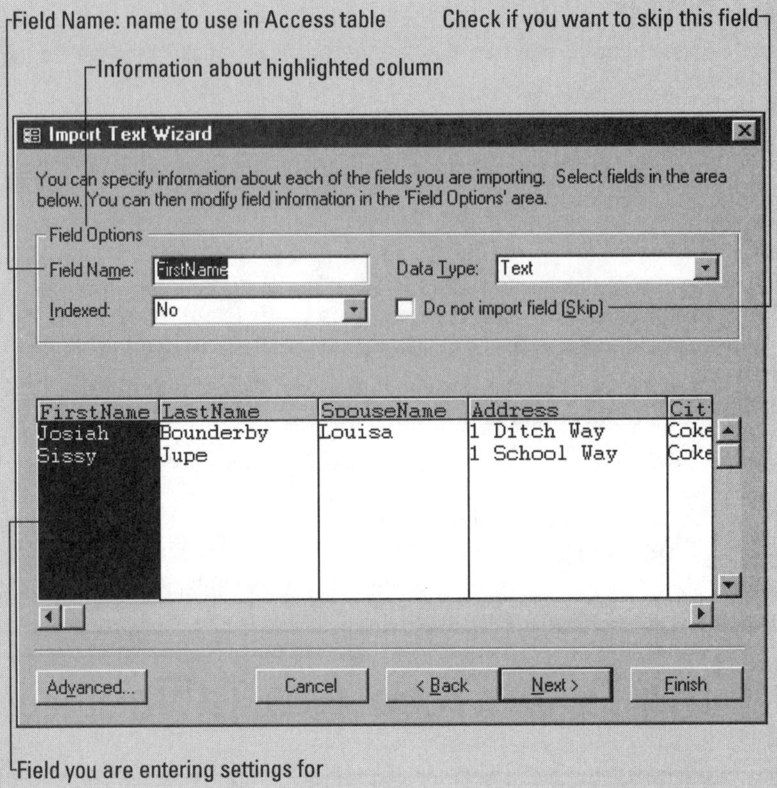

Field Name: name to use in Access table   Check if you want to skip this field

Information about highlighted column

Import Text Wizard

You can specify information about each of the fields you are importing. Select fields in the area below. You can then modify field information in the 'Field Options' area.

Field Options

Field Name: FirstName   Data Type: Text

Indexed: No   ☐ Do not import field (Skip)

FirstName	LastName	SpouseName	Address	Cit
Josiah	Bounderby	Louisa	1 Ditch Way	Coke
Sissy	Jupe		1 School Way	Coke

Advanced...   Cancel   < Back   Next >   Finish

Field you are entering settings for

Figure 5-6

Notes:

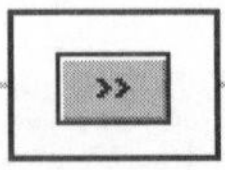

>>

Select All button

2 Click the Queries tab and the New button in the database window.

You see the New Query window with a list of the options for creating different types of queries.

3 Choose Simple Query Wizard and click OK.

As shown in Figure 5-7, the wizard allows you to grab any fields from one or more tables or queries. You are spoilt for choice here (as they say in Britain).

Make this query take its records from the Addresses1 table, the one you imported from the Dickens Extras database in Lesson 5-1.

4 Click in the Tables/Queries box and choose Table: Addresses1 from the list that appears.

The Available Fields list now shows all the fields in the Addresses1 table.

5 Click the Select All button (double arrow pointing to the right) to choose all the available fields. Then click Next.

The wizard moves all the available fields into the Selected Fields list. The Available Fields list is empty — you have no more fields to select. Don't panic if the Selected Fields list looks a little different from the Available Fields list. The wizard has actually positioned you at the bottom of the Selected Fields list. Scroll to the top of the list, and the list appears just as the same as it was in Available Fields.

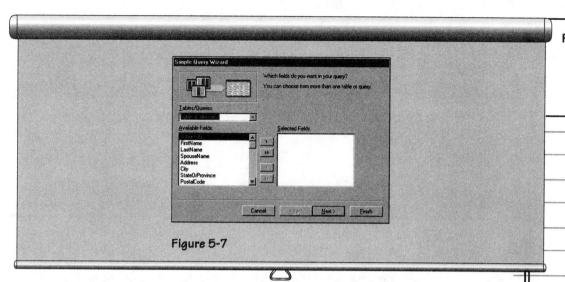

Figure 5-7

Figure 5-7: The Simple Query Wizard lets you choose which tables or queries contain the fields you want.

If you didn't want to copy all the fields from the Addresses1 table into the Addresses table, you could use the Select and Deselect buttons between the two lists to allow you to move all the fields or individual fields back and forth between the lists. To move an individual field, click it to highlight it and then click one of the single-arrow buttons to move it in the direction you want.

6 **Choose Detail (if it's not already selected) and then click Next.**

You don't want any of your addresses summarized. Do you? *Summarizing fields* means that you want totals, counts, or averages of the values in the field, instead of the values themselves.

The Simple Query Wizard wants to know what name to give the new query.

7 **Leave the Query name alone — it's just fine the way it is. Click Modify the query design and then Finish.**

By choosing to modify the query design, you tell the Simple Query Wizard to show you the query in Design view, which you may remember from Unit 4. Say thank you and good-bye to the wizard. You're now going to complete the design without its aid.

8 **From the menu bar, choose Query⇨Append Query to change this query from a select query to an append query.**

Access wants to know what table to add the records to and displays the Append dialog box shown in Figure 5-8.

9 **Click the list button at the right end of the Table Name box and choose the Addresses table. Then click OK.**

The name of the query changes in the title bar of the query window. You're adding the data to a table in the current database — that is, the Dickens Address Book database. If you wanted, you could add this data to a table in another database.

Access also adds an extra row (Append To) to the design grid window for the query, as shown in Figure 5-9. The Append To row represents the fields with which to match your query field names in the row labeled Field. In other words,

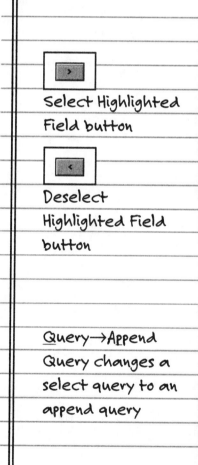

Select Highlighted Field button

Deselect Highlighted Field button

Query→Append Query changes a select query to an append query

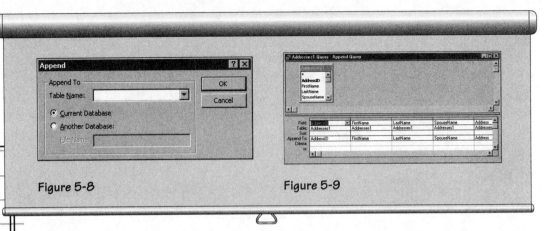

Figure 5-8: You tell Access which table to add these records to.

Figure 5-9: The Append Query window shows how fields will be copied into another table.

Figure 5-8   Figure 5-9

Append To row = field to put the data into

Run button

☑ Progress Check

If you can do the following, you've mastered this lesson:

❑ Use the Simple Query Wizard to create a query.

❑ Turn a simple query into an append query in Design view.

❑ Match fields in the query with those in the table that you're adding to.

what field in the Addresses table should receive the values from the FirstName field in the query? This row appears only in append queries. Access has matched up identical field names. If a field name was misnamed, you can click the list button at the end of the Append To field and select from the list of fields in the Address table.

10 **Because the field names match perfectly, choose Query⇨Run from the menu bar or click the Run button on the toolbar.**

A message tells you that what you are about to do is permanent and that you cannot undo it later. Right now, you know that the query will work because you have followed our instructions very closely. In the real world, take the time to read the message and ensure that Access is doing what you expect.

heads up

When you append records using an append query, Access applies its various rules regarding what information you can enter into a table. Access complains if you import information that violates its rules. For example, if you try to append a record that has the same value for the primary key field as an existing record, Access won't do it — Access refuses to allow two records to have the same primary key value. Similarly, Access may refuse to append records that violate other types of rules.

11 **Click OK.**

You're done, but clean up before you dash off to see what's happened.

12 **Close the Addresses1 Query window, choose Yes to save it, and leave it with that name.**

You don't *need* to save it — it's already done its job — but you may want to use it again some other time.

13 **Open the Addresses table in Datasheet view and look at what you've done.**

Look! The records from the Addresses1 table have appeared at the end of the table!

14 **Close the database.**

Tip: When appending records to a table that has an AutoNumber field, you may want to let Access number the records automatically. That is, don't import any field into the AutoNumber field.

Recess

Thank heavens that you now know how to import information into Access! Now you won't have to retype all the information that you've already got in other types of files. Close your eyes and meditate briefly on how much time importing will save you and then get ready for the Unit 5 Quiz.

That's it. You can take data from just about anywhere and bring it, as a new table, into your database. You can take it as it comes, or you can skip a few fields. After the data is in your database as a table, you can use an append query to add it to an existing table. As you get more comfortable with Access and more knowledgeable about its capabilities, you'll find yourself bringing all sorts of data into Access databases. Once you have the information in Access, it is truly at your mercy.

Unit 5 Quiz

For each of the following questions, circle the correct answer or answers:

1. **Importing data means . . .**

   A. Buying data from overseas and bringing it into this country.

   B. Using data from someone else's computer.

   C. Copying data from another file into your Access database.

   D. Copying data from your Access database into another file.

   E. Dragging a file into Access.

2. **Which is true when you are importing a delimited file?**

   A. Commas are the only valid delimiters.

   B. A space can be used as a delimiter.

   C. Tabs can be used as delimiters.

   D. You can specify your own delimiter.

   E. You can specify more than one delimiter for a single import.

3. **What can you import to Access?**

   A. Excel spreadsheets

   B. Access tables

   C. Tables on Web pages

   D. Comma-delimited files

   E. All of the above

4. **To add the records from one table to another table, you can . . .**

    A. Create an append query.

    B. Print the first table and then type the records back into the second table.

    C. Open both tables and use Windows Cut and Paste commands to copy records from one to the other.

    D. All of the above.

5. **In Dickens's classic *A Christmas Carol*, Ebenezer Scrooge is visited by . . .**

    A. His mother.

    B. Three ghosts.

    C. His nephew, inviting him to a Christmas party.

    D. Two men asking for charitable contributions.

    E. An IRS auditor.

6. **To create an append query, you can . . .**

    A. Use the Simple Query Wizard to create a select query and then change it into an append query.

    B. Use Design view to create a query from scratch and then change it into an append query.

    C. Choose Insert⇨Append Query from the menu.

    D. Click the Append Query button on the toolbar.

    E. Clip one out of this book and paste it onto the front of your monitor.

Unit 5 Exercise

1. Open the Dickens Address Book 4 database in Access.

2. Import the More Dickens Extras Web page (More Dickens Extras.htm).

3. Add the imported addresses to the Addresses table, using an append query.

Part II Review

Unit 3 Summary

▶ **Viewing records:** You can look at records in a table in Datasheet view or in a form in either Form view or Datasheet view.

▶ **The record selector:** *Triangle:* You have selected this record. *Pencil:* You are editing this record. *Asterisk:* This is a new record. *Do not enter:* You can't edit this record because someone else in your network is using it.

▶ **Movement commands:** Pressing Tab or Enter moves to the next field. F2 moves to the beginning of the field. Home moves to the first field of the current record. End moves to the last field of the current record. PgDn moves to the next record. PgUp moves to the previous record. Ctrl+↓ moves to the current field in the last record. Ctrl+↑ moves to the current field in the first record. Ctrl+Home moves to the first field in the first record. Ctrl+End moves to the last field in the last record.

▶ **Edit commands:** Ctrl+' duplicates the value of a field from the prior record. Ctrl+; inserts the current date. Ctrl+Z or Esc undoes what you typed in the current record. Ctrl+Enter enters a newline character in a text field. Backspace deletes the character to the left or the high-lighted text. Delete deletes the character to the right or the highlighted text.

▶ **Cut and Paste commands:** Ctrl+C copies data to the Clipboard. Ctrl+V pastes data from the Clipboard.

▶ **Special entry fields:** Combo boxes let you choose a value from a list by clicking the list button or pressing F4. Radio buttons let you choose a single option from the choices pre-sented.

▶ **Deleting records:** Select a record or group of records by clicking in the record selector field. Then press Delete.

▶ **Finding stuff:** Use the Find button or Ctrl+F to see the Find window. Find First starts at the beginning of the table; Find Next starts at the current record. To restrict your search and speed it up in large tables, select the Search Only Current Field box. You can also restrict your search by using the Match box and choosing to match using Whole Field, Any Part of Field, or Start of Field.

Unit 4 Summary

▶ **Creating a query:** To create a query, click New in the Queries tab of the database window, click the New Object button on the Toolbar and choose Query, or choose Insert⇨Query from the menu bar.

▶ **Simple Query Wizard:** This wizard creates queries based on one table and lets you choose which fields to include in the query.

▶ **Design view for queries:** The top half of the window shows a list of fields for each table for which information is to be included. The bottom half of the window shows the design grid that includes rows showing the field selected, the table that the field comes from, what type of sort is applied to this column, whether the column should show in the query results, and the criteria used to select records that match certain parameters.

▶ **Copying a query:** Select the query in the database window, press Ctrl+C to copy, and press Ctrl+V to paste a copy into the database. Enter a new name when prompted.

▶ **Switching between views:** In Datasheet view, choose View⇨Design View from the menu bar. In Design view, choose View⇨Datasheet View. In either view, click the View button on the toolbar.

▶ **Sorting records:** In the Sort row of the design grid, specify whether a column is to be sorted in ascending order, sorted in descending order, or not sorted at all. If more than one column has a sort selected, Access sorts the records starting with the left-most sorted column and finishing with the right-most sorted column.

Part II Review

Unit 5 Summary

▶ **Files you can import information from:** Other Access databases, Excel spreadsheets, 1-2-3 spreadsheets, Word tables, dBASE files, FoxPro files, Paradox databases, Web pages (that is, HTML files), and comma-delimited and fixed-width text files.

▶ **Importing data:** Choose File⇨Get External Data⇨Import and then select the Files of type setting. When you import data, you end up with two separate copies of the data: one in your database and one in the data's original location.

▶ **Importing from another Access database:** You can import tables, queries, forms, and reports from another Access database.

▶ **Importing delimited text files:** The delimiters can be commas, tabs, semicolons, spaces, or something else that you specify yourself.

▶ **Importing Web pages:** You can import tables from Web pages. Each row of the table becomes a record, and each column becomes a field.

▶ **Using the append query to add records to a table:** Choose Query⇨Append Query, select the tables that you want to add to, and match up fields by using the Append To row in the design grid. Then click the Run button to run the query. You don't need to save the query if you don't plan to use it again.

Part II Test

The questions on this test cover all the material presented in Part II, Units 3 through 5.

True False

T　F　1. Press F4 to edit the contents of a field.

T　F　2. To create a new record, you click the New Record button on the navigation bar.

T　F　3. You don't have to type the same field value over and over for subsequent records; press Ctrl+' instead.

T　F　4. To enter today's date, type **@date**.

T　F　5. Combo boxes and radio boxes are both useful when a field can accept only certain values.

T　F　6. The gray box in the left margin of a form or datasheet is called the *record selector.*

T　F　7. The little binoculars icon on the Toolbar is for scanning the database for errors.

Part II Test

T   F   8. Once you have used a Wizard to create a query, you cannot change that query yourself.

T   F   9. You can use the Windows Cut (Ctrl+C) and Paste (Ctrl+V) commands to copy a query.

T   F   10. The Import Text Wizard allows you to specify that the column headings in the first row of the text file be used as field names in the new table being created.

Multiple Choice

For each of the following questions, circle the correct answer or answers. Remember, each question may have more than one right answer!

11. **A combo box is . . .**

  A. A combination of a table and a query.

  B. A box that you can click to combine two records.

  C. A box that you can click to see a list of possible values for a field.

  D. Two tacos, fries, and a shake.

  E. One from column A and one from column B.

12. **Using the Find dialog box, you can . . .**

  A. Search anywhere in the table for a field that matches your search condition exactly.

  B. Search for a field that begins with your search condition.

  C. Search for the meaning of life.

  D. Search for a SWF who enjoys dining out and walks in the rain.

  E. Start searching back at the beginning of the table when you are positioned partway through the table.

13. **Which of the following is/are *not* a type of query?**

  A. Select query.

  B. Analyze query.

  C. Append query.

  D. Simple query.

  E. Make table query.

14. **Which of the following criteria statements is/are correct?**

  A. *>23* means greater than 23.

  B. *<=10* means less than or equal to 10.

  C. *Between 600 and 800* includes 600 and 800 in the results.

  D. *Is Null* means does not contain a value.

  E. All of the above.

15. **Dickens's *A Tale of Two Cities* is about . . .**

  A. New York and London during the great financial collapse.

  B. London and Edinburgh during the wars between England and Scotland.

  C. London and Paris during the French Revolution.

  D. London and Madrid during the Spanish Armada.

  E. New York and Atlanta during the 1996 World Series.

Part II Test

Matching

16. Match the Toolbar or navigation bar button with its name.

A. Find button   1.

B. New Record button   2.

C. Run button   3.

D. New Object button   4.

E. View button   5.

17. Match the following keys with what they do.

A. Ctrl+Z   1. Displays the Find dialog box

B. Esc   2. Undoes the changes that you've made to the current record or, if you're editing a field, to the current field

C. Ctrl+;   3. Enters today's date in the current field

D. Ctrl+"   4. Enters the same thing that you typed in the current field of the previous record

E. Ctrl+F

18. Match the Criteria row entry with what it does.

A. Between 1 and 10   1. Matches values from 1 to 10, not including 1 and 10

B. Is Not Null   2. Matches the value *VT*

C. "VT"   3. Matches any value except a blank

D. >="S"   4. Matches values from 1 to 10 (inclusive)

E. >1 And < 10   5. Matches values that start with the letter *S* or later

19. Match the design grid row with what it's for.

A. Field   1. Tells Access whether to sort on this field

B. Table   2. Specifies the table that the information comes from

C. Sort   3. Selects records

D. Show   4. Indicates whether to include this column in the query results

E. Criteria   5. Specifies the field that the information comes from

20. Match the *Star Wars* character with his, her, or its description.

A. Han Solo   1. Guy learning to be a Jedi warrior

B. Leia   2. Yucky monster

C. Jabba the Hut   3. Princess

D. Luke Skywalker   4. Jedi master

E. Yoda   5. Reluctant hero

Part II Lab Assignment

on the CD

In this lab, you take data from the database that you created in the Part I Lab Assignment and import it into another database that you create here. If you skipped that lab, you need to go back and do it now. You import the records from the Books table in the Dickens Books database into the database you created.

Step 1: Open your Books database

Open the database that you created in the Part I Lab Assignment.

Step 2: Import another Books table

Import the Books table from the Dickens Books database in the *Dummies 101* Access 97 folder.

Step 3: Add the new records to your Books table

Use an append query to add the newly imported table to the existing Books table. Because the field names are the same, no changes should be required.

Step 4: Review the information in the Books table

Look at the information in the Books table however you like: Either look at the table in Datasheet view or print out a report, using the Main Switchboard.

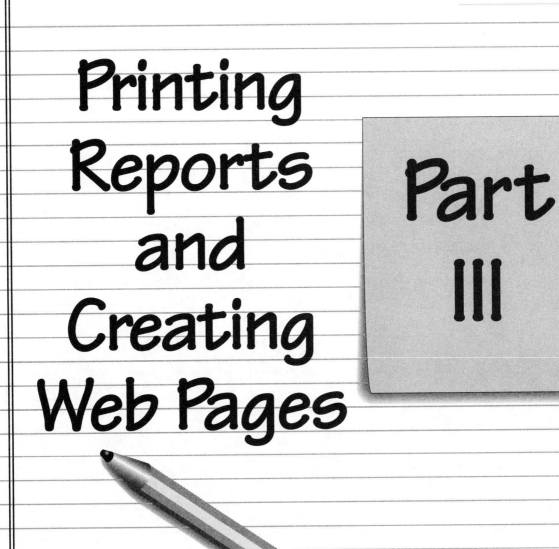

Printing Reports and Creating Web Pages

Part III

In this part . . .

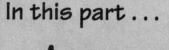fter you get information in your database, you are ready to do something with it. For example, you'd probably like to print some reports that you can show other people. Even before finding out about how to create and use reports, there's an easy way to make some nice-looking printouts — print tables or queries in Datasheet view. When you print a datasheet, as you'll see in Unit 6, the printout shows a grid or rows and columns in the same layout you see on the screen.

If you want a report with subtotals, totals, and other amenities, a datasheet can't cut the mustard. Instead, you can create a report, as you do in Unit 7. The Report Wizard steps you through the process, asking what fields should appear and what order the records should be sorted in. Mailing labels, the bane of most database users, are also a type of report, and they are a breeze in Access — you just run the Label Wizard to produce great-looking labels!

A newfangled way to let other people see the information in your database is to publish the information as a Web page, either on the Internet's World Wide Web or on your organization's intranet. Either way, creating a Web page showing information from your Access database is just as easy as creating a report. Access comes with the Publish on the Web Wizard, which does all the hard work. You'll learn all about the fabulous Web Wizard in Unit 7.

Formatting and Printing Datasheets

Objectives for This Unit

✓ Making your datasheet look pretty by eliminating big white gaps

✓ Switching the order of the columns on the datasheet

✓ Selecting which columns appear on the datasheet by hiding unwanted columns

✓ Choosing which field to sort the records in a datasheet

✓ Previewing your document before you click the Print button

✓ Printing selected pages or multiple copies

✓ Printing both table and query results as datasheets

Prerequisites

▶ A working printer attached to your computer (either directly or via a local area network), with all required supplies (ink cartridge, paper)

▶ Working knowledge of the buttons, knobs, switches, and flashing lights on your printer

▶ Looking at a table in Datasheet view (Lesson 1-3)

▶ Looking at the result of a query in Datasheet view (Lesson 4-2)

on the CD

▶ US Senate Database (US Senate.mdb)

▶ Dickens Address Book 4 database (Dickens Address Book 4.mdb)

▶ Dickens Address book5 database (Dickens Address book 5.mdb)

Creating a database is usually pointless if you can't get the information out on paper. Luckily, Access lets you print all kinds of paperwork — reports, datasheets, and forms are the most common documents to print. This unit describes how to get Access to print datasheets, as well as how to make a datasheet look good before you print it. If all you need is a straightforward list of information from one of your tables or queries, you can print it directly from Datasheet view. You can even spruce up the appearance of your datasheet by changing column widths, printing sideways on the paper, adjusting the font, or sorting the records in a different sequence.

A datasheet is simply a window into a table or the results of a query. So printing information from either of these sources is essentially the same: Display the datasheet, dress it up a bit, and then print it. If you want the datasheet to contain all the fields and records in a table, open the table in Datasheet view. If you want your printout to contain selected fields and records, create a query (as described in Unit 4) and then open the query in Datasheet view.

In Unit 7, you will learn how to create your own reports so that you can print information in ways that datasheets can't display. Why go to the trouble of creating reports if you can just print datasheets? The truth is that reports are much more flexible than datasheets. In a report, you aren't limited to the rows-and-columns grid layout of a datasheet, and you can add subtotals, pictures, lines, and boxes. Using reports, you can even print labels and envelopes. Unit 7 will also tell you how to create Web pages (for use on the Internet or on your organization's intranet) using information from your database.

If you have been using your computer for a while and have been printing other stuff, like word-processing documents, spreadsheets, or graphics downloaded from the World Wide Web, then printing datasheets from an Access database is a piece of cake. All the hard work needed to connect your computer to a working printer has been done already. However, if you have never printed a thing before, you may need to jump through a few printer configuration hoops first. What's more, we can't help much because each configuration and printer is unique. We recommend cultivating a friendship with someone who can help. Plan on acquiring some pizza or warm chocolate chip cookies to use as a bribe. The nice thing is that once you're set up, the only thing you need to worry about is replacing the paper and ink supplies.

In this unit, you use the US Senate database, which contains a list of the 100 members of the U.S. Senate as of the election of 1996.

on the CD

*printing
datasheets =
easy way to
create printout*

*datasheet can
show contents of
table or results of
query*

Lesson 6-1

Adjusting Datasheet Columns

Printing a datasheet may be the simplest way of getting your data onto paper. But for a datasheet to meet your needs, you may need to make it look better. You can

on the test

- **Change the column width:** In this lesson, you make columns narrow and wider.

- **Move a column around on the datasheet:** You can drag a column to another location, to change the order in which the columns appear. You'll try this technique later in this lesson.

- **Hide a column:** If you don't want to print a particular field, you can "hide" its column. See Lesson 6-3.

- **Sort the datasheet:** In Lesson 6-2, you'll sort the records in a datasheet into different orders.

- **Change fonts:** Don't like Arial? No problem! You'll try some other fonts later in this lesson.

▶ **Filter records:** If you don't want to include all the records in the table and you're too busy to make a query that selects the records you want, you can filter the datasheet instead. A *filter* is a temporary query that specifies the records you want. When you close the datasheet, Access forgets the filter. We don't teach filters in this course — use a query instead.

To make many of these changes, you use the column headings at the top of the datasheet. In Microsoft parlance, the column headings are known as *field selectors,* which is not a bad name: You use them to select the fields whose columns you want to fool around with. When you point your mouse at a field selector, the mouse pointer changes shape to show you that clicking field selectors has an effect.

You can also do things to columns in a datasheet by right-clicking the column's field selector. A little menu, called a *shortcut menu,* appears, listing things that you can do to the column. In this lesson, you use a shortcut menu to change the width of a column. (Of course, if you've told Windows 95 to swap the meanings of your two mouse buttons, perhaps because you are left-handed, then you've been using the right mouse button all along, and you have to use the *left* mouse button to bring up the shortcut menu.)

Now for the fun part: Put on your painter's cap because what happens now is more art than science. As you follow the instructions, remember that tastes differ, so what we think looks good is not necessarily the same as what you think looks good.

Changing column widths

First step: Make some of those columns wider or narrower!

on the CD

1 Run Access, open the US Senate database, and then open the Senators table in Datasheet view.

The Senators table looks like Figure 6-1. We made this database ourselves, without the help of the Database Wizard, so no Switchboard form pops up.

2 Run the mouse pointer over the field selectors (column headings) in the Senators table.

When you point to a field selector, the mouse pointer turns into a downward-pointing arrow, indicating that if you click the field selector, you select the whole column below it.

As the pointer crosses the border between two field selectors, the mouse pointer turns into a strange little thing with arrows pointing in two directions. This mouse pointer shows where to click to adjust the column width. Notice that you don't need to be exactly on the border for the mouse pointer to change shape — a lucky thing!

on the test

3 Click the border between the State and Last Name field selectors and drag the border leftward to make the State column narrower.

Make the column narrow but still big enough to fit the two-letter state abbreviations in the column and the word State in the field selector. You probably won't be satisfied with your first try, so keep moving the border until you're happy with the result.

---

field selectors = datasheet column headings

shortcut menus appear when you right-click with mouse

↔
mouse pointer when changing column widths

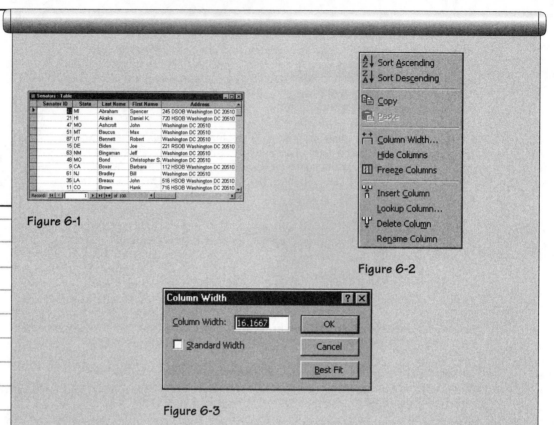

Figure 6-1: The Senators table looks okay as a datasheet, but it could look better. Why is that State column so wide?

Figure 6-2: A shortcut menu appears when you right-click the field selector.

Figure 6-3: You can enter an exact width for a column, measured in characters.

Figure 6-1

Figure 6-2

Figure 6-3

Notes:

right-click field
selector to see
menu of column-
related commands

4 Repeat Step 3 for the Senator ID column.

If you make the column too narrow, the field selector gets truncated. The column widths don't affect the way that the information is stored in the table, by the way — even if a field value doesn't fit in the datasheet, it is still stored in its entirety in the table.

5 Right-click the State field selector.

Access turns the whole State column black to show that the whole column is selected. At the same time, you see a shortcut menu, shown in Figure 6-2.

Access has another way to change the width of a column: You can type the exact width you want, in inches or centimeters (see the next step).

6 Choose Column Width from the shortcut menu.

You see the Column Width dialog box showing the current width of the column in characters (see Figure 6-3). This number is useful if you're using a fixed-width font like Courier, but it doesn't mean much when you use a variable-width font — in most fonts, *LEAHY* is wider than *Leahy*.

Entering a number in the Column Width box is useful if you want to make several columns exactly the same width — you can type the same number as the width for each column.

7 Type 7.5 in the Column Width box and click OK.

This width fits both the field name and the state abbreviations.

8 **Double-click the border between the First Name and Address field selectors.**

Alternatively, you can right-click the First Name field selector, choose Column Width from the shortcut menu, and click Best Fit in the Column Width window. Either way, this neat feature tells Access to set the column width just wide enough to fit the longest entry for the field. Letting Access choose the best fit is great when you have a long list of data so that you don't have to search for the longest entry yourself. If the column heading (the field name) is longer than the longest value in the field, Access sets the column width so that the column heading fits. Best Fit is not helpful if you have short data with wordy field names.

9 **Repeat Step 8 for the Address, Party, E-mail, and Web Page columns.**

10 **When you're happy with the layout, close the datasheet window. When Access (or the Office Assistant) asks whether to save changes to the layout of the table, click Yes.**

You return to the database window. Access saves the changes you made to the column widths so the next time you open that table, the column widths will be as you just set them.

Changing the widths of columns in the datasheet is easy: Drag the right edge of the field separator, double-click the right edge of the field separator, or use the Column Width dialog box.

Swapping columns around

Try one or two other formatting tricks:

1 **Open the Senators table again.**

The column widths remain as you set them. You'd like to move the State column between the First Name and Address columns.

2 **Click the State field selector.**

The whole column turns white-on-black.

3 **Drag the State field selector between the First Name and Address field selectors.**

When you release the mouse button, the whole State column moves to the left between the First Name and Address columns. Next, try selecting several columns at the same time and moving them as a group — how about moving the two Phone columns to the left of the Address and Party columns?

4 **Click the Phone field selector. Then Shift+click the Phone2 field selector.**

Both columns are selected.

5 **Drag the two selected columns leftward between the State and Address columns.**

When dragging the columns, your mouse pointer must be in one of the selected field selectors.

double-click column border to get best fit

Access saves datasheet column widths

Figure 6-4: What font would you like the entire datasheet to appear in?

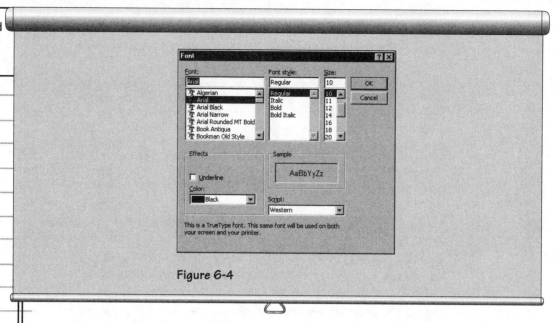

Figure 6-4

So much for moving columns around! By the way, moving columns in the datasheet has absolutely no effect on the way the information in the table is stored. So don't worry that you are messing up your Senators table.

Changing the datasheet font

You like the columns in the datasheet just the way they are. But how about using a more serious and dignified font than Arial, the font currently in use?

1 Choose Format➪Font from the menu bar.

You see the Font dialog box, shown in Figure 6-4. This dialog box controls the font used in the entire datasheet.

2 Set the Font option to Times New Roman and then click OK.

Scroll way down the list of fonts until you find it. When you click OK, the datasheet changes to Times New Roman.

3 If any of the column widths look wrong, reset them by double-clicking the right edge of the field selector for the column.

Because the widths of characters in Times New Roman are different from those in Arial, the information in the fields may no longer fit right using the column widths you chose earlier.

4 Close the Senators datasheet window and tell Access to save changes to the layout.

Now you know how to change the order of columns in the datasheet, as well as change the font.

heads up

When you change the order of the fields in the datasheet, you don't change the order of the fields in the table itself.

☑ Progress Check

If you can do the following, you've mastered this lesson:

❑ Change the width of a column of data by dragging the field selector border.

❑ Set the width of a column to a specific number of characters by using the Column Width dialog box.

❑ Change the order of the columns in a datasheet by dragging field selectors.

❑ Make Access choose the width of a column based on the longest entry for that field.

❑ Change the font used for a datasheet.

Recess

Your datasheet looks good — long entries aren't cut off, and the font looks nice. Take a break, do some calisthenics, and when you're ready, come back to do some sorting.

Sorting Datasheets Lesson 6-2

If you've ever spent hours slaving over a list for someone, you know what it feels like when you proudly present your work only to be told, "That's perfect, but could you list them by date instead of alphabetically?" It's all you can do to resist becoming a Disgruntled Computer User and fantasizing about *Getting Promoted to Your Boss's Job For Dummies.*

Fortunately, Access makes it easier to resist that urge. This lesson shows how you can quickly sort the data in a table. When you sort a column of data in a table, Access sorts the whole record, using the selected column as the *key* — that is, as the field to sort by.

If you don't have the US Senate database open, run Access and open the database before starting these steps.

1 Open the Senators table.

You see the Senators table in Datasheet view.

2 Click anywhere in the State column.

If you click the field selector, Access turns the whole column black. Either way is fine!

3 Click the Sort Ascending button on the toolbar.

The button shows an A sitting on top of a Z next to a downward-pointing arrow. Another way of choosing this sort option is to right-click the I-age field selector and choose Sort Ascending from the shortcut menu.

Access sorts the records in the table, showing the senators from Alaska (AK) at the top and those from Wyoming (WY) at the bottom. If Wyoming is at the top and Alaska at the bottom, you mistakenly clicked the Sort Descending button. That's easy to do because it's right next to the Sort Ascending button but has a Z sitting on top of an A. If you clicked the wrong button, just click the correct button, and things will be fine.

Put the senators into alphabetical order by last name.

4 Click anywhere in the Last Name column and click the Sort Ascending button.

Access sorts the senators back into last name order. Hey, look: John Kerry and Bob Kerrey have almost the same last name.

5 Close the datasheet, saving the changes to its layout.

---

key = field to
sort by

Sort Ascending
button

☑ Progress Check

If you can do the following, you've mastered this lesson:

❏ Sort a table in alphabetical or numerical order, based on a chosen field.

❏ Sort a table in reverse alphabetical or reverse numerical order, based on a chosen field.

Nothing could be easier than sorting the records in a datasheet — just click in the column to sort by and then click the Sort Ascending or Sort Descending button.

The next step is to see how the datasheet will look when printed.

Lesson 6-3   Looking Before You Print

Print Preview shows what printout will look like

You can look at your datasheet in Print Preview before you take the drastic step of printing it out on real paper (*hard copy,* as geeks call it). The *Print Preview* feature shows you exactly what the printer is going to spit out *before* you print. If you're in an office and your printer is on the other side of the building, you don't want to walk all the way over there only to find that you have made one of your rare mistakes and the printout is useless. Or perhaps your printer is right next to your PC, but it prints at 1 inch per century, or seems to. You can save at least a California redwood per year by using the neat little Print Preview option.

WYSIWYG = What You See Is What You Get

What you see in Print Preview is exactly what will print out — *WYSIWYG* (pronounced *wizzy-wig*), meaning *what you see is what you get.* Actually, Print Preview shows you a picture of your printout reduced to fit in a window on-screen, so some of the image, lettering especially, is a little fuzzy. Don't worry — on paper, the text will look fine. Your aim is to look at the general layout, not the exact text.

Print Preview button or choose File⇨Print Preview

To see a datasheet in Print Preview, open a table or query so that you see the datasheet. Then choose File⇨Print Preview from the menu or click the Print Preview button on the toolbar. (It's the one with the dog-eared sheet of paper and a magnifying glass.)

on the test

You can print your datasheet (or other report) in one of the following two orientations on the page:

portrait = normal way to print on paper

- ◆ **Portrait:** The way most people use a piece of paper — each line of text runs parallel to the short edge of the paper.

- ◆ **Landscape:** Sideways — each line of text runs parallel to the long edge of the paper.

If a datasheet is wider than it is long (for example, the datasheet contains a lot of columns), printing in landscape orientation may let your datasheet fit across one page. Of course, you'll have to tip your head sideways to read the printout.

landscape = printing sideways, with lines of text parallel to long edge of paper

To control whether your printer uses portrait or landscape orientation, you choose File⇨Page Setup to see the Page Setup dialog box. The Margins tab lets you change the top, bottom, left, and right margins for the printout. The Page tab lets you choose the print orientation.

heads up

When printing large datasheets, you may be tempted to set the margins very close to the edge of the paper, but keep in mind the following caveats:

File→Setup
controls portrait
versus Landscape
and margins

▶ Don't print too close to the edge. If the datasheet is going into a binder, the punched holes may create a gaping void where some vital information should be. If the datasheet is to be photocopied, the information may bleed off the edges because most photocopiers enlarge slightly. And in general, tiny margins aren't good design. (Everyone needs margins to doodle in!)

▶ Your printer is unlikely to be able to print right up to the edge of the paper. Some printers warn you if you try margins that are too small, and they allow you to correct the problem. Others just keep the problem a secret and ignore what they can't print.

In this lesson, you look at a large datasheet in Print Preview and try some strategies for fitting it onto your paper.

Previewing a datasheet

Take a look at a datasheet that is too wide to print in portrait orientation and too long to print in landscape orientation. You use the Senators table in the US Senate database again.

on the CD

1 **Run Access, open the US Senate database, and open the Senators table in Datasheet view, as shown in Figure 6-1.**

2 **Choose File⇨Print Preview from the menu bar or click the Print Preview button on the toolbar.**

You see a little picture of a page containing the Senators datasheet, shown in Figure 6-5. The print is too small to read, but you can see the general layout — six columns of information running across the page.

But wait! The table has ten fields, so there should be ten columns in the datasheet. Where are the other four? Because all the information in a record can't fit across a single page in portrait orientation, Access decides to put the last four columns on the next page. Using landscape orientation you could fit more columns across the page, but you'd fit fewer records.

3 **Click the Next Page button on the navigation bar in the lower-left corner of the window to move to the next page of information.**

The Next Page button, the one with the right-pointing triangle, is near the lower-left corner of the window. You see the second page of the printout, with the next three columns of information for the senators listed on the first page.

Next Page button

4 **Click the Next Page button again: You see the last column of information about the senators listed on the first page.**

If you print this datasheet, you can tape the pages together in sets of three to make a huge table of senators three sheets of paper wide.

Figure 6-5: The Print Preview window shows the general layout of the whole page.

Figure 6-6: You can choose which columns appear in the datasheet by clicking the boxes on the Unhide Columns dialog box.

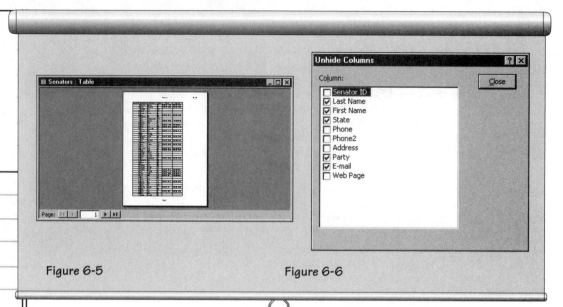

Figure 6-5   Figure 6-6

Notes:

5 **Click inside the Print Preview window, somewhere near the column headings at the top of the page.**

Access zooms in on the image of your datasheet. You can no longer see the whole page, but now you can read the text. You can also see that Access formats the column headings nicely, with boldface text and a gray background. Ah — the column on the third page is the Web Page column.

6 **Click inside the Print Preview window again.**

Access zooms back out to the full-page view.

7 **Close the Print Preview window.**

You return to the database window.

This listing will never fit across one page with all those columns. What can you do?

Hiding columns in a datasheet

You may not want to include all the columns in the datasheet when you print it. Luckily, you can tell Access to hide a column temporarily. Hiding columns doesn't delete any information from the table: Hiding just makes the column invisible, or too narrow to see, in the datasheet.

on the test

Hidden columns aren't deleted, though. The information is still safe and sound in your table, completely unaffected by getting hidden in the datasheet.

Here's how to hide columns and then "unhide" them later:

- Hide a selected column from view by choosing Format⇨Hide Columns or by right-clicking the field selector and choosing Hide Columns.

- Show columns again after they have been hidden by choosing Format⇨Unhide Columns. You see a list of fields — check off which ones you want to see or hide. (No check mark means that the column is hidden.) Then click Close.

Perhaps you don't need to include all the columns when you print this datasheet. Hide some so that the columns you do want fit across one page.

1 Open the Senators table in Datasheet view.

It still looks more or less like Figure 6-1.

2 Right-click the field selector for the Senator ID column and choose Hide Columns from the menu that appears.

The column disappears! How about hiding the phone numbers and mailing address columns, too, to make an e-mail directory of senators?

3 Click the Phone field selector and then Shift+click the Address field selector to select all three columns. Next, right-click anywhere in the selected (black) columns and choose Hide Columns.

All three columns disappear.

4 Repeat Step 2 for the Party and Web page columns.

Wait a minute — the Party columns is narrow. How about putting it back?

5 Choose Format⇨Unhide Columns from the menu.

You see the Unhide Columns dialog box (shown in Figure 6-6), listing the fields in the table. The columns that appear have check marks, and the hidden columns don't.

6 Click the box to the left of the Party field so that it contains a check mark.

You should have check marks for the Last Name, First Name, State, Party, and E-mail columns.

7 Click the Close button.

The Unhide Columns dialog box goes away.

8 Click the Print Preview window to see how the datasheet looks.

The five remaining columns fit across the page. Now when you click the Next Page button, you see the save five columns for the next pageful of senators.

Hiding and unhiding columns lets you choose which columns to include in your datasheet. It's a good way to create a columnar report that fits across one page.

---

hide columns you don't want to appear in the datasheet

to hide selected column, right-click field selector and choose Hide Columns

to unhide columns, choose Format→Unhide Columns

☑ **Progress Check**

If you can do the following, you've mastered this lesson:

❑ Use Print Preview to take a sneak peek at your printout before it goes to the printer.

❑ Move from page to page in Print Preview.

❑ Hide columns on the datasheet.

❑ Unhide columns so they appear.

Telling Access about orientation and margins

You can control the margins and page orientation of your printout, too. Choose File⇨Page Setup to display the Page Setup window. The window has two tabs: Margins and Page. The Margins tab shows the margins around the edge of the page: 1 inch all the way around, which is the usual amount.

You can try to fit more information on this page by decreasing the margins, but don't decrease them too much — having type go very close to the edge of the page isn't aesthetically pleasing. The Page tab lets you choose between Portrait (normal) and Landscape (sideways) orientation.

Lesson 6-4

Printing the Datasheet

You've done the hard part: formatting the datasheet the way you want it. As long as you have a working printer, the rest is easy. If your printer isn't ready to print, then it's time to make friends with a local techno-nerd. We suggest that you call that person "sir" or "ma'am" or "your majesty" or something along those lines. Or cut through all that sycophancy and simply use a bribe. Pizza usually gets a computer guru's attention. While you've got someone setting up your printer, you may as well hand out an extra slice or two and ask for a quick lesson on how to connect to and use your printer so that you don't have to ask again.

In this lesson, you'll use the Print dialog box (shown in Figure 6-7), where you can tell Access to print several copies or only an individual page or to use a different printer. You display the Print dialog box by choosing File⇨Print from the menu bar or pressing Ctrl+P when you're looking at whatever you want to print — in this case, your datasheet.

Here are settings that you can change in the Print dialog box:

- **Printer Name:** If you have more than one printer connected to your computer (or local area network, if you're on one), you can choose which printer to print on. Click the downward-pointing-triangle button at the right end of this setting to see a list of the available printers.

- **Print Range:** You usually print All the pages in the datasheet or report, but if you want to print only certain pages, click the Pages option in the Print Range box. Then fill in the starting and ending page numbers in the From and To boxes.

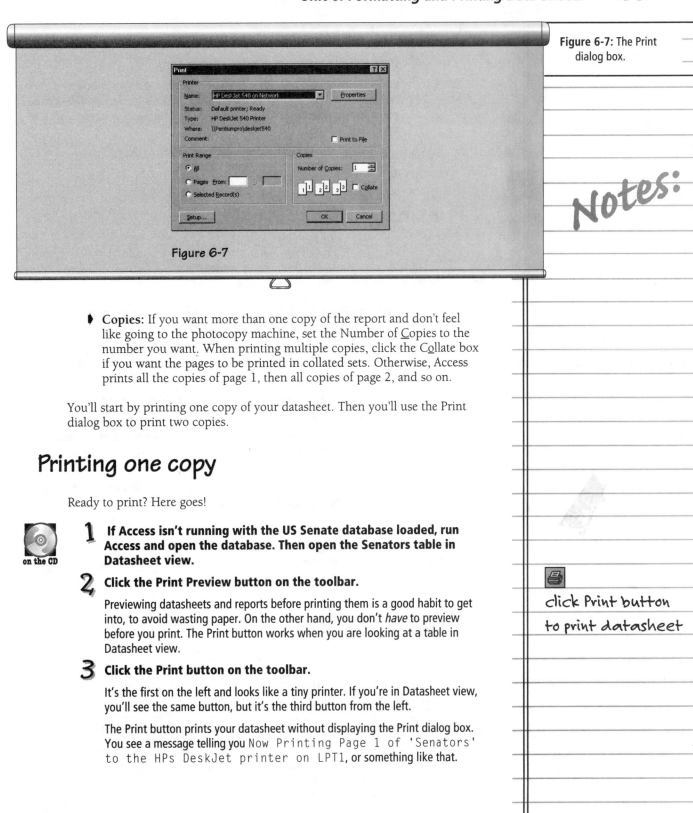

Figure 6-7: The Print dialog box.

Figure 6-7

Notes:

▶ **Copies:** If you want more than one copy of the report and don't feel like going to the photocopy machine, set the Number of Copies to the number you want. When printing multiple copies, click the Collate box if you want the pages to be printed in collated sets. Otherwise, Access prints all the copies of page 1, then all copies of page 2, and so on.

You'll start by printing one copy of your datasheet. Then you'll use the Print dialog box to print two copies.

Printing one copy

Ready to print? Here goes!

1 **If Access isn't running with the US Senate database loaded, run Access and open the database. Then open the Senators table in Datasheet view.**

2 **Click the Print Preview button on the toolbar.**

Previewing datasheets and reports before printing them is a good habit to get into, to avoid wasting paper. On the other hand, you don't *have* to preview before you print. The Print button works when you are looking at a table in Datasheet view.

3 **Click the Print button on the toolbar.**

It's the first on the left and looks like a tiny printer. If you're in Datasheet view, you'll see the same button, but it's the third button from the left.

The Print button prints your datasheet without displaying the Print dialog box. You see a message telling you `Now Printing Page 1 of 'Senators' to the HPs DeskJet printer on LPT1`, or something like that.

click Print button
to print datasheet

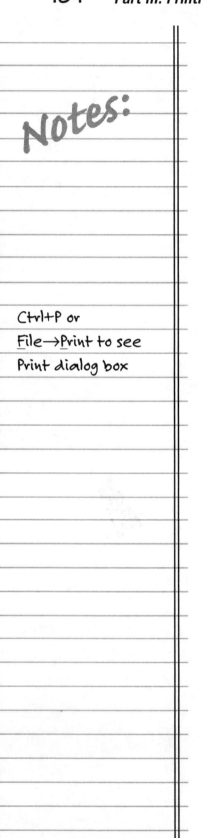

4 **Dash to your printer and collect the output.**

If you share your printer with a bunch of other people, this step is a very important task because all too often, if you don't pick it up straightaway, you may find your treasured printout buried underneath reams and reams of other uncollected reports.

You've printed a very nice list of the 100 members of the United States Senate with e-mail addresses. Nice work!

Printing multiple copies

Of course, there's more than one way to peel a banana (although we can think of only one offhand). You can use the Print dialog box to change some of your printing options.

1 **With the Print Preview of the table still on-screen, choose File➪Print from the menu bar or press Ctrl+P.**

You see the Print dialog box (shown in Figure 6-7). The default is printing all the pages, but you can print individual pages by specifying the page numbers in the Pages box.

2 **Type 2 in the Number of Copies box and then click OK. (Click Cancel if you want to save paper.)**

If you clicked OK, you see the same message as when you used the Print button to print: Now Printing Page 1 of 'Senators' to the 'Your Printer' on LPT1, or something similar.

3 **Check that Access printed both copies (if you clicked OK); then close the Print Preview or datasheet window.**

Now that you've learned how to print a datasheet, you'll be happy to hear that you can use the same Print button, File➪Print command, Ctrl+P keystroke, and Print dialog box when you print reports in Unit 7! You're already ahead of the game.

Printing the results of a query

Printing the results of a query is just as straightforward as printing a table. Treat the results of a query exactly as you would a table — open the query, look at its datasheet, adjust the format, and print it. Printing a datasheet is the same whether the datasheet is a view of a table or the results of a query.

on the CD

1 **Open the Democratic Senators query in Datasheet view.**

That is, click the Queries tab in the database window and double-click the Democratic Senators query. The query has only one field: Name. (***Note:*** This book takes no political position. You could use that list of Democratic senators for letters of support or of criticism.)

Notes:

Ctrl+P or
File→Print to see
Print dialog box

2 Click the Print button on the toolbar.

3 Collect the output.

4 Close the Democratic Senators query.

What more could you want? You can now print a datasheet for a table or a query.

Recess

Print Preview is a wonderful feature and is probably responsible for saving thousands of trees annually. Use it to save yourself a lot of trips to the printer and lots of time listening to the whirring and chattering of the printer. Printing becomes a few simple clicks of the mouse or a handful of keystrokes. If you wore yourself out on that trip to the printer, go lie down for a while to recover.

Good going! You've finished this unit about formatting and printing datasheets. Jump right into the Unit 6 Quiz!

☑ Progress Check

If you can do the following, you've mastered this lesson:

❑ Print directly from Print Preview using the Print button on the toolbar.

❑ Use the Print dialog box to choose which pages to print or to print more than one copy.

❑ Print the results of a query.

Unit 6 Quiz

For each of the following questions, circle the letter of the correct answer or answers. Remember, there may be more than one right answer for each question.

1. **Which kinds of formatting can you do with datasheets?**

   A. Sort the records into alphabetical order.

   B. Choose which columns (fields) appear.

   C. Choose the order of the columns.

   D. Adjust the widths of each column individually.

   E. Set the font used to display and print the datasheet.

2. **To change the width of a column on a datasheet, you . . .**

   A. Choose Column⇨Make It A Lot Wider from the menu.

   B. Choose Column⇨Make It A Lot Narrower from the menu.

   C. Choose Format⇨Column Width from the menu.

   D. Drag the column divider left or right with the mouse.

   E. Right-click the field selector for the column and choose Column Width from the shortcut menu that appears.

3. **What does this button do?**

   A. Zooms in on the datasheet.

   B. Displays the datasheet as it will appear when printed.

100% ▾

C. Looks at the datasheet through a magnifying glass.

D. Checks the spelling on the datasheet.

E. Starts a small fire on the datasheet by holding the magnifying glass at just the right angle to the sun.

4. **The computerese terms for printing letter-style (the normal, straight-up way) and sideways on the page are . . .**

A. Portrait and landscape.

B. Normal and sideways.

C. Skinny and wide.

D. Tree and shrub.

E. Head, shoulders, knees, and toes.

5. **In *James and the Giant Peach,* James' two nasty aunts are named . . .**

A. Spider and Fly.

B. Chip and Dale.

C. Sponge and Spiker.

D. Gulch and Grinch.

E. Portrait and Landscape.

6. **After you've hidden a column in a datasheet . . .**

A. You can never see it again.

B. The column is permanently deleted from the table.

C. The column is unaffected in the table and reappears in the datasheet when you use the Format⇨Unhide Columns command.

D. The column is unaffected in the table, but you can never see it in the datasheet again.

E. You can still see it under a microscope.

Unit 6 Exercise

on the CD

1. Open the Dickens Address Book 5 database.

2. Open the Addresses table.

3. Change the datasheet so that you can print all the addresses on one page. (Adjust column widths and hide columns, if needed.)

4. Sort the addresses by last name.

5. Preview your printout.

6. Print.

7. Close the Addresses window, saving your layout changes.

Making Reports and Web Pages

Objectives for This Unit

✓ Creating a report by using a Report Wizard

✓ Printing a report

✓ Creating reports that contain selected records from a table

✓ Creating reports with groups and totals

✓ Printing mailing labels by using reports

✓ Making Web pages using data from an Access database

Prerequisites

▶ Using the database window (Lesson 1-2)

▶ Using the navigation bar to move around in a window (Lesson 2-1)

▶ Making queries (Lesson 4-3)

▶ Printing a datasheet (Lesson 6-4)

on the CD

▶ Dickens Address Book 7 database (Dickens Address Book 7.mdb)

Printing datasheets is all well and good. They look pretty good, especially after you fool around with the widths and order of the columns. But what about reports that are in some other format? What about printing totals? What about mailing labels?

This unit talks about reports of many kinds — columnar reports, reports with totals, reports that summarize the information in a table, even mailing labels. You can print reports, save them in files, or even fax them (if you have a faxmodem). Finally, Access 97 lets you create a Web page using information from your database, as you'll learn in Lesson 7-5.

To make a report, you create a report design, which is stored as part of your database. The information included in the report comes from the *record source,* which can be any table or query in the database. When the Database Wizard makes a database for you, the database usually includes a report or two, just to get you started. You can make more reports with help from the Report Wizard by answering a series of questions that tell the wizard what you want on the report. The truly courageous among you can create a report with your bare hands or change the design of an existing report using Design view.

record source = table or query that contains report records

After you've created a report, you can look at it on-screen or print it anytime. Each time you open a report, Access updates it so that it includes the latest information from the table or query that is the source for the report.

on the CD

In this unit, you use the Dickens Address Book 7 database, a copy of the Dickens Address Book database that you've used in preceding units, but with one additional field in the Addresses table. This field, Invitations, contains the number of people attending the upcoming Dickens Society Meeting for each household.

Lesson 7-1 Printing a Report

Printing a report that already exists is easy — just open it. If you're using a database created by the Database Wizard, a choice on the Main Switchboard displays another Switchboard, called the *Reports Switchboard*. The Reports Switchboard contains one button for each of the reports that the Database Wizard creates. You click the button to preview the report. Then you can click the Print button to print it. You can also use the database window to see and print reports. You'll see the Reports Switchboard in this lesson, because the Database Wizard created the Dickens Address Book 7 database.

When you open a report, Access displays the report in Print Preview — that is, the report looks as it will when you print it. Print Preview works the same for reports as for datasheets (see Unit 6).

on the test

Here are things that you can do with a report in Print Preview:

▶ Print the report by clicking the Print button on the toolbar (the leftmost button), pressing Ctrl+P, or choosing File➪Print from the menu bar.

▶ Zoom out to see the whole page by clicking the report.

▶ When you see a whole page of the report, you can zoom in on part of the report by clicking that part.

▶ See two pages of the report by clicking the Two Pages button.

▶ Move from page to page of the report, using the same navigation bar that you see on forms (you used it in Lesson 2-1, when entering records in the Dickens Address Book database).

In this lesson, you'll use the Reports Switchboard to print a report and the database window to see another report.

Looking at the Database Wizard's reports

First, take a look at the Reports Switchboard.

Reports Switchboard lists reports created by Database Wizard

Two Pages button

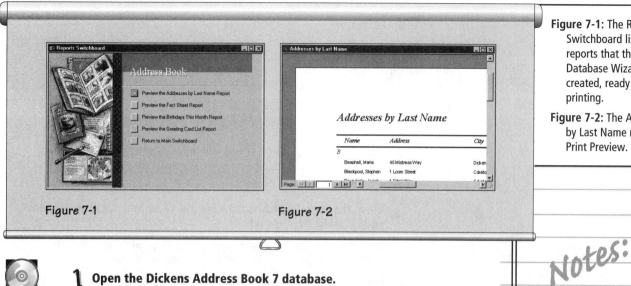

Figure 7-1

Figure 7-2

Figure 7-1: The Reports Switchboard lists the reports that the Database Wizard created, ready for printing.

Figure 7-2: The Addresses by Last Name report in Print Preview.

on the CD

1 **Open the Dickens Address Book 7 database.**

The database is in the usual place — the *Dummies 101* Access 97 folder in your My Documents folder.

2 **Click the Preview Reports button on the Main Switchboard.**

When the Database Wizard created this database, the magic spells resulted in several reports. You see the Reports Switchboard window, which lists the reports that the wizard made (shown in Figure 7-1). You can preview each report by using a button on the Reports Switchboard and then print it by using the Print button on the toolbar.

3 **Click the Preview the Addresses by Last Name Report button on the Reports Switchboard.**

Access displays the report in Print Preview (shown in Figure 7-2).

4 **Click the Two Pages button, the fifth icon from the left on the toolbar.**

You see the first two pages of the report. The print is too tiny to read (unless you've got an amazingly big monitor), but you get an idea of the report layout. For example, you can probably tell that this is a *landscape* report — that is, the text runs sideways, with the lines parallel to the long edge of the paper.

5 **Click anywhere in the report.**

Access zooms in on the report so you can read the text again.

6 **Click anywhere in the report again.**

Access zooms back out.

7 **Close the report.**

You've got your choice of two Close buttons: the usual Windows 95 Close button in the upper-right corner of the report window and the button labeled Close on the toolbar. Decisions, decisions!

8 **On the Reports Switchboard, click the Return to Main Switchboard button.**

The Reports Switchboard is replaced by your old friend the Main Switchboard.

Notes:

Two Pages button

To look at a report in Print Preview, choose it from the Reports Switchboard, which you display by clicking the Preview Reports button on the Main Switchboard.

Looking at any report

But what if you want to open a report that didn't come from the Database Wizard? You can find all the reports in your database, regardless of where they came from, in the database window.

1 **Close the Main Switchboard window, open the database window, and click the Reports tab.**

When you click the Reports tab, you see the list of all the reports in the database, including those created by the Database Wizard.

2 **Double-click the Fact Sheet report, or click it and then click Preview.**

Access opens the Fact Sheet report in Print Preview (shown in Figure 7-3). This report contains all the information about each person in the Addresses table, one person per page.

3 **Click the Next Page button on the navigation bar at the bottom of the Fact Sheet window.**

It's the right-pointing-triangle button near the lower-left corner of the window. You see the next page of the report. You can use the buttons on the navigation bar to move from page to page of a long report or to see the first or last page. If you type a number in the Go to page box and press Enter, you see the page that corresponds to that number.

When Access displays a report, you start by looking at its upper-left corner. In fact, most of the window is usually occupied by the top and left margins of the report; as a result, you don't see much of the text of the report. (Some people refer to this feature of Access as "user-hostile.") You can use the scroll bars on the report window to see other parts of the page.

4 **Click the button (with the right-pointing triangle) at the right end of the horizontal scroll bar along the bottom of the Fact Sheet window.**

The window pans left along the report, so you can see more text and less left margin. Click the button again if you want to move your view farther right.

5 **Click the button (with the downward-pointing triangle) at the lower end of the vertical scroll bar along the right side of the Fact Sheet window.**

Your view pans down the page.

The report looks the same, and Print Preview works the same, whether you open the report from the Reports Switchboard or from the database window.

[handwritten margin note:] open a report from database window to see Print Preview

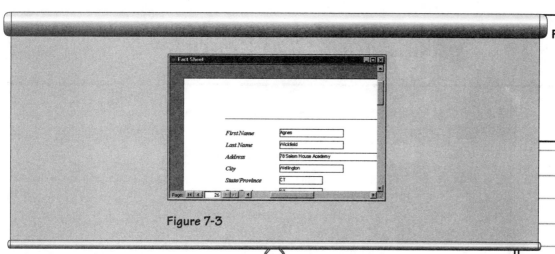

Figure 7-3

Figure 7-3: You can use the navigation bar along the bottom edge of the Print Preview window to move to another page of the report.

Notes:

Printing a report

While you're looking at a report in Print Preview, you can print it by clicking the Print button on the toolbar, pressing Ctrl+P, or choosing File⇨Print from the menu bar. The Print button prints the report immediately. Pressing Ctrl+P or choosing File⇨Print from the menu bar displays the Print dialog box, which you learned about in Lesson 6-4.

If you've been following the steps in this lesson, you're looking at the Fact Sheet report in Print Preview.

Print button

1 Press Ctrl+P to display the Print dialog box.

You last saw the Print dialog box in Lesson 6-4. This report has as many pages as the Addresses table has records — 26 — so to save paper, choose to print only page 3.

2 Click the Pages option in the Print Range box and type 3 in both the From and To boxes.

Printing from page 3 to page 3 prints just one page — page 3.

3 Click OK.

A message appears, telling you that Access is sending the page to the printer. If you decide not to print after all, you can click the Cancel button in the message box. After Access is done printing, you return to Print Preview.

4 Close the report window.

If you want to print just one copy of the entire report to your usual printer, you can click the Print icon on the toolbar and skip the Print dialog box. If you want to change any print settings, press Ctrl+P (or choose File⇨Print) instead.

☑ Progress Check

If you can do the following, you've mastered this lesson:

❑ Look at a report in Print Preview.

❑ Print one or more copies of the report.

Lesson 7-2   # Making Your Own Reports

on the test

When you create a report, you have to tell Access a bunch of things:

- ◆ Which report or query supplies the records to include in the report (that is, what's the *record source*)?

- ◆ Which fields should Access include in the report, and where do they appear on the page?

- ◆ What order should the records be in?

- ◆ What should Access print at the top and bottom of each page? Do you want headings or page numbers?

- ◆ Do you want the records to be grouped in any way? For example, do you want the people in each town to be grouped together? And if you group records, do you want counts or totals for each group?

- ◆ Would you like any lines, boxes, or graphics on the report?

A report can include other kinds of formatting information, too, but this list gives you enough to think about!

To make a new report, click the Reports tab in the database window and click the <u>N</u>ew button. Or you can choose <u>I</u>nsert⇨<u>R</u>eport from the menu bar anytime — the database window doesn't have to be open and displaying the list of reports. Yet another method is to click the downward-pointing-arrow button at the right end of the New Object button on the toolbar and choose New Report from the menu that appears. You see the New Report window, shown in Figure 7-4.

The easiest way to create a report is (you've guessed it already) by using either a wizard or an AutoReport. An *AutoReport* is like a very simple wizard that creates a quick report with very little input from you. From the New Report window, the following wizards and AutoReports are at your beck and call:

- ◆ **Report Wizard:** Asks a series of questions so you can tell it what table(s) or query(ies) the information comes from, which fields to include, how to sort them, how to group them, and what general style to use for the report. You'll meet this wizard in this lesson.

- ◆ **Columnar AutoReport:** Makes a quick but ugly report without asking any further questions. The report lists all the fields in each record of the source table or query. You have to select the table or query that the report will be based on *before* summoning up the New Report window, or the wizard will refuse to do any magic. Click the Tables or Queries tab in the database window, click the table or query that you want a report about, choose <u>I</u>nsert⇨<u>R</u>eport from the menu bar, and choose AutoReport: Columnar from the New Report window.

- ◆ **Tabular AutoReport:** Works like the Columnar AutoReport, but makes a quick but ugly tabular report, with a column for each field in the source table or query.

---

record source =
table or query
from report gets
information

to create a report,
click New button
on Reports tab of
database window

AutoReport =
report created by
a simple AutoReport
Wizard

use Report Wizard
to make new
columnar report

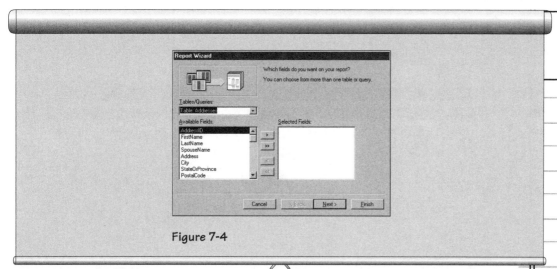

Figure 7-4

Figure 7-4: How would you like to create your new report?

Notes:

extra credit

Tabular versus Columnar

When you create a report, you can choose Columnar or Tabular AutoReports, among others. What's the difference between *tabular* and *columnar*, anyway? Most of us use the two words to mean the same thing (something that is like a table, or in columns), if we use them at all!

Here's what they mean to our pals at Microsoft, as far as we can tell:

▶ *Columnar* means just one column. A Columnar AutoReport has one page per record (if all the fields fit on a page). On each line, you see the name of the field and its entry for that record. Ugly and basic, but it could be useful.

▶ *Tabular* means a table with multiple columns. A Tabular AutoReport has one column per field and one row per record. It looks a bit like a datasheet, actually.

Don't worry about remembering the difference between these two terms in Access — you can always look it up in this book!

▶ **Chart Wizard:** Makes a graph of the information in a table or query.

▶ **Label Wizard:** Creates a report that prints names on mailing labels. You'll use this wizard in Lesson 7-4.

You'll use the Report Wizard to make a good-looking columnar report with information from the Addresses table in the Dickens Address Book 7 database.

Making a columnar report with the Report Wizard

The Report Wizard can create a wide variety of columnar reports, with one column for each field that you choose to include. You can sort the records by any field in the table, group the records, and choose how to format the report.

Figure 7-5: You tell the Report Wizard which fields from the table you want to appear on the report.

Notes:

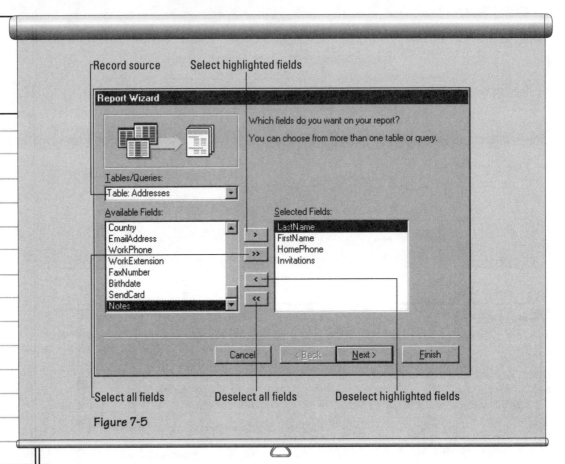

Record source   Select highlighted fields

Select all fields   Deselect all fields   Deselect highlighted fields

Figure 7-5

Here's how to get the Report Wizard to work on your report. You're organizing the Dickens Society Meeting, and you need a listing of the invitees (everyone in the Addresses table) with the number of people expected for each record. You decide to include phone numbers, too, in case you need to call people to confirm how many are coming.

on the CD

1 **If you aren't already looking at the database window in the Dickens Address Book 7 database, open the database, close the Main Switchboard window, open the database window, and click the Reports tab.**

You see the list of reports that are already in the database. Maybe the report that you want already exists? No? Then make one!

2 **Click the New button in the database window.**

You see the New Report window, shown in Figure 7-4, listing your options for creating reports.

3 **Click Report Wizard and then click OK.**

The Report Wizard asks its first question, shown in Figure 7-5: Which fields should appear in the report? The Tables/Queries box is already set to use the Addresses table as the record source, although you could use one of the queries that you created in Unit 4 instead. For example, if you wanted to create a listing of people whose phone numbers you don't have, you could set the Tables/Queries box to the Missing Phone Number query that you created in Lesson 4-3.

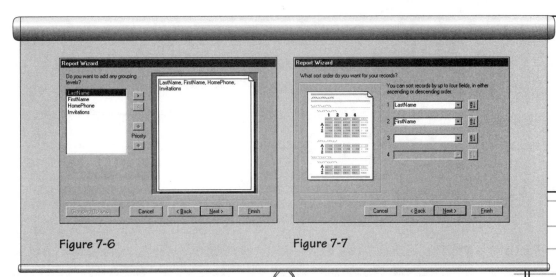

Figure 7-6: You can tell the Report Wizard to group the records based on the value of a field.

Figure 7-7: Here's where you tell the Report Wizard whether to sort the records in the report.

Figure 7-6   Figure 7-7

The Available Fields box lists the fields in the table or query that you selected. The Selected Fields box lists the fields that you have decided to include in the report. The fields will appear on the report in the same order in which they appear on the Selected Fields list. You use the buttons between the two lists to move fields from one list to the other.

4 **Click LastName in the Available Fields list and click the right-pointing arrow button between the two lists.**

The field jumps over into the Selected Fields list. (Double-clicking the LastName field also makes it jump into the Selected Fields list.)

5 **Move the FirstName, HomePhone, and Invitations fields to the Selected Fields list the same way.**

These four fields will appear on your report.

6 **Click Next.**

You see the Report Wizard's next question: Do you want to group the records together based on the value of one or more fields (see Figure 7-6)? For example, do you want all the records from each town grouped together or all the records with the same number of people coming to the meeting?

"No, thanks!" you reply. "Just a plain listing, thank you very much." (You'll make a report with groups in Lesson 7-3.)

7 **Click Next.**

Now the Report Wizard wants to know whether you want to sort the records (see Figure 7-7). You can sort on up to four fields (which is almost always more than enough). To get a listing sorted by last name, and first name within last name, use LastName for the first sort field and FirstName for the second.

8 **Click the list button at the right end of sort field number 1 and choose LastName from the list that appears.**

The little A-to-Z button to the right of the sort field indicates that the records will be sorted in ascending order (A, B, C, . . .). If you wanted them in descending order (Z, Y, X, . . .), you would click the button so that it says Z-to-A.

fields appear on report as on Selected Fields list

Select highlighted field button

tell Report Wizard whether to group or sort records

Sort order button

Figure 7-8: You can control the page orientation and layout of the report.

Figure 7-9: Here's the report you created with help from the Report Wizard!

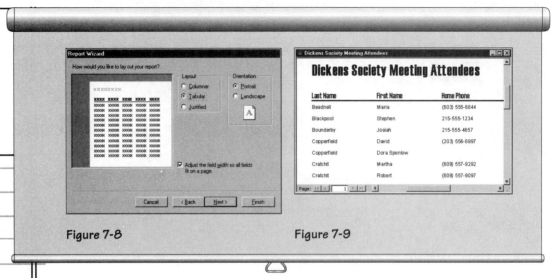

Figure 7-8

Figure 7-9

Notes:

choose between
portrait and
landscape
orientation

9 **Set sort field number 2 to FirstName.**

Leave sort fields 3 and 4 blank.

10 **Click Next.**

It's time for the wizard's next question (shown in Figure 7-8): How do you want the report arranged on the page? The Report Wizard window actually contains two questions, one in the Layout box and the other in the Orientation box.

- **Layout:** Do you want the field values for each record to appear listed down the page, with one record following the next? (Probably not — it looks lousy.) If you do, choose Columnar. Or do you want one row for each record and one column for each field? If you do, choose Tabular. In tabular layout, if you chose a lot of fields to appear in the report, the columns for the fields may not fit across the page. Or do you want one row for each record, with field names above each row? If you do, choose Justified. (It looks strange — try it sometime.)

- **Orientation:** Do you want to print the report the usual way on the paper (Portrait) or sideways on the paper (Landscape)?

If the Adjust the field width so all fields fit on a page box is selected, the Report Wizard shrinks the columns of a tabular report so that all the fields fit across the page. If it's not selected, your report may be two or more pages wide.

11 **Leave Tabular and Portrait selected and click Next.**

The Report Wizard asks what graphic design style you would like to use. As you click the various choices — Bold, Casual, Compact, Corporate, Formal, and Soft Gray — the wizard shows an example of each style when you select it.

12 **Click the style you like best and then click Next.**

We like Compact, but they all look pretty classy.

The Report Wizard waves the flag at the finish line (are we mixing our metaphors here, or what?). You see the last window that the Report Wizard displays before it retires to its cave to create the report. This time, you are called upon to decide on the title that appears at the top of the report. This title is also the name that the report has in the database window.

13 **In the box at the top of the Report Wizard window, type** Dickens Society Meeting Attendees.

You can see what the report looks like in Print Preview, or you can see the report in Design view, where you can modify its design. You'll find out about changing the design of a report in Unit 10. For now, leave the <u>P</u>review the report option selected.

14 **Click <u>F</u>inish.**

Disks whir and windows flash — the wizard is concocting your report. (You can think of yourself as the sorcerer's apprentice!)

At last, your report appears from the mists in Print Preview. It looks something like Figure 7-9.

15 **Admire your creation and close the report window.**

The Report Wizard already saved the report, using the title you entered.

The Report Wizard leads you through the process of making a columnar report by asking a series of questions. You can use this wizard to create many useful columnar reports. Each time you run the wizard, you can choose different fields to include, a different sort order, or different record groupings, to create a different report. After the Report Wizard creates a report, the wizard disappears, leaving a new report. As with all reports, these reports are updated each time you open them, so they always contain up-to-date information. You can print the report the same way you learned in Lesson 7-1.

Recess

The Report Wizard is a powerful ally in the World of Access. Now you know how to work with him, her, or it to create reports. With the Report Wizard at your side, you can create lots of useful tabular reports.

If you want to take a break, go ahead and clear your head after all this wizardry!

type report title

Access updates information in report when opening or printing it

☑ **Progress Check**

If you can do the following, you've mastered this lesson:

❑ Create a tabular report using the Report Wizard.

❑ Choose which fields to include in the report.

❑ Specify how to sort the records.

❑ Choose the paper orientation and style for the new report.

❑ Look at your new report.

Making Fancier Reports

Lesson 7-3

on the CD

If your table contains more than a few records, you may want to arrange similar records together when you print a report. For example, if you were the product manager at the Middlebury Tours company, you might want a report that listed your tours by month or by target group. In this lesson, you'll create a listing of people in the Dickens Address Book who plan to come to its upcoming meeting, and you'll group the people by state.

to select records for report, create query and then use query as record source

when creating queries, * in Field row on query grid means all fields in table

On query grid, Show box controls whether column appears in query result

A report doesn't have to contain all the records in a table. If you want a report to contain only a selection of the records in a table, first create a query that includes only the records that you want in the report. Then create a report that uses the query as its record source. That's how you'll create a list of people who are intending to come to the Dickens Society Meeting, omitting those who don't plan to come. You can tell who they are because their Invitations field contains a zero (zero people from this family plan to come).

When you make a query on which to base a report, you frequently want the query to include all the same fields as the original table. To include all the fields from a table in a query, use the * entry in the field list for the table. Drag the * entry from the field list at the top of the query window to the design grid, and *presto!* The query includes all the fields from the table. You see only one column in the design grid, with a * in it, representing all the fields in the table.

on the test

However, what if you want to enter criteria for one of the fields? For example, to make a report that includes only those people who are planning to come to the Dickens Society Meeting, you can select records that don't have a zero in the Invitations field of the Addresses table. (The Invitations field contains the number of people attending the meeting from each household.) To enter the criteria for Invitations, you need a column in the design grid for the Invitations field. You can make a column for the Invitations field by dragging the field name from the field list to the design grid, but then the Invitations field would appear in the query results twice! To prevent two Invitations columns from appearing in the query results, click the box in the Show column of the Invitations column so that the check mark disappears from the Show box. Now you'll just see Invitations once in the query results, not twice, and you can enter the selection criteria in the Criteria row. Figure 7-10 shows a query that includes all the fields in the Addresses table but only those records that have at least one person coming to the party.

Selecting records to include

First, make a query that includes only people who are coming to the meeting.

on the CD

1 **Open the Dickens Address Book 7 database. Close the Main Switchboard window and open the database window.**

2 **Click the Queries tab and then click New.**

3 **When you see the New Query window, with Design View selected, click OK.**

Access opens a new, blank query and displays the Show Table window so you can decide which tables to base the query on.

4 **In the Show Table window, with the Addresses table selected, click Add and then click Close.**

Access adds the Addresses table to the query, displaying a field list in the top half of the query window.

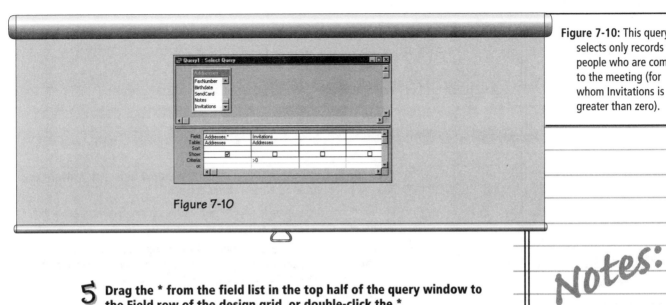

Figure 7-10

Figure 7-10: This query selects only records for people who are coming to the meeting (for whom Invitations is greater than zero).

Notes:

5 **Drag the * from the field list in the top half of the query window to the Field row of the design grid, or double-click the *.**

The * in the field list represents *all* the fields in the Addresses table. In the design grid, you see `Addresses.*` in the Field row. Now the query contains all the same fields as the Addresses table, including the Invitations field. But how can you enter a criterion for Invitations to omit people who aren't coming to the meeting?

6 **Drag the Invitations field name from the field list to the Field row of the design grid (or double-click it).**

You have to scroll the field list right down to the end because Invitations is the last field in the Addresses table.

on the test

7 **Click the check box in the Show row of the Invitations column so that the check mark disappears.**

Otherwise, the Invitations column would appear twice in the query result.

click Show box to omit column from query result

8 **In the Criteria row of the Invitations column, type >0 to have Access include records for which Invitations is greater than zero. Then press Enter or Tab.**

Be sure to type a zero, not a capital O (the letter). The query is done; your query should look like Figure 7-10.

9 **Click the View button on the toolbar (the leftmost button) to see the results of the query.**

The query includes 18 of the 26 records in the Addresses table. (Not too many wallflowers on the list!)

View button

10 **Close the query, click <u>Y</u>es to save it, and name it** Meeting Attendees.

This query contains the records to include in a report on who's coming to the meeting.

Using a query as the record source for a report

Now you can use this query as the record source for a new report. You'll also tell the Report Wizard to group the records in the report by city and to total the Invitations field.

1 **Click the Reports tab in the database window and click New. In the New Report window, click Report Wizard.**

Before clicking OK, tell the Report Wizard which table or query to use as the record source.

2 **Click the list button (the downward-pointing triangle) at the right end of the box in the lower box on the New report window and choose the Meeting Attendees query from the list that appears. Then click OK.**

The Tables/Queries box shows Query: Meeting Attendees as the record source for the report. Now you can choose which fields to include in the report, the same way you did in Lesson 7-2.

3 **Move the LastName, FirstName, City, StateOrProvince, HomePhone, and Invitations fields onto the Available Fields list. Then click Next.**

The Report Wizard asks whether you want to add any grouping levels, which is its techno-speak way of asking whether you'd like to group the records together based on the values of a field.

4 **Click StateOrProvince in the list of the fields in the report and then click the right-pointing-arrow button.**

The Report Wizard displays a little diagram of the report (shown in Figure 7-11), with the StateOrProvince field at the top of each section of the report. (You'll see how this looks in a minute, when you see the actual report on-screen.)

5 **Click Next.**

The Report Wizard wants to know how you want the records sorted. The records will be grouped by state, but you can sort them within each state group.

6 **Enter LastName for the first sort field and FirstName for the second sort field.**

Have you noticed the Summary Options button in this window? This button is how you tell the Report Wizard that you want to print some totals.

7 **Click the Summary Options button.**

You see the Summary Options window shown in Figure 7-12. The window lists all the numeric fields to be included in the report — only the Invitations field for this report. Because it doesn't make much sense to total date or text fields, the Report Wizard doesn't list them.

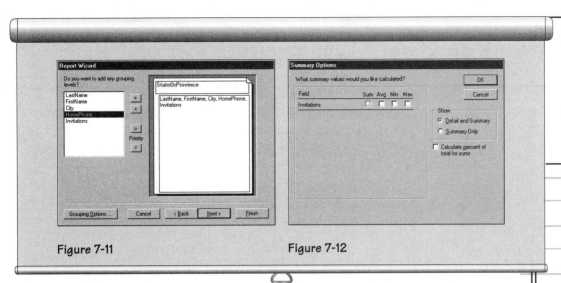

Figure 7-11

Figure 7-12

Figure 7-11: At the top of the diagram of the report you can see that the records will be grouped by StateOrProvince.

Figure 7-12: You can choose which numeric fields you want totaled.

8 **Click the Sum box for the Invitations field.**

The report will include totals of the numbers of people who will be attending the meeting. Because the report is grouped by city, you'll see subtotals of the total number of attendees from each city and a grand total at the end of the report.

If you wanted only the totals by group and the grand totals, without listing each record individually, you would click the Summary Only option.

9 **Click OK.**

You return to the Report Wizard window that asks about sorting the records.

10 **Click Finish.**

The Report Wizard makes a report to your specifications and calls it Meeting Attendees. If you prefer, you can click Next and look at each of the rest of the Report Wizard windows, making changes to the settings as you go.

The wizard may take a few minutes to create this report. The report contains a summary section that appears after the list of people from each city and shows the sum of the Invitations field. The format is a little geeky, but the information is there. At the end of the report is the grand total of people attending the meeting.

11 **Take a look around the report (and print it, if you want) and then close the report window.**

heads up

If you use the Close button on the toolbar, you see the report in Design view, an interesting but confusing set of headers, footers, and boxes. You'll learn more about the Design view of reports in Unit 10. If you see the Design view window, close it without changing anything.

The Report Wizard can create a report with selected records from a table — just make a query to use as the report's record source. The Report Wizard can group the records in the report as well as calculate totals — that's as easy as clicking the Summary Options button.

☑ Progress Check

If you can do the following, you've mastered this lesson:

❏ Create a query to use as the record source for a report.

❏ Include all the fields from a table in a query, using the * option in the design grid.

❏ Control which columns from the design grid appear in the query result, using the Show check box.

❏ Create a report that uses a query as its record source.

❏ Create a tabular report with groups, subtotals, and totals.

Lesson 7-4   # Making a Mailing Label Report

Label Wizard creates reports to print on mailing labels

labels have Avery number on box

If you want to store a list of people's names and addresses, you'll want to mail something to them once in a while. There's no point hand-addressing envelopes, because Access makes printing mailing labels easy — you just conjure up the Label Wizard!

on the test

Before you get started, buy the labels that you plan to print on. On the box, you should see the *Avery number* of the labels — that is, the part number used by the Avery company to describe labels of this particular size. Even labels made by companies other than Avery usually have the Avery number on the box. Avoid boxes of labels without Avery numbers if you can, because it's easier to create a report if you know the Avery number!

Different labels can fit different numbers of lines on each label. Make sure to buy labels that are at least one inch high so that you can fit addresses that have a two-line street address or a country name.

on the CD

1 **Open the Dickens Address Book 7 database and then open the database window. Click the Reports tab in the database window and then click New.**

2 **Click the Label Wizard.**

3 **Click the list button at the right end of the lower box in the New Report window, the box in which you can tell Access which table or query is the record source for the report. Choose Addresses and then click OK.**

You see the Label Wizard window, shown in Figure 7-13.

on the test

4 **Choose the Avery number of the labels that you're using.**

In case your labels don't have an Avery number, choose the labels that have the same dimensions as your labels and the same number of labels across the sheets.

If you are just following this lesson to learn about mailing labels but you don't have any labels on hand, choose Avery number 5161, the number for labels that are one inch high and four inches wide. If you have a dot-matrix printer and continuous labels rather than cut sheets, click Continuous for the Label Type.

5 **Click Next.**

The Label Wizard wants to know what fonts to use on the labels. It suggests 8-point Arial, which is rather small.

6 **Change the Font size to 10 and then click Next.**

You see a window in which you decide which fields appear on the labels. Figure 7-14 shows how the window will look when you're done.

7 **Click FirstName and then click the Select highlighted field button.**

Or double-click the FirstName entry. {FirstName} appears in the Prototype label box.

»

Select highlighted field button

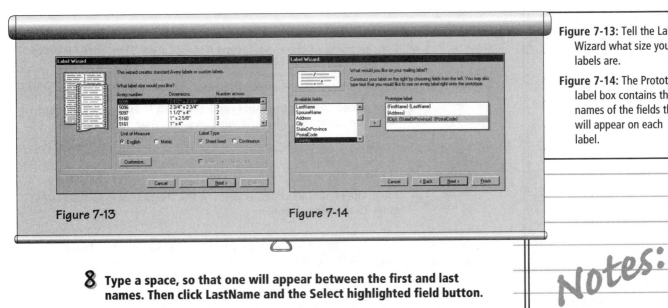

Figure 7-13

Figure 7-14

Figure 7-13: Tell the Label Wizard what size your labels are.

Figure 7-14: The Prototype label box contains the names of the fields that will appear on each label.

8 **Type a space, so that one will appear between the first and last names. Then click LastName and the Select highlighted field button.**

If you put the wrong fields or characters on the label, you can use the Backspace or Delete key to delete what's wrong.

9 **Press Enter to move to the next line of the mailing label.**

10 **Using the right-pointing-arrow button, put the Address field on the label. Press Enter to move to the next line of the label.**

The next line contains the City, StateOrProvince, and PostalCode fields, with appropriate punctuation.

11 **Put the City field on the label and type a comma and a space. Put the StateOrProvince field on the label, type two spaces, and put the PostalCode field on the label.**

Because all the addresses are in the U.S., you can omit the Country field if you are in the U.S., too. (Otherwise, press Enter to start a new line, and then put the Country field on the fourth line of the label.)

Your label looks like this:

```
{FirstName} {LastName}

{Address}

{City}, {StateOrProvince} {PostalCode}
```

12 **Click Next.**

The Label Wizard wants to know how to sort your labels. Sorting labels is always a good idea. For example, if you are mailing hundreds of letters, you may want to hike down to the post office and get a bulk mail permit, which saves you lots of money on postage but requires that the letters be sorted into zip code order.

13 **Choose the PostalCode and LastName fields to sort by, in that order. Then click Next.**

Use the Select highlighted field button to move these fields to the Sort by list.

Notes:

always sort mailing labels

print mailing list report on plain paper first to check for errors

☑ **Progress Check**

If you can do the following, you've mastered this lesson:

❑ Create a report formatted to print on mailing labels.

❑ Sort the mailing labels.

❑ Control which fields appear on the labels.

14 **For the name of the report, type** Address Labels. **Then click** **Finish to see the label report in Print Preview.**

The Label Wizard creates a report that prints the mailing labels as you specified.

15 **Take a look around the label report in Print Preview. If you want, print the report on labels (if you have them) or on plain paper.**

It's not a bad idea to print a mailing-label report on plain paper to test it out. That way, if you made a mistake somewhere, you don't waste expensive sheets of labels.

16 **Close the report window. If you see the Design view of the report, close that window, too.**

Each time you print the mailing label report, Access updates it to use the latest information from the table. If you want to print labels for only selected records, create a query that includes only those records and select the query in Step 3.

Lesson 7-5

Creating a Web Page from Your Database

Web pages are all the rage these days. Everyone's got to have a home page on the Internet, and lots of organizations are creating their own internal Webs, or *intranets*. With all the hype, how can you resist making your own Web pages?

Easily, we're sure! There's no point making Web pages that aren't useful. Luckily, Web pages created from databases are among the most useful Web pages there are. Many major Web sites, from the Yahoo! Directory (at http:// www.yahoo.com) to the Amazon.com online bookstore (at http:// www.amazon.com) are created using data from huge databases. IDG Books Worldwide's own . . .*For Dummies* Web site (at http://www.dummies.com) pulls information from a database of . . .*For Dummies,* . . .*For Teachers,* and *Dummies 101* books.

If you maintain a database and would like to publish information from the database on the Web, on either the Internet or an intranet, Access makes it simple. You can create Web pages automatically from datasheets, forms, or

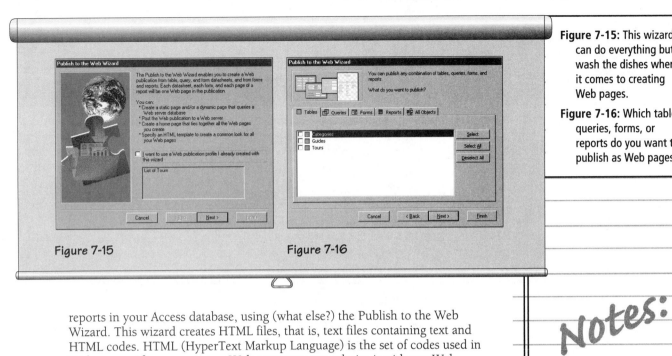

Figure 7-15

Figure 7-16

Figure 7-15: This wizard can do everything but wash the dishes when it comes to creating Web pages.

Figure 7-16: Which tables, queries, forms, or reports do you want to publish as Web pages?

reports in your Access database, using (what else?) the Publish to the Web Wizard. This wizard creates HTML files, that is, text files containing text and HTML codes. HTML (HyperText Markup Language) is the set of codes used in Web pages. After you create a Web page, you can admire it with any Web browser.

on the CD

In this lesson, you'll use the Middlebury Tours database, the same database you looked at in Unit 1. You'll create a Web page that lists the tours that this company offers so that the Middlebury Tours Web site can show the latest list of available tours.

Tip: We've found that when we turn reports into Web pages we get strange-looking pages, since the columns don't line up very well on the Web page. Instead, we recommend turning datasheets (either tables or queries) into Web pages instead. Web pages based on datasheets use the HTML tables feature and look pretty sharp.

To create a Web page, you use the <u>F</u>ile⇨Save As <u>H</u>TML command to run the Publish to the Web Wizard. There are zillions of options, bells, whistles, and fancy features, but this lesson shows you how to get started. You'll need a Web browser (like Netscape Navigator or Microsoft Internet Explorer) to see your finished Web page.

1 Run Access and open the Middlebury Tour database.

If you don't remember what the information in the Tours table looks like, open it and take a peek.

2 Choose <u>F</u>ile⇨Save As <u>H</u>TML from the menu.

The Publish to the Web Wizard appears, as shown in Figure 7-15.

3 Click <u>N</u>ext.

You see a window (Figure 7-16) that lets you choose one or more tables, queries, forms, and reports as Web pages. The Tables tab is selected, listing the tables in the database. If you choose a table or query, the wizard creates a Web page that looks a lot like the table or query Datasheet view.

Notes:

File→Save As HTML creates Web pages

Figure 7-17: You can see the records from the Tours table in a Web page!

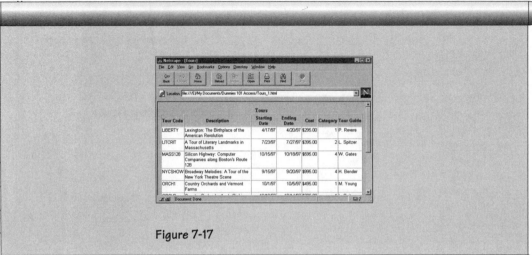

Figure 7-17

Notes:

4 **Click the Tours table and then click the Select button.**

A check mark appears in the little box to the left of the Tours table.

5 **Click Finish.**

Alternatively, you can click Next to see the rest of the pages that the wizard displays. These dialog boxes show you advanced settings, such as HTML templates to control the design of the finished Web page, whether to create the Web page once or to make a page that updates automatically in response to requests from people browsing the Web, where to store the finished Web page, and whether to store all your answers to make it easy to create an updated page the next time you give the File⇨Save As HTML command. Leave these settings on these pages alone, and keep pressing Next until the Next button turns gray and doesn't work. Then press Finish.

Access creates a Web page containing the information that you specified. Nothing seems to have happened, but an HTML file is sitting on your hard disk, stored in the same folder as the Middlebury Tours database. To see it, you need to run your favorite Web browser. We'll give instructions for Netscape Navigator and Microsoft Internet Explorer, the two most popular browsers.

6 **Run Netscape Navigator, Microsoft Internet Explorer, or your favorite Web browser.**

Next, you open the Web page you just created.

7 **In Netscape Navigator, press Ctrl+O or choose File⇨Open File from the menu. In Microsoft Internet Explorer 3.0, press Ctrl+O or choose File⇨Open from the menu, and then click the Browse button on the dialog box that appears. In either program, you then move to the *Dummies 101* Access 97 folder (or wherever the Middlebury Tours database is stored) and open the Web page named Tours_1.html.**

If you use another browser, give the command to open a Web page that is stored on your own computer. The Web page looks like Figure 7-17.

☑ Progress Check

If you can do the following, you've mastered this lesson:

❑ Run the Publish to the Web Wizard.

❑ Create a Web page that displays a table or query in Datasheet view.

❑ Display the Web page you created.

8 **Close your browser.**

That's all it takes to create a Web page from the records in a table. If you have a Web site on which you can store the Web page, you can make the page accessible to other people on the Internet or on your intranet. Now that you know how to create and print reports and mailing labels and create Web pages, all using the information in your Access database, you're more than ready for the Unit 7 Quiz.

Unit 7 Quiz

For each of the following questions, circle the letter of the correct answer or answers. Remember, each question may have more than one right answer.

1. **When you are displaying a report in Print Preview, you can . . .**

   A. Press Ctrl+P to print the report.

   B. Click in the report to zoom in and out.

   C. Click the Two Pages button to see two pages of the report side by side.

   D. Click buttons on the navigation bar to move to other pages of the report.

   E. All of the above.

2. **When you create a tabular report by using the Report Wizard, you specify . . .**

   A. Which table(s) or query(ies) to use as the record source for the report.

   B. Whether the records should be grouped together based on the value of one or more fields.

   C. Which fields should appear in the report and in which order.

   D. What color paper to print the report on.

   E. How the records should be sorted.

3. **When creating a query, what is the Show box on the design grid for?**

   A. Choosing your favorite TV show.

   B. Playing "Show and Tell."

   C. Playing "I'll Show You Mine If You'll Show Me Yours."

   D. Choosing whether to show the column in the query results.

   E. Practicing your clicking.

4. To create a report that prints mailing labels, you have to tell the Label Wizard . . .

   A. How many ounces the letters will weigh.

   B. What fields should appear on the labels.

   C. How many labels run across the page.

   D. The Avery number of the labels that you plan to use.

   E. Which table or query to use as the record source.

5. In *James and the Giant Peach* (both the children's classic book by Roald Dahl and the recent Disney movie), James makes friends with a bunch of huge . . .

   A. Peaches.

   B. Aliens.

   C. Giants.

   D. Bugs.

   E. Politicians.

6. What is an Avery number?

   A. The number of Averies that can dance on the head of a pin.

   B. The number of molecules in one gram of Avery labels.

   C. The number on the outside of a box of mailing labels that identifies the size and shape of the labels in the box.

   D. The easiest way to tell Access what kind of labels you've got.

   E. The number of mailing labels in the box.

Unit 7 Exercise

1. Open the Dickens Address Book 7 database.

2. Create a query that selects people who have e-mail addresses. (For the selection criterion, enter **Is Not Null** for the EmailAddress field.)

3. Save the query as People with E-Mail Addresses.

4. Create a columnar report, using your new query as a record source, that includes people's names and e-mail addresses, sorted by last name.

5. Name the report E-Mail Addresses.

6. Print your new report.

Part III Review

Unit 6 Summary

▶ **Changing column width in a datasheet:** Drag the column divider with the mouse or right-click the field selector (column heading) and choose Column Width from the shortcut menu.

▶ **Adjusting column width automagically:** Double-click the column divider to the right of the column to ask Access to adjust the column width just wide enough to fit the widest entry in the column.

▶ **Changing the order of columns in a datasheet:** Select the column to move by clicking its field selector and then drag the column left or right to its new location. To select a range of columns, click the first field selector and then Shift+click the last field selector.

▶ **Setting the font for a datasheet:** Choose Format⇨Font from the menu. Check column widths again after changing fonts.

▶ **Sorting records in a datasheet by the values in a column:** Click anywhere in the column and then click the Sort Ascending or Sort Descending button on the toolbar.

▶ **Print Preview:** Choose File⇨Print Preview from the menu bar or click the Print Preview button.

▶ **Formatting the page:** Choose File⇨Page Setup from the menu bar to choose between portrait and landscape orientation and to set margins.

▶ **Moving around in Print Preview:** Use the navigation bar buttons to move from page to page.

▶ **Hiding columns before printing:** To temporarily hide a column in a datasheet (without deleting the information from the table), select the column and choose Format⇨Hide Columns. To unhide them, choose Format⇨Unhide Columns and click column boxes to choose which columns should appear.

▶ **Printing a table or query in Datasheet view:** Click the Print button on the toolbar or choose File⇨Print from the menu bar.

▶ **Printing selected pages or multiple copies:** Set options in the Print dialog box. (Choose File⇨Print.)

Unit 7 Summary

▶ **Where reports come from:** The Database Wizard creates reports when creating a database. You can make your own reports from scratch or with help from the Report Wizard by clicking New on the Reports tab of the database table.

▶ **Previewing reports created by the Database Wizard:** Click the Preview Reports button on the Main Switchboard.

▶ **Previewing any report:** Click the Reports tab on the database window and double-click a report.

▶ **Printing reports:** Preview the report with Print Preview; then click the Print button on the toolbar, choose File⇨Print from the menu bar, or press Ctrl+P. Use the Print dialog box to choose the number of copies or the pages to print.

▶ **Creating a report:** Click the New button on the Reports tab of the database window. Double-click the Report Wizard to create a columnar (tabular) report with help from the Report Wizard. Tell the Report Wizard which fields to include in the report, record order, page orientation, and other report specifications.

▶ **Selecting which records to include in a report:** Create a query that selects the records you want on the report. Then create a report that uses the query as its record source.

Part III Review

▶ **Including all the fields from a table in a query:** When creating the query, drag the * from the field list to the Field row. If you want to select records based on the value of field, drag the field name to the Field row and then click the Show box for that field to remove the check mark. Type a criterion as usual.

▶ **Creating a report that prints mailing labels:** Click the New button on the Reports tab of the database window and then double-click the Label Wizard. When possible, buy labels with the Avery number on the box to simplify report creation.

▶ **Creating a Web page from a table or query:** Choose File⇨Save As HTML from the menu to run the Publish to the Web Wizard. Select a table or query to publish. Access creates a Web page in a file with the .html extension in the same folder as the database. Use your Web browser to see it.

Part III Test

The questions on this test cover all the material presented in Part III, Units 6 and 7.

True False

T F 1. You can't print datasheets. You can only print reports.

T F 2. Portrait orientation is for printing reports the usual way on the page: with the lines of text parallel to the short side of the paper.

T F 3. To adjust the width of a column, drag the column divider left or right.

T F 4. There's no place like home.

T F 5. You have to look at a datasheet or report in Print Preview before you can print it so that Access can format the report for the printer.

T F 6. The Database Wizard and the Report Wizard both create reports.

T F 7. To create a report, click the Reports tab on the database window and then click the New button.

T F 8. If you want to sort the records in your report, you must design it yourself because a Wizard won't do that for you.

T F 9. To include all the fields from a table in a query, you have to drag each field name to the Field row of the design grid individually.

T F 10. To create a Web page from the information in an Access database, you choose File⇨Save As HTML from the menu.

Part III Test

Multiple Choice

For each of the following questions, circle the correct answer or answers. Remember, there may be more than one right answer for each question!

11. **How do you sort the records in a datasheet?**

   A. Click in the column you want to sort by and then click the Sort Ascending button.

   B. Click in the column you want to sort by and then choose Records➪Sort from the menu.

   C. Print the datasheet, cut the printout into strips with one record per strip, sort the strips, tape them back together, and photocopy the result.

   D. Make a query that sorts the records and then open the query in Datasheet view.

   E. Click in the column you want to sort by and then click the Sort Descending button.

12. **In Print Preview of a datasheet or report, you can . . .**

   A. Move from page to page, using the navigation bar.

   B. Print the datasheet or report.

   C. Zoom out so you can see the whole page.

   D. Zoom even farther out so you can see two pages at the same time.

   E. Zoom so far out that you can see the entire Earth spinning through space like a luminous marble.

13. **When looking at a table or query in Datasheet view, you can . . .**

   A. Change the widths of the columns.

   B. Sort the records in the datasheet by the values in a column.

   C. Take a break and get a glass of water.

   D. Switch the order of the columns.

   E. Close the datasheet.

14. **What body of water is on the east end of the Panama Canal?**

   A. The Atlantic Ocean.

   B. The Pacific Ocean.

   C. Panama Bay.

   D. The Gulf of Panama.

   E. The Caribbean.

15. **The Report Wizard lets you . . .**

   A. Choose which table or query is the record source for the report.

   B. Choose which fields appear on the report.

   C. Sort the records by one or more fields.

   D. Eat as much ice cream as you want and not get fat.

   E. Print totals for numeric fields on the report.

Part III Test

16. **When creating a report to print on mailing labels, you should. . .**

    A. Use the Label Wizard.

    B. Know the Avery number or dimensions of the labels you plan to print on.

    C. Get someone else to do it because it's a pain.

    D. Set the font to at least 10 points so that letter carriers and sorters have some hope of reading the addresses.

    E. Include the ZIP or postal code on the labels.

17. **Which of the following are good reasons to create a Web page from a table or query in your database?**

    A. Because your friends are doing it.

    B. Because everyone who's anyone has a Web page.

    C. Because you want other people on the World Wide Web or your organization's intranet to be able to see information in your database.

    D. Because you have nothing better to do.

    E. Because it's a brand new command and you've just *got* to try it out.

Matching

18. **Match each of the following buttons with its name.**

    A. 1. Database Window

    B. 2. Sort Descending

    C. 3. Print Preview

    D. 4. Sort Ascending

    E. 5. Print

19. **Match the movie with the actors who appeared in each.**

    A. Julie Andrews   1. *Casablanca*

    B. Robin Wright   2. *Peter Pan* (the 1960 stage version)

    C. Humphrey Bogart   3. *Star Wars*

    D. Mary Martin   4. *The Sound of Music*

    E. Mark Hamill   5. *The Princess Bride*

20. **Match each of the following actions with what it does.**

    A. Double-clicking column divider   1. Adjusts the width of the column to its left to "best fit"

    B. Clicking Print button   2. Displays the Print dialog box

    C. Clicking Sort Ascending button   3. Opens Print Preview window

    D. Clicking Print Preview button   4. Sorts records by the current column

    E. Pressing Ctrl+P   5. Prints without displaying the Print dialog box.

Part III Lab Assignment

In this lab, you will print two lists of the characters in the Dickens Address Book: a datasheet and a report. Don't worry if you haven't done Labs 1 and 2 because this lab uses a different database.

Step 1: Open the Dickens Address Book 7 database

This is the database you last used in Unit 7, so you might still have it open.

Step 2: Create a query that selects everyone who lives in the town of New London

Include all the fields in the Addresses table or at least the FirstName, LastName, Address, and HomePhone fields.

After checking out the query in Datasheet view to make sure it looks right, close the query and name it New London Inhabitants.

Step 3: Create a report that prints the names, street addresses, and phone numbers of everyone who lives in New London

Use the Report Wizard to help you. Sort the people by last name. After previewing the report, close it and name it New London Address List.

Step 4: Print the new report

When you're done, exit Access.

Creating and Using Multitable Databases

Part IV

In this part . . .

You've come a long way since you started to learn about Access. You know how to use tables, queries, forms, and reports. But sooner or later, you're going to want to make your own database or to make some major changes to the databases you use.

The last three units in this book tell you how to do just that. Unit 8 explains the basics of database design so that you can figure out what tables and fields belong in your database. Part of database design is learning how tables relate and how to design tables that will relate to other tables.

Unit 9 describes how to make queries, forms, and reports that use more than one table, and Unit 10 tells you what you need to know to make changes to an existing database, including adding new fields, changing the specs of existing fields, and deleting fields you don't plan to use.

Making Databases with Related Tables

Objectives for This Unit

✓ Learning the principles of relational database design

✓ Understanding how tables in a multitable database relate to one another

✓ Taking a peek at the design of a multitable database

✓ Looking at the relationships in a multitable database

Prerequisites
- Creating a database by using the Database Wizard (Unit 2)
- Looking at tables and queries in Design and Datasheet views (Unit 4)

on the CD
- US Senate database (US Senate.mdb)

The beauty of Access is that it is a *relational database program,* and you can use it to create *relational databases.* Yikes! Sounds like a serious programming project. But what is it, exactly?

on the test

A *relational database* is a database that contains more than one table, where the tables are related. Are the tables cousins? Aunt and nephew? Not quite. Two tables are *related* if they contain fields that match. For example, remember the Middlebury Tours database (from Units 1, 3, and 7)? The database contains a Tours table with one record for each type of tour that the company offers. The Tours table contains a field named Tour Guide, with the name of the guide for the tour. It also contains a Guides table, with the name and phone number for each tour guide. The Tour Guide field in the Tours table contains information that relates to the Tour Guide field in the Guides table. Figure 8-1 shows how this relationship works.

relational
database =
database with
related tables

Figure 8-1: The Tour Guide field in the Tours table relates to the Tour Guide field in the Guides table. Each record in the Guides table can relate to no, one, or many records in the Tours table. Each record in the Tours table can relate to exactly one record in the Guides table.

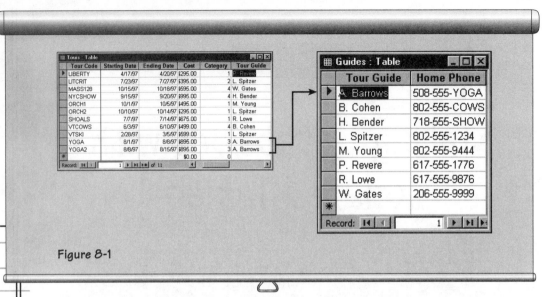

Figure 8-1

one-to-many relationship = record in one table relates to many records in related table

Lots of records in the Tours table can have the same entry in the Tour Guide field — that is, a guide can lead a bunch of tours, just not at the same time. A relationship between two tables in which one record in one table relates to a bunch of records in the other table is called a *one-to-many relationship*. For example, one record in the Guides table can relate to none of the records, one of the records, or many records in the Tours table: You can have no tours, one tour, or many different tours led by a particular guide.

When you create a database, how do you figure out what tables to create and how the table should be related? This is the topic of many advanced computer science courses. In this unit, you'll learn the principles of designing a relational database. Then you'll look at a multitable database created by the Database Wizard.

Lesson 8-1   Database Design 101

This lesson doesn't require using Access at all. In fact, you don't even have to use the computer. Why not put your feet up on your desk (take your shoes off first), or take your book outside or down to the cafeteria?

Why use related databases at all?

For some projects, you need to maintain several different lists of items. For example, suppose you run a congressional watchdog group and you need to keep track of which U.S. senators are on which Senate committee. Your database will include a list of senators, a list of political parties, and a list of committees.

To track senators, parties, and committees, you need three different tables. The Senators table contains one record for each member, the Parties table contains one record for each party, and the Committees table contains one record for each committee.

You could store all this information in one big table, but you would be sorry. For example, you could add fields to the Committees table to record the name, address, and phone number of each member. But a senator can be on more than one committee, so you'd have many senators appear in the Committees table more than once. Storing the same information over and over is a waste of time and disk space, and it makes the tables harder to maintain.

don't store same information more than once

Here's a way to tell when you should create multiple tables: Count how many instances of each field you've got. You have 100 senators, and you track 12 committees. You have 100 different senator names, addresses, and phone numbers; two different major political party names; and 12 different committee names. This is an indication that you should store the information in three different tables: a Senators table with 100 records, a Parties table with two records, and a Committees table with 12 records.

The Senators and Parties tables are related in a one-to-many relationship. One record in the Parties table can relate to none of the records, one of the records, or many records in the Senators table. (If there's no record in the Senators table for a record in the Parties table, the party hasn't fielded any successful candidates yet.) The table on the "one" end of the one-to-many relationship (in this example, the Parties table) is frequently called the *master table*. The table on the "many" end of the relationship (the Senators table) is called the *detail table*.

master table = "one" end of one-to-many relationship

detail table = "many" end

Linking tables with key fields

If you use master and detail tables in a one-to-many relationship, you need to link the tables together to create reports. For example, the Parties table contains the Party Code (*R* or *D*, or *I* for independents) and the full name of the party. If you want to print the full name of a senator's political party on a name tag, you need to include the name fields from the Senators table and the Party Name field from the Parties table. To link the two tables, you need one field (or a set of fields) in each table that *links* or *relates* the two tables, indicating which records in one table are linked to which records in the other table. These fields are called *key fields*.

master and detail tables are linked by key field(s)

For example, the Senators and Parties tables can each contain a field called Party Code that contains a one-letter code identifying a political party. When Access prints a name tag for a senator, it looks at a record in the Senators table and sees what the senator's party code is (*D*, *R*, or *I*). Then it looks in the Parties table for a record with the same entry in its Party Code field and prints the Party Name for that record. This process is called a *relational lookup*, and Access can perform this kind of lookup automatically.

relational lookup = looking up matching record in related table *primary key field = key field in master table*

foreign key field = key field in detail table

many-to-many relationship requires additional table

Relational lookups work only when key fields relate the two tables. The key fields need not have the same names in the two related tables, but the whole business is less confusing if they do. For example, the key field could be called Party in the Senators table and Party Code in the Parties table. However, the two fields must have the same field type (text, number, date, or whatever) and the same length. Access lets you use a combination of fields as the key field to relate two tables, but we don't use this feature in this unit. The key field in the master table is called the *primary key field,* and the key field in the detail table is called the *foreign key field.*

With a one-to-many relationship, the master table (Parties, in our example) must have a primary key field that uniquely identifies each record. That is, the Party Code must be different for each record in the Parties table. Otherwise, when Access does the relational lookup, it won't know which Party Code is the one you want. In the detail table (Senators, in our example), you can have many senators from one party, so you can have many records with the same value in the foreign key field.

on the test

Tip: The AutoNumber field is perfect for uniquely identifying each record in many tables.

Many-to-many relationships

What if two tables are related but *many* records in one table relate to *many* records in the other table? Here's an example: The US Senate database contains a table of Senators and a table of Committees. One senator can be on many committees. One committee can contain many senators. It's a *many-to-many relationship.*

The problem is that Access (and most other database programs) can't handle many-to-many relationships. Access refuses to accept that these relationships exist. (Don't you know people like that?) But don't worry — there's a way around this problem. You can create an additional table that saves the day.

on the test

Take a look at Figure 8-2. The Committee Members table stores the connections between the Senators and Committees tables. For each position on each committee, the Committee Members table has a record that indicates which senator holds the position and which committee it is by specifying the Member ID of the person and the Committee ID of the committee. So a member can be the subject of more than one record — if a member is on three committees, he or she has three records in the Committee Members table.

There's a one-to-many relationship between the Committees table and the Committee Members table. There's another one-to-many relationship between the Senators table and the Committee Members table. This new table turns a many-to-many relationship into two one-to-many relationships so that Access can handle it.

The Committee Members table contains two foreign keys: one that matches the primary key field in the Senators table and another that matches the primary key field in the Committees table.

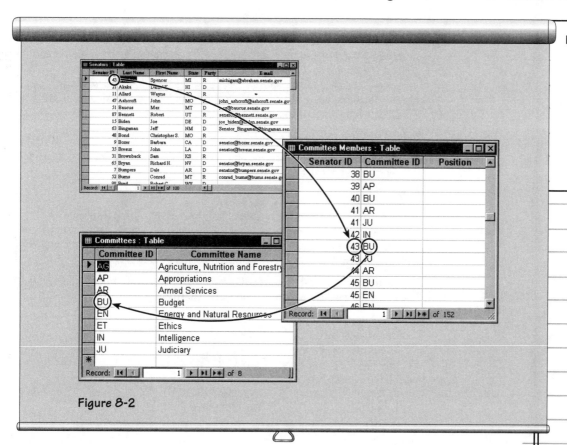

Figure 8-2: You store the many-to-many relationship between the Senators and Committees table in a new tables, the Committee Members table. Senator Abraham Spencer is on the Budget Committee, according to this relational lookup.

Notes:

Figure 8-2

Eight steps for database design

on the test

When you need to create a database, follow these steps to determine what the tables should be and how they should be related:

1 State the problem.

State what kind of information you want to handle and what output you want to produce. For example, if you're creating a system to track a Senate committee so that you can spot illegal lobbying activities or inappropriate campaign donations, the statement might be "Track senators, parties, and committees so I can print lists of who's on what committee."

Make a list of the things that you want the database to do. For example:

- ◆ Keep a list of senators' names, addresses, and telephone numbers.
- ◆ Keep track of what committee each senator is on.
- ◆ Track who's in what party.
- ◆ Print e-mail address lists and telephone lists by committee or by party.
- ◆ Print mailing labels for all or selected senators.

state purpose of database

find available
data

choose field types

don't store
unnecessary
information

divide fields into
tables

Tip: To get a clear picture of what you need, make *mockups* of the reports you need — examples of what the reports will look like, with real data. For example, sketch out what an address or phone list would look like. For an order entry database, figure out what information your invoices, packing slips, and purchase orders would contain.

2 **Identify the available data.**

Find out what information is available, who maintains it, what it looks like, and how it is used. Make a list of the possible fields.

3 **Decide what type of information each field contains.**

Some fields look like numbers but ought to be text. For example, phone numbers and zip codes may be composed of a bunch of digits, but they don't represent quantities. Use number fields only for numbers you'd do math with — who ever heard of totaling a bunch of phone numbers or zip codes?

You might end up with this list of fields for your US Senate database (field type codes: T for text, N for number, and D for Date/Time):

First Name (T)	Date Elected (D)
Last Name (T)	Birthdate (D)
Street Address (T)	Age (N)
City (T)	Party Code (T)
State/Province (T)	Party Name (T)
Postcode (T)	Committee Name (T)
Phone (T)	Committee Members (T)
Fax (T)	

4 **Review the data, eliminating unnecessary items.**

Remove any data items that are redundant or that don't appear in any of the reports you think you'll need.

For example, if you store each senator's birth date, storing the senator's age is redundant because you (or Access) can calculate people's ages from their birth dates. You might also decide to eliminate senators' social security numbers and election dates because you don't need them on any report.

5 **Organize the information into groups of related items.**

Look at the information to see whether it falls into groups. One indicator that you can use groups is when some fields occur more often than others. In this example, more member names appear than committee names, and more payment dates than members.

The groups in this example might be as follows:

Senators	**Parties**
First Name (T)	Party Code (T)
Last Name (T)	Party Name (T)
Street Address (T)	
City (T)	**Committees**
State/Province (T)	Committee Name (T)
Postcode (T)	Committee Members (T)
Phone (T)	
Fax (T)	

Each group will be a table, and the items will be fields.

6 **Choose a primary key field (or combination of fields) for each table.**

For most of the tables in your database, you need a *primary key field* that uniquely identifies the record. Any table on the "one" side of a one-to-many relationship needs a primary key field for the relationship to work. For other tables, a primary key field can be useful: If a table has a primary key field, Access displays its records sorted into order by the primary key. Also, searching by primary key is fast because Access creates an index for the field.

If the table already contains a field that uniquely identifies the record, use that field as the primary key. For example, seat numbers in the Senate would be perfect as the primary key of the Senators table, unless senators routinely sit in each other's laps.

If no field or combination of fields in a table uniquely identifies each member, add an AutoNumber field to the table — this new field will be the table's primary key. In the Senators table, add an AutoNumber field named Senator ID. In the Parties table, use the Party Code, a one-letter abbreviation of the political party's name.

Your database design looks like this:

Senators

Senator ID (AutoNumber) - *key*
First Name (T)
Last Name (T)
Street Address (T)
City (T)
State/Province (T)
Postcode (T)
Phone (T)
Fax (T)

Parties

Party Code (T) - *key*
Party Name (T)

Committees
Committee Name (T) - *key*
Committee Members (T)

7 **Link the tables, adding fields and tables as needed.**

The Senators and Parties tables have a one-to-many relationship (one party with many senators). You can't tell by looking at a senator's record what party he or she is in. You need to add a foreign key field to the Senators table to match the primary key field of the Parties table and to contain the party code of the party the senator belongs to. Add a field to the Senators table called Party, a one-character text field.

The Committees table has one record for each committee. But something is wrong with the Committee Members field in the Committees table — for one committee name, there can be lots of Committee Members. You could use one long text field to contain a list of senators' names, but doing so would prevent you from easily looking up committee members' addresses and phone numbers for a committee phone list. A better idea is to make each member's name a separate record.

Because one member can be on many committees and one committee can have many members, you want a many-to-many relationship between the Senators and Committees tables. As explained in the section "Many-to-many relationships" earlier in this unit, you need to create a new table to store this relation-

Notes:

choose primary key fields, adding AutoNumber field as primary key where necessary

add foreign key fields to relate tables

add new tables to store many-to-many relationships

ship; call it Committee Members. Give each record in the Committees table a two-letter code, stored in a Committee ID field in the Committees table, and make this code the primary key field. The new Committee Members table can contain a matching foreign key field to identify the committee that senators are members of.

Your new database design might look like this:

Senators
Senator ID (AutoNumber) - *key*
First Name (T)
Last Name (T)
Street Address (T)
City (T)
State/Province (T)
Postcode (T)
Phone (T)
Fax (T)
Party (T)

Parties
Party Code (T) - *key*
Party Name (T)

Committees
Committee ID (T) - *key*
Committee Name (T)

Committee Members
Committee Code (T) - *key*
Senator ID (N) - *key*

8 Look at your database design and make adjustments as needed.

You've got a bunch of tables, with fields in each one. Consider each table in turn; think about what each record signifies. Is there any other information you want to store in that table? Are all the fields in the table needed?

For example, in this design, the Committee Members table contains one record for each combination of committee and senator. You may want to add a field called Position to store what position that person has on that committee, or maybe a field called Start Date to store the date when the person started serving on the committee.

Congratulations! You've designed a database. If you've been lolling under a tree or munching a snack in the cafeteria while reading this lesson, it's time to get back to your computer — the next lesson requires Access.

Progress Check

If you can do the following, you've mastered this lesson:

❏ List the fields you might want to use.

❏ Exclude fields that you don't need.

❏ Divide fields into tables.

❏ Choose appropriate primary and foreign key fields to relate the tables.

extra credit

Using AutoNumber fields

When you add records to a table that contains an AutoNumber field, Access automatically fills in the field with the next available number, starting with 1 for the first record. You can't modify the contents of an AutoNumber field. When you delete a record, that record's number is retired forever — Access doesn't reuse the values of an AutoNumber field.

You cannot use an AutoNumber field as the foreign key field — Access will not allow it. Instead, use a number field with size Long Integer. (AutoNumber fields are so-called *Long Integer* numbers — that is, integers that can be as long as approximately 2 billion. So please don't plan to have any Access tables with more than 2 billion records.)

Opening a Multitable Database

You're about to look at the US Senate database supplied on the *Dummies 101* CD-ROM. We created the database with information that we found on the Senate Web site at `http://www.senate.gov`. Aren't we nice — we're not making you build the database yourself and type all that data!

Looking at the tables

Now, go snooping around and see whether the database matches the one we designed in Lesson 8-1.

on the CD

1 **Run Access, open the US Senate database, and click the Tables table on the database window.**

Because we made this table ourselves, it doesn't have a Switchboard.

In the database window, you see the four tables we built: Committee Members, Committees, Parties, and Senators. It's the same design (more or less) as the one we came up with in Lesson 8-1.

In the rest of this lesson, you'll open each of the tables in Datasheet view, review the entries, and then switch to Design view as we discuss salient points about each table.

2 **Open the Senators table in Datasheet view. To reveal the hidden columns (the result of datasheet formatting that you did in Unit 6), choose Format⇨Unhide Columns from the menu, click the little boxes so they all contain check marks, and click Close.**

Now all the fields appear in the datasheet.

3 **Review the entries and then switch to Design view (by clicking the View button, the leftmost button on the toolbar).**

As you would expect, this table contains all the information associated with an individual senator, with one record per member. The fields include name, office address, and telephone number, as well as each senator's e-mail address and Web page. Figure 8-3 shows the table in Design view; the table has too many fields to fit in the window, so you scroll down to see the rest.

The Senator ID field is an AutoNumber field and has been set as the primary key because each member has a unique Senator ID. Using meaningless keys, such as assigned numbers, as the primary key for your table is a good idea. If you use a meaningful key (you may have thought of using FirstName and LastName for this database), problems arise when that piece of data changes or when two senators have the same name (two current senators are named Kerry and Kerrey, which are awfully similar).

4 **Close the Senators window, clicking Yes to save changes to the layout (namely unhiding the hidden columns). Open the Parties table in Datasheet view, review the entries (all three of them), and switch to Design view (shown in Figure 8-4).**

The Party Code field (a one-letter abbreviation) is the primary key field and relates to the Party field in the Senators table.

Notes:

Figure 8-3: Senator ID is the primary key field for the Senators table.

Figure 8-4: Each party has a unique one-letter abbreviation.

Notes:

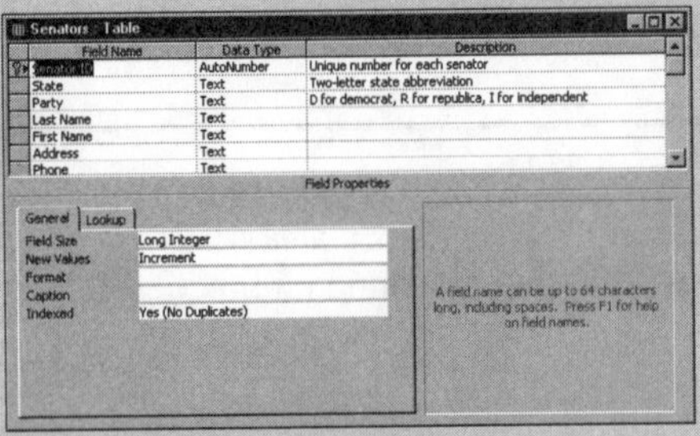

Figure 8-3

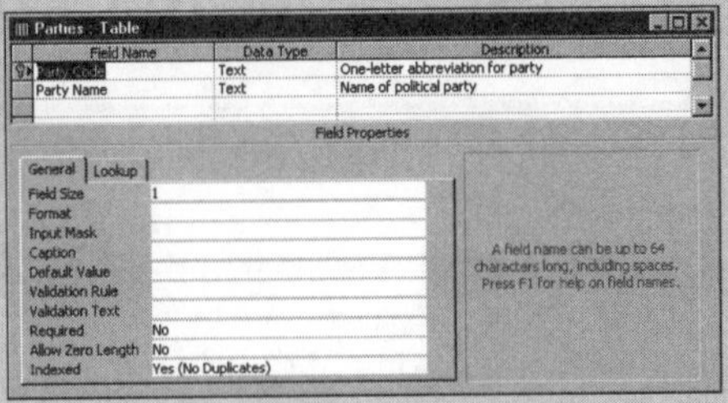

Figure 8-4

5. **Close the Parties table. Open the Committees table in Datasheet view, review the entries, and switch to Design view (shown in Figure 8-5).**

   The Committee Name is a standard text field, and the primary key field, Committee ID, is a two-letter text field.

   You may want to add other fields that describe each committee, like MeetingTime (to contain when the committee usually meets, like the third Wednesday of each month) or Standing? (a Yes/No field that indicates when the committee is a standing committee). You'll learn how to add fields to a table in Unit 10.

6. **Close the Committees table. Open the Committee Members table in Datasheet view, review the entries, and switch to Design view.**

   This table (shown in Figure 8-6) links a member with a committee. Each record stores the fact that a particular person is on a particular committee. The Committee ID field specifies which committee you're talking about (it's a foreign key field that corresponds to the Committee ID field in the Committees table), and the Senator ID field specifies which senator is on that committee (it's a foreign key field that corresponds to the Senator ID field in the Senators table).

   The relationship between Senators and Committees is a many-to-many one, as we described in Lesson 8-1. The Committee Members table converts the many-to-many relationship into two one-to-many relationships so that Access can handle it.

   One other piece of information is stored in each record: the position that the person holds on the committee — for example, *Chair.*

7. **Close the Committee Members table.**

So far, you've seen the tables used to store information in a membership database. There are more tables than you expected, aren't there? Every list of values — including lists of types of membership or who's on what committee — should be stored in a table.

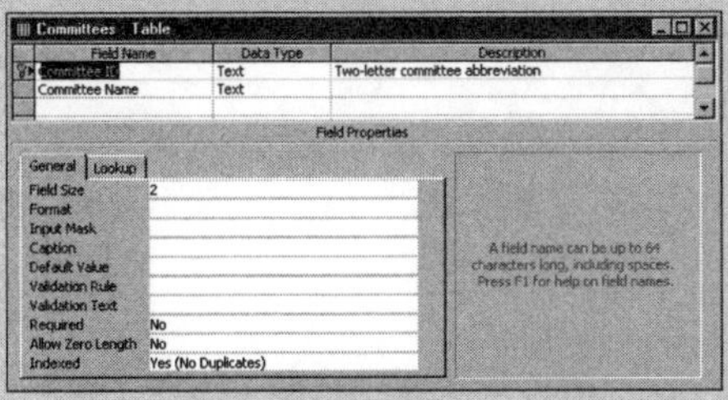

Figure 8-5 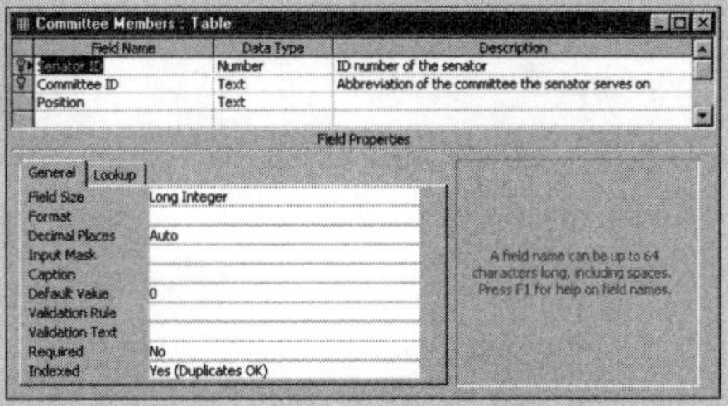 | Figure 8-6

Figure 8-5: Each committee has a code and a name.

Figure 8-6: Each record in the Committee Members table connects one senator (via the Senator ID field) to one committee (via the Committee ID field).

Looking at other database elements

Tables do not a database make, as Shakespeare said. (Okay, maybe someone else said it.) Take a look at the other items in the US Senate database, such as queries, forms, and reports.

1 **In the database window, click the Queries tab.**

You see a list of the queries in this database. You can make queries in a multitable database just the same way you would in a single-table database: Click the <u>N</u>ew button. In Unit 9, you'll learn to make queries that include fields from more than one table.

2 **Click the Forms tab.**

You see a list of forms, two of which are subforms (Committees Senators Are On and Senators On Committees). You'll see what subforms look like in a minute.

3 **Open the Committees form and look it over.**

The Committees form, shown in Figure 8-7, displays information about one committee (one record in the Committees table).

This form uses a subform in Datasheet view to list the senators who are on the committee. A *subform* is a form that appears inside another form. You generally use subforms to show a list of information from a table related to the record being displayed on the regular form. In a one-to-many relationship between two tables, a form can display information from the "one" table, and a subform can display information from the "many" table.

This form uses the Committee Members table to find out the Senator IDs of the people on the committee and the Senators table to find out the full names of the senators.

When you look at a form, what part of it (if any) is a subform isn't always obvious. If you see what looks like a little datasheet on the form — as you do on the Committees form — the datasheet is a subform.

heads up

subform = form within a form

Figure 8-7: The Committees form combines information from one record in the Committees table (at the top of the form) and from related records in the Committee Members and Senators tables (in the datasheet in the rest of the form).

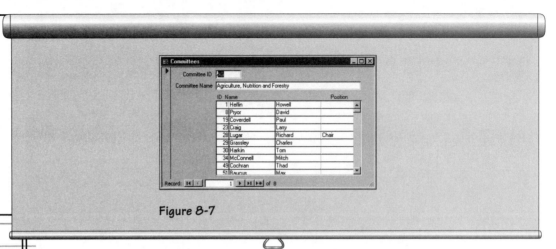

Figure 8-7

make multitable reports by creating multitable queries and then creating reports based on those queries

☑ **Progress Check**

If you can do the following, you've mastered this lesson:

❑ Open a multitable database.

❑ Search an existing database to get hints on how to set up a database for your own needs.

4 **Close the Committees form.**

You see the database window again. The Senators form works the same way as the Committees form, with information about one senator and a list of the committees he or she is on.

5 **Click the Reports tab.**

This database doesn't contain any reports (yet). You'll create one in Unit 9, though! To create a report that includes information from multiple tables, you usually create a query that combines information from the tables and then create a report that uses the new query as its record source.

6 **Click the Macros and Modules tabs.**

Phew! Thank goodness nothing is in either place. Macros and modules are a little too complex a topic for this book. For more information about the programming capabilities of macros and modules, check out *Access Programming For Dummies* by Rob Krumm (IDG Books Worldwide, Inc.).

Of course, we haven't told you everything that you can do with multitable databases. Instead, you have seen some interesting sights, and we hope you will revisit them on your own one day without needing us as a tour guide.

In Unit 9, you'll learn how to combine information from two or more tables into one query, which is the single most powerful feature of multitable databases. And in Unit 10, you'll learn to make changes to a database, including creating a table that uses the automatic lookup feature of Access!

Don't forget that you always have help close at hand: Check out the Extra Credit sidebar near the end of Unit 1 to learn more about online help.

Lesson 8-3   Mapping Out Relationships

In life, relationships are tough, and when they start on the wrong foot, making them work is even tougher. As goes life, so go databases (another Shakespeare quote).

Relationships between tables can be complex, and you need to think about them carefully as you build the database. The more you think about relationships up front, the better they work out in the end, and although we can't help out much with your personal relationships, we can give some hints on planning table relationships. In this lesson, you take a close look at the relationships between the tables in the US Senate database. You will see some of the special relationships we created, and we'll explain why we set them up this way. Prepare yourself for a surprise — when we say that you'll see the relationships, we aren't kidding.

Here's how to see relationships: When you're looking at the Database window, click the Relationships button on the toolbar (the button with three connected boxes, third from the right). Or choose Tools⇨Relationships from the menu bar. Either way, you see the Relationships window, shown in Figure 8-8.

In the Relationships window, you can see to following: every table in the database that is joined to another table; a list of the fields in each table; the primary key field for each table, highlighted with a bold font; and *join lines* (lines that join related tables). Join lines show which fields in the tables are related, and they show what type of relationship it is. For example, a line joins the Senator ID field (the foreign key field) in the Committee Members table to the Senator ID field (the primary key field) in the Senators table. The 1s and lazy 8s (a.k.a. infinity signs) identify the "one" (1) and "many" (lazy 8) sides of one-to-many relationships.

Using the Relationships window, you can see how tables are related, and you can choose when to ask Access to enforce referential integrity. *Referential integrity* means that Access prevents you from adding a record to the detail table if you don't already have a corresponding record in the master table. For example, you can't add records to the Committee Members table without having a corresponding entry in the Committees table — you can't add people to a committee that doesn't exist. Think of it as a parent with children: You can have a parent before the children, but not the other way around. Referential integrity also frowns on orphans, so although orphans unfortunately exist in real life, this relationship between tables prevents you from deleting a record from the master (Committees) table that would leave orphans in the detail (Committee Members) table.

Peeking in the Relationships window

Take a look at the Relationships window.

1 **Make sure that the US Senate database is open.**

2 **Choose Tools⇨Relationships from the menu bar or click the Relationships button on the toolbar.**

What you see, as shown in Figure 8-8, is a pretty cool picture of all the tables in the database and the relationships between them all. We make no bones about it — this is a great picture. Although we're going to look at some of the supporting design structure that sits behind this awesome picture, the most important information about all the tables and their relationships is right here on one fantastic-looking screen. Did we mention that we like this picture?

Margin notes:

Relationships button or Tools→Relationships displays Relationships window

join lines = lines between fields that relate tables

referential integrity = each record in detail table must have matching record in master table

Relationships button

Relationships window displays fabulous pictue

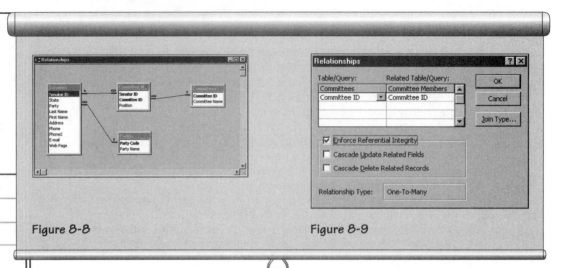

Figure 8-8   Figure 8-9

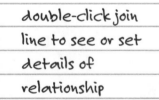
right-click background of Relationships window and choose Show **T**able to add tables to window

3 Choose Relationships⇨Show **T**able from the menu bar. Or right-click the gray background of the Relationships window and choose Show **T**able from the menu that appears.

on the CD

You see the Show Table window, listing all the tables and queries in your database. This window is where you can choose other tables that you want to add to the Relationships window. We've done all the work, so you don't need to add any tables to the Relationships window — but we thought you'd want to know how to add tables just in case. Besides, in the next few steps, you're likely to be clicking in the gray background accidentally, and we want you to know what's down this route even though we don't want you to take it.

4 Close the Show Table window.

So far, you've seen a nice diagram that explains how the tables in the database are related.

Looking at join lines

Next, look at the properties behind the join lines.

double-click join line to see or set details of relationship

1 Double-click the join line linking the Committees and Committee Members tables, or right-click the line and choose Edit **R**elationship from the pop-up menu.

If you accidentally right-click in the background instead of on the line, you see the pop-up menu for the background that you saw in the last step. Try again. If you find it hard to double-click a join line, click the line once to make sure that your mouse pointer is pointing to the line itself; if you click the line, the line gets darker. Then double-click without moving the mouse.

The new, smaller Relationships window you see is shown in Figure 8-9. The fields that join the two tables together are listed side by side. The window tells you that the Committees table relates to Committee Members by using fields called Committee ID in both tables. At the bottom of the window, you see that the Relationship Type is one-to-many. The "one" table is on the left in this window (the Committees table), and the "many" table is on the right (the Committee Members table).

This relationship specifies that referential integrity be enforced. Because referential integrity is enforced, the join line between the two tables shown back in Figure 8-8 shows the one-to-many relationship by displaying a 1 on the join line next to the master table and a lazy 8 (it's actually the symbol for infinity) next to the detail table. Click and drag the window if you need to move it to see the join line in the Relationships picture.

2 **Cick Cancel to close the Relationships window showing referential integrity and relationship type.**

3 **Close the remaining Relationships window.**

Now you've seen how relationships look in Access, as diagrammed in the Relationships window. You'll see relationships in action in Unit 9.

Recess

You've just absorbed lots of complex information about the structure of the database. If you're feeling a little bit unsure of things, take a sanity break and come back and run through the unit again.

☑ Progress Check

If you can do the following, you've mastered this lesson:

❏ Understand the components making up the Relationships picture.

❏ Add tables to the Relationships window.

❏ Know how to look at the properties of the join lines to see the specifics of the relationship between two tables.

Unit 8 Quiz

For each of the following questions, circle the letter of the correct answer or answers. Remember, a question may have more than one right answer.

1. **When designing a database, you should think about . . .**

   A. Which pieces of information you will use in reports and forms.

   B. How to group pieces of information into tables.

   C. What the database will be used for.

   D. Whether pieces of information are text, numbers, or dates.

   E. All of the above.

2. **A relational database is . . .**

   A. A database containing information about your relatives.

   B. A database containing information about relativity.

   C. A database containing information that is relative to other information.

   D. A group of tables that are related by matching fields.

   E. A group of tables you can really relate to.

3. **Which of the following is true?**

    A. Master and detail tables are related by a one-to-many relationship.

    B. The primary key field is one that uniquely identifies records in a master table.

    C. An AutoNumber field is useful as a primary key.

    D. To store a many-to-many relationship, you need to create a new table.

    E. Geese fly north for the winter.

4. **Which of the following can you see by simply looking at the Relationships picture?**

    A. Your family tree.

    B. Which table sits on the "many" side of a one-to-many relationship (that is, which is the detail table).

    C. Primary key fields.

    D. A full list of fields in a table.

    E. The type of join used to link two tables.

5. **To see a map of the relationships between the tables in your database, you can . . .**

    A. Get a big piece of paper and a ruler and start drawing.

    B. Choose Tools⇨Relationships from the menu bar.

    C. Click the Relationships button on the toolbar.

    D. Click the Map button on the Relationships window.

    E. Choose File⇨Relationships from the menu.

Unit 8 Exercise

In this exercise, you'll use the Database Wizard to create a new multitable database. Then you'll snoop around in it so you understand its design.

1. Create a new database using the Database Wizard. Use a template that you haven't used so far. When you create the database, tell the Database Wizard to include the sample data supplied.

2. Before you look at the design, give some thought to how you would design the database.

3. Try out the database by clicking all the Switchboard buttons and printing all the reports.

4. Review the design and compare it with the one you came up with.

5. Pay special attention to how table relationships are structured.

6. Close the database.

Making Multitable Queries

Objectives for This Unit

✓ Creating a query that includes fields from two related tables

✓ Creating calculated fields in a query

✓ Renaming columns in a query

Prerequisites

▶ Creating a select query by using the design grid (Unit 4)

▶ Understanding the concepts of joining related tables (Unit 8)

on the CD

▶ US Senate database (US Senate.mdb)

In Unit 8, you found out what multitable databases look like, and you learned the theory behind related tables. Now that you have a database with related tables (the US Senate database, which we'll use again in this unit), how do you create queries and reports that combine information from more than one table? For example, how do you print name tags for senators with the full name of their party on each name tag? The names come from the Senators table, and the party names come from the Parties database. Here's another example: How do you print a listing of the names of the senators on the Budget Committee? The senator names are in the Senators table, and the information about who's on that committee is in the Committee Members table.

Easy: You make a query that contains two or more related tables. In the top part of the Query window, you put a field list for each table you want to pull information from. In the design grid, you include fields from the various tables. No sweat! Once you've got a query that combines information from several tables, you can print the query in Datasheet view or use that query as the record source for a report.

In this unit, you use much of the information that you've learned about Access so far. You build a multitable query without the aid of the Query Wizard. You don't use the Query Wizard because you're going to create queries that the wizard doesn't know how to create. See — you're already smarter than the wizards!

Notes:

Suppose that in your work for a Senate watchdog organization, you decide that you need a listing of senators who are not on any committee so that you can call them and nag them to get to work. This unit steps you through this process.

Note: The US Senate database includes information on only a few committees. Senators who look lazy in our database may be on lots of committees in real life. Check the Senate Web site at http://www.senate.gov for latest committee assignments.

Although building a query that includes information from two or more tables presents some special challenges, the process is not that different from building a query based on a single table. If you were playing hooky during Unit 4, we recommend that you at least review that material now, especially Lessons 4-2 and 4-3.

Lesson 9-1

Starting a Multitable Query

Where on Earth do you start? You start at the end, of course — where else? You have to know what you want to get out of your query before you can make any sensible decisions about which tables you need to use. As you learned in Unit 4, you need to ask yourself the following before you begin:

- Which records do you want to see?
- How can you identify these records?
- Which fields in those records do you want to see?

Because the information you need is in two tables, you also need to know how the tables are related.

What might you need to get a useful list of inactive senators? The Senators table has the telephone numbers and the senators' names, but to determine whether a senator is on a committee, you need to use the Committee Members table, too. To make a query that contains fields from more than one table, you include field lists for each table in the query. In this lesson, you start creating the query and get the necessary field lists to appear.

Adding field lists

Make a new query in the US Senate database that includes field lists for two tables: Senators and Committee Members. The query will eventually show you all the people in the Senate who aren't on any committee, so you need information about people and who's on what committee.

on the CD

1 In the US Senate database, open the database window and click the Queries tab. Then either click the <u>N</u>ew button or choose <u>I</u>nsert➪<u>Q</u>uery from the menu bar.

You see the New Query dialog box. If you can't remember having seen this dialog box or you skipped some of the earlier units, review Unit 4.

2 Double-click Design View, or click it and click OK.

You see the Show Table dialog box, which wants to know which tables contain the information that you want to include in the query. In the background, you also see the blank Design view window for the query that you're starting to create — it's entitled Query1 at this point.

3 If it's not already selected, click the Tables tab in the Show Table dialog box.

heads up

The Show Table dialog box lets you select the tables or queries that contain the information you want to include in your query. Although you're using only tables in this lesson, you can use the results from other queries, too. Use the query results option with care, however — you could end up with queries built on queries built on queries built on queries. If you want to slow your machine to a crawl, base queries on queries with large amounts of data.

4 Double-click the Senators table, or choose Senators and click the <u>A</u>dd button.

A field list box pops up in the upper pane of the Design view window for the query you're creating. This field list box represents the Senators table, and in the box is a complete list of the fields in the Senators table. The box is too short to list all the fields without scrolling and too narrow to fit the full field descriptions, but other than that, Microsoft has made good use of space here. Unfortunately, good use of space is of little use to you when you're just learning how to build queries, especially when you're working with multiple tables. So take a little time to rearrange the Design view window and make it a little easier to work with before adding the other table you'll need, the Committee Members table.

5 Close the Show Table dialog box.

You now see the Design view window for your query. The window's lower half has space for some heavy-duty selection criteria in the design grid. In the narrow upper part of the window, you still have this itsy-bitsy box with the field list for the Senators table. The following steps show you how to make it bigger so you can see the fields better.

6 Maximize the Design view window (the window entitled Query1: Select Query) by clicking its Maximize button.

Click the Maximize button for the query window, not for the Access window. Now the window for the query takes up the whole inside of the Microsoft Access window.

Tip: If you run your mouse pointer over the separator line dividing the upper and lower halves of the Design view window, you see that the pointer changes shape to a horizontal bar with one arrow pointing up and another pointing down. When your pointer looks like this, you can drag the separator up or down and so change the relative sizes of the two halves.

add tables from Show Table window to query by clicking Add

click Maximize button on Query window to expand it to fill Access window

adjust query window divider to make space for field lists

expand field lists
to see more fields

add all tables
that hold fields
for query

Notes:

🗗

Restore button

7 **Click and drag the window separator downward so that the upper part fills about two-thirds of the window.**

Now you have an itsy-bitsy field list box in a huge empty window, like the proverbial pea in a drum. Move your mouse pointer over the bottom-right corner of the field list box. The pointer changes shape again to a double-headed diagonal arrow.

8 **Click and drag the bottom-right corner of the field list box for the Senators table down and to the right until you like its size.**

Your field list should be looking a little easier to read and work with now.

9 **Right-click the background of the upper window pane and choose Show Table from the shortcut menu that appears.**

You see the same Show Table dialog box that you used in Steps 3 and 4.

10 **Double-click the Committee Members table, or choose Committee Members and click Add.**

A field list for the Committee Members table appears in your Query window. The relationship between the two tables is also included in the picture, shown as a *join line* connecting the related fields in the two tables (see Figure 9-1). Access already knows that the two tables are related, as you saw in Unit 8.

11 **Close the Show Table dialog box — you've added all the tables you need.**

Okay, everything looks clear, but those two field list boxes seem to be awfully friendly, snuggling up so close on one side of the upper pane.

12 **Click and drag the Committee Members field list box to the right by clicking in the title portion of the box.**

We'll admit that moving the boxes around is, perhaps, a little frivolous in this situation, but in the future, when you're building a query from several tables, you'll find that being able to move the tables around in the window pane can be very helpful. The ability to see a visual representation of what you're doing is invaluable.

You aren't done with this query, but you've got the field lists set up for the tables that contain the information you need. It's time to save the query and take a break.

13 **Close the query by clicking the Close button for the query — it's the X button just below the Close button for the Microsoft Access window, in the upper-right corner.**

Access asks whether you want to save the query — but of course!

14 **Click Yes, type Inactive Senators in the Query Name box, and click OK to save the query.**

You return to the database window. Because you maximized the Design view window for the query, Access figures that you want all your windows big and maximizes the database window, too. To return to your regular-size database window, you can always click its Restore button, the button with two overlapping boxes, in the second row of little buttons in the upper-right corner of the window.

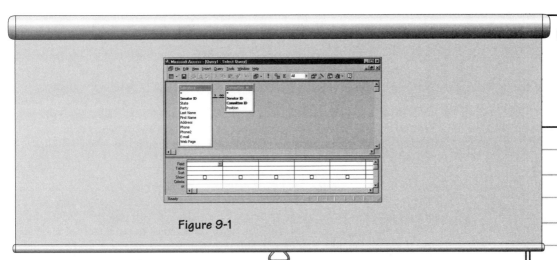

Figure 9-1

Figure 9-1: This query can include fields from the Senators and Committee Members fields, which are related by Senator ID fields.

You've started building a query with two tables. You added field lists for the two tables that contain information that you want in your query. The Design view wasn't very well laid out, but you've changed that so you can see field lists from the two tables more clearly. You're all ready to go!

Tip: Another way to add the field list for a table to a query is to drag the table name from the database window into the Design view window for the query. Switch to the database window (by clicking the Database Window button on the toolbar or clicking the database window itself if part of it is visible), click the Tables tab, and drag the name of the table to the top half of the query window. A field list appears.

Recess

Wiggle your fingers and wave your mouse arm around a bit to limber up for the next lesson. A few neck exercises might be a good idea, too. Who cares who might see you?

☑ Progress Check

If you can do the following, you've mastered this lesson:

❑ Use the Show Table window to add multiple tables to the Design view window for a query.

❑ Change the layout of the Design view window to make things easier to see.

Adding Fields from Multiple Tables to the Design Grid

Lesson 9-2

In this lesson, you use the design grid to build your query with fields from both tables. You then run the query and inspect the results to see how they compare to what you expect.

While you're at it, you'll use a few advanced tricks in the design grid. You learn to create a *calculated field* — that is, a field that exists in the results of the

calculated field = field not stored in any table, but calculated by Access based on values of other fields query and is calculated from one or more fields from the tables that provide input to the query. When we say *calculated*, we mean that Access does something to the values in the field — it doesn't have to be a mathematical calculation.

In this query, you'll create a calculated field called Name that combines the information in the FirstName and LastName fields of the Senators table. Instead of seeing the first and last names in separate columns, you'll see them separated by a space in one column.

To tell Access to create a calculated field in your query, you type an expression into the Field row of the design grid in Design view. An *expression* is composed of field names, numbers (if you're doing a calculation with number fields), text in quotes (if you're doing a calculation with text fields), and operators. Table 9-1 lists a few of the most common operators.

Table 9-1	Operators Used in Expressions
Operator	**What It Does**
+	Addition
-	Subtraction
*	Multiplication
/	Division
&	Concatenation (strings two text values together)

If the field names in the expression include spaces, you have to enclose the field names in square brackets ([ ]), so that Access can tell where field names begin and end.

For example, in an order entry database with fields named Unit Price and Quantity Ordered, you could create a field that contains the amount of the order by using an expression like this:

```
[Unit Price] * [Quantity Ordered]
```

To create a field that contains each person's first and last names, you might use this expression:

```
[First Name] & [Last Name]
```

The ampersand (&) strings together two text fields, one after the other. Oops! That expression doesn't leave a space between the two names, so the result looks like *RodneyLowe*. This expression works better:

```
[First Name] & " " & [Last Name]
```

This expression strings together the first name, a space, and the last name.

Handwritten margin notes:

expression = field names, numbers, text, and operators that specify calculated field

* multiplies numbers

& concatenates (strings together) text

Finally, you can give the calculated result a name by typing the name at the beginning of the expression, followed by a colon. This formula creates a field named Name with the first and last names:

```
Name: [First Name] & " " & [Last Name]
```

If you don't provide a name, Access calls the new field something creative, like Expr1.

Now you know how a query can contain fields that aren't even in the original tables!

Creating calculated fields

To create a query that includes fields from more than one table, just drag field names from more than one table to the design grid in the lower half of the Design view window. Access keeps track of which fields come from which table.

on the CD

1 **If you're not already looking at the US Senate database, open it and open the database window.**

2 **Click the Queries tab, click the Inactive Senators query, and click the Design button. If the query is in a window, click the Maximize button so that the query takes up the whole Access window.**

The query looks just the way it did when you saved it in Lesson 9-1.

3 **Type the following into the Field row in the first column of the design grid and press Enter or Tab:**

```
Name:[First Name]& " "&[Last Name]
```

That is, type **Name**, then a colon (not a semicolon), then **[** (an open square bracket) **First Name**, then **]** (a close square bracket), then an ampersand, then a double quote (not a single quote), then one space, then another double quote, then another ampersand, and then **[Last Name]**. This formula creates a calculated field called Name. Of course, no field called Name exists in either of the tables that you've selected to be included in this query. In fact, there isn't a field called Name in any of the tables in this database. Name is a new field that you're setting up in this query by typing an expression.

When you press Enter or Tab, Access adds spaces that make the expression more readable.

4 **Drag the very top end of the column divider on the right edge of the Name column to the right until you can see the whole Name expression.**

heads up

Notice that the Table row is empty. It's empty because Name doesn't come from either of the tables used in your query. You didn't specify where Access picks up First Name and Last Name, but Access uses the Senators table because it's the only one of the two selected tables to hold these fields. If you use two tables that have the same field name, you need to qualify the field names with

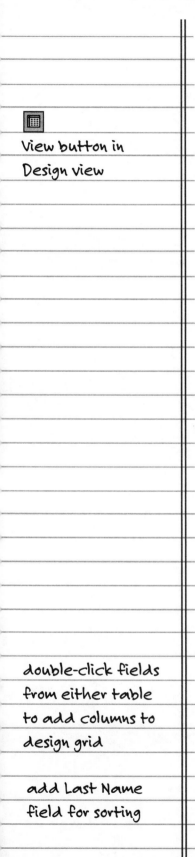

View button in
Design view

double-click fields
from either table
to add columns to
design grid

add Last Name
field for sorting

the table name to avoid ambiguous references. Although this example doesn't need qualified field names, you could have typed the following expression to specify which table the First Name and Last Name fields come from:

```
Name: Senators.[First Name] & " " & Senators.[Last
        Name]
```

5 **Click the View button (the leftmost button on the toolbar).**

You see the results of the query, which contains only one column at this point. Make the column wider if you need to. (Making the column wider in Design view doesn't affect the column width in Datasheet view, and vice versa.)

Tip: If you see a little box called Enter Parameter Value, that means you spelled First Name or Last Name wrong in your expression. Click Cancel and fix the Name expression.

For some of the records in the Senators table, Access took the First Name and Last Name fields and glued them together, separated by a space. That part looks just fine. However, lots of senators appear several times! Hmm . . . this isn't right yet.

6 **Click the View button on the toolbar to return to Design view.**

The View button is still the leftmost button on the toolbar, but when you're in Datasheet view, the button shows a picture of drafting tools (a T-square and a right triangle).

So far, you've got one column in your query, containing information from the Senators table. Next, you'll include fields from both the Senators and Committee Members tables. Then you'll fix the query so it contains the right senators — those who aren't on any committee.

Adding fields from both tables

You're not done with the query yet — keep adding fields!

1 **Double-click Senator ID in the field list for the Senators table or click and drag Senator ID to the second column.**

Either way, Senator ID appears in the Field row of the second column of the design grid. The Table row shows Senators to indicate which table this information comes from. The Senator ID will be useful in checking the results of your query.

2 **Double-click Committee ID in the Committee Members table or click and drag Committee to the next column.**

The Table row for this column shows that this information comes from the Committee Members table.

3 **Double-click Last Name in the Senators table or click and drag Last Name to the next position.**

You'll need this field later to sort the records alphabetically by last name.

4 **Click the View button on the toolbar.**

You see the datasheet with the results of the query. Is this what you want? Nope! What's wrong?

Well, for one thing, the list you have in front of you shows all senators who are on a committee, and it lists them once for each committee each senator is on. Sen. Jon Kyl is on three committees, so he appears three times! The query results omit people who aren't on a committee — and what you want is people who *aren't* on a committee! Also, the list isn't sorted in alphabetical sequence.

You fix these problems, one at a time, in the rest of this unit. First off, you just need the Name column to appear in the query result, not the Last Name and Committee ID fields. You'll use the Last Name column for sorting the names and the Committee ID for omitting the names of senators who aren't on any committee, but these two columns don't have to appear in the query results. You get rid of them in the next section.

Sorting records and omitting fields

In this last part of the lesson, you sort the query results and omit the fields that you don't want to see — the Last Name and Committee ID fields.

Back in Design view, you can make a few more changes to the design grid.

1 **Click the View button on the toolbar to return to Design view.**

First, remove the last two columns from the query results. You need the columns in the design grid but not in the query results.

2 **Click the Show boxes for the Last Name and Committee ID fields to prevent these columns from being shown in the query results.**

By default, the boxes start off with check marks in them; you need to remove the check marks in these two columns.

3 **Choose Ascending in the Sort row for the Last Name column.**

When you click the Sort row in the Last Name column, a menu of sort options appears, from which you pick Ascending.

Now you see the reason for including the Last Name field separately from the Name field in the first column. If you sort on the Name field, you're sorting by first name. By adding this extra column, you can sort by last name while still producing a query that lists people's names in a friendly format.

4 **Type Is Null into the Criteria row for the Committee ID column.**

Is Null is technobabble meaning that the field is absent or missing or empty or blank. This entry lets you select only those senators who do not have any Committee ID.

It's time to grit your teeth and see whether the query works now. This process is known as debugging a query, and it's similar to debugging programs — you use trial and error and a big dose of head-scratching and puzzlement.

Notes:

*clear Show boxes
to omit columns
from query results*

*Is Null = including
records where this
field is blank*

Progress Check

If you can do the following, you've mastered this lesson:

❑ Create columns that have data calculated from any table in the query.

❑ Sort the information by using the Sort row.

❑ Select the contents of a query by using the Criteria row.

❑ Omit columns from the results by using the Show row.

extra credit

Using expressions to mix, manipulate, and mangle your data

You can create all kinds of cool and useful calculated fields in your queries. The following examples give you a flavor of the power of Access expressions.

Suppose you want to know the year in which each senator was first elected, so you add a Date Elected field to the Senators table. To calculate the year, use the DatePart function to extract the year in *YYYY* format (that is, the year as a four-digit number) from the Date Elected field. The expression you'd type in the Field row would look like this:

```
Year Joined:
  DatePart("yyyy", [Date
  Elected])
```

Or suppose you want to print people's first and last initials rather than their names. Use the Left function to extract one character starting at the leftmost end of the First Name field. Do the same for the Last Name field and glom the two results together.

```
Initials: Left([First
  Name],1) & Left([Last
  Name],1)
```

Or you might decide to print a report of each senator's e-mail address, but you want to print *None* for those who don't have one. Use the IIf function to check

whether the e-mail address IsNull (blank). If it is, print *None;* otherwise, print *Address: ####.* (Don't ask why Microsoft has decided to spell *if* with two *i*'s.) The first item in parentheses is the condition you want to test for. What you want to happen when the condition is true is specified after the first comma. What you want to happen if the condition is false is specified after the second comma.

```
Email Address:
  IIf(IsNull([E-mail]),
  "None", "Address: " &
  [E-mail])
```

Say you want a list of new senators with the dates they were elected. If the current date minus 365 days is less than the Date Elected, print *New;* otherwise, print *Old.* Use the Date() function. You can put whatever date you like in the parentheses; when the parentheses are empty, Access uses today's date.

```
New Member:IIf(Date() -
  365 < [Date Elected],
  "New", "Old")
```

If you're hungry for more of these fancy expressions, choose Help from the menu bar and ask about expressions — or ask the Office Assistant!

 Click the View button on the toolbar.

Drat, the result contains nothing — the datasheet is completely empty! Something is obviously still wrong.

The problem is that Access has done one thing for you that is not what you want: The query uses the relationship between the Senators and Committee Members tables that is specified in the Relationships table, and therein lies the problem. You'll solve that in the next lesson.

 Close the query and click <u>Y</u>es to save the changes to the query.

You've used the design grid to construct a query that uses fields from both of your selected tables. You've added a new field that doesn't come from either table directly but is instead built from two separate fields. You've sorted the query results based on a field from one table and set up some criteria to filter the information based on the information in another. In addition, you indicated which fields you actually want to see in the results window and which ones you don't want to see because they're just used for controlling the appearance of the results and are of no intrinsic visual value in themselves. Not bad for one lesson. Take a break, and when you're ready, you'll fix that one irritating problem with the relationship between the two tables that is preventing you from seeing the results you want.

Setting Relationship Options

Lesson 9-3

Relating (or joining) tables is like marriage — it's got to be done right. Joining tables is a very important task, and if it isn't done correctly, things can get very confusing very quickly.

Back in Lesson 9-1, when you added the Committee Members table to the query and Access displayed the join line automagically, you probably said, "That's great. I don't have to worry about joining these two tables now." Wrong! Unfortunately, this relationship doesn't work quite right for this query. This lesson tells you more about the types of joins you can create and how to change them for a query in Design view.

You can tell from the join line in the Inactive Senators query that a one-to-many relationship connects the Senators and Committee Members tables and that referential integrity is enforced. How can you tell? The 1 and infinity signs appear at either end of the join line (refer to Figure 9-1).

For each relationship between two tables, there are three ways that a query containing the two tables can decide which records to include:

▶ Only include information for which records exist in both tables. For example, in the query we've been making, include senators who have records in the Committee Members table.

▶ Include all the records from the first table and only records that match from the second table. For example, include all the senators and include only Committee Members records that match senators (which will be all of them).

▶ Include all the records from the second table and only records that match from the first table. For example, include all records from the Committee Members table and include only senators that match them (senators who are on at least one committee).

You can tell by looking at the join lines between tables in the Relationships window or Design view of a query which of these three options the relationship uses. A line with no arrow head uses option 1, and a line with an arrowhead at one end uses option 2 or 3.

Notes:

relationships also define how queries determine which records to include

inner join = queries
include only
records that
match in both
tables

outer join = queries
include records for
which no record
exists in one of the
tables

double-click join
line to change join
properties

Most relationships use Door Number 1: They include only information where records exist in both tables. In the Design view of the query you've been working with, the join line doesn't have an arrowhead — the line doesn't point in either direction. This tells Access aficionados that any query that includes these two tables will include only senators for which there are records in the Committee Members table. Access won't include records in the Senators table for which there are no related records in the Committee Members table, and (conversely) it won't include records in the Committee Members table for which there are no records in the Senators table. You see only records that exist in both tables. In geeky database-ese, this kind of relationship is called an *inner join*.

This way of including records is precisely what you don't want for this particular query. Because you're looking for noncommittee members, you want to see records in the Senators table for which there are *no* rows in the Committee Members table. Access omits these records from the query. Bummer!

In older database programs, you would be Out Of Luck. Tough Luck Charlie. No Way, José. (You get the idea.) But Access can do another type of relationship between tables, called an *outer join*. In fact, you have two options when you create an outer join between these two tables:

 ♦ Access can include all the records in the Senators table, whether or not the Committee Members table has matching records.

 ♦ Access can include all the records in the Committee Members table, whether or not the Senators table has matching records. (All Committee Members records match a Senators record, so this option doesn't do you any good.)

You're going to look at the join between the two tables and change it to fulfill your requirements. Take each step slowly and understand what you see and why before moving on to the next step.

on the CD

1 **If you're not already looking at the US Senate database, open it and open the database window.**

2 **Open the Inactive Senators query in Design view and maximize the query window.**

3 **Double-click the join line between the Senators and Committee Members field lists to display the Join Properties window, shown in Figure 9-2.**

heads up

Clicking the join line can be hard. The mouse pointer doesn't change when it is pointing at a join line. If you think you're pointing at the line, click once. The line should get darker, showing that it's selected. If the join line doesn't get darker, move the mouse a bit and try again. When you've got the mouse pointer in the right place, double-click.

Option 1 is the type of join in effect between these two tables — an inner join. The fact that the results from the last lesson showed no records is not surprising, then. You specified that you wanted only records that had no Committee ID information (with *Is Null* in the criteria row for the Committee ID column). But this join omits all senators for which there is no Committee Members record.

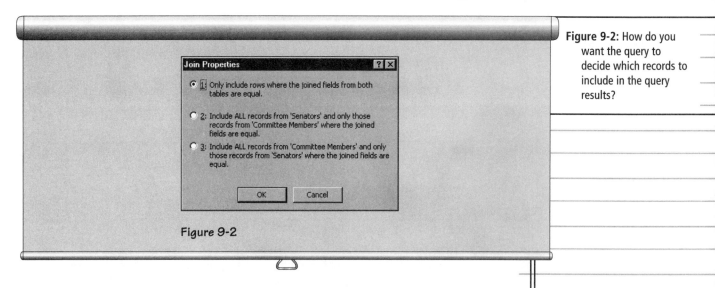

Figure 9-2

To fix this problem, you must change the join to include all records from the Senators table regardless of whether they have matching Committee Members records. The criterion entered in the query will then work correctly.

 Choose option 2 to include all records from the Senators table; then click OK.

Now the join line between the two tables points from the Senators table to the Committee Members table.

Your final Design view looks something like Figure 9-3, depending on how you rearranged your display in Lesson 9-1. (We adjusted column widths in the design grid to make it more readable.) The outer join selects all records from the Senators table whether or not the Committee Members table has a matching record.

Do you have that feel-good feeling? Are you confident that the results are going to give you what you want? Good — now check it out.

 Click the View button to review the query results.

Lo and behold, you see the 26 records showing senators who do not have a position on any of the committees that we included in this database. (Before rushing to the phone to hound your congressperson, please recall that this database doesn't include all the Senate committees, just a few. We can assure you that Sen. Jesse Helms is on a committee or two. Also, 15 senators had just been elected to the Senate when we constructed this database and had not yet received committee appointments.) The join now includes records for all senators, and your Committee ID criterion in the design grid selects only senators with null values — that is, no matching information in the Committee Members table.

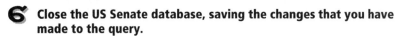 **Close the US Senate database, saving the changes that you have made to the query.**

Notes:

Figure 9-3: Will this
query work to list
only senators who
aren't on any
committee? The
suspense is killing us!

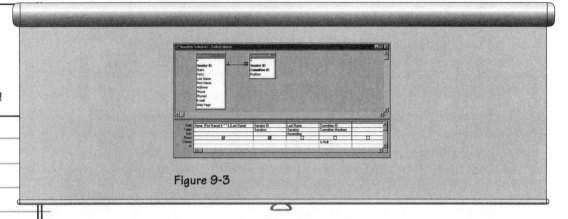

Figure 9-3

You're done! Pat yourself on the back — you have just mastered some of the most complex concepts in Access. Take a much-deserved rest before you try the quiz.

extra credit

Copying tables or the results of a query to a word-processing document

So you've created a nifty list of the people in the Senate who aren't on any committee. What if you want to include this list in a memo you're writing? Yes, you can print the query in Datasheet view or create a report that includes information from the query, but you have one other way: You can copy the query into your word-processing document. This method works for tables, too.

Make sure that both Access and your word processor are running at the same time. In Access, open the database window, click the Tables or Queries tab, select the table or query, and press Ctrl+C to copy the table or query to the Windows Clipboard. Press Alt+Tab to switch to your word pro-

cessor (you may need to press Alt+Tab several times if you're running several programs, as we usually are). Put your cursor at the point in the document where you'd like the table or query results to occur; then press Ctrl+V.

Windows, Access, and your word processor are so smart that they figure out that you don't want the table or query design in your document — you want the Datasheet view of the table or query. The results appear in a table in your document.

Warning: If you update the query or table later, the document doesn't change. You have to copy it again.

☑ Progress Check

If you can do the following, you've mastered this lesson:

❑ Identify relationships by looking at join lines.

❑ Understand inner joins versus outer joins.

❑ Adjust join properties.

Unit 9 Quiz

For each of the following questions, circle the letter of the correct answer or answers. Remember, a question may have more than one right answer.

1. **To create a report with information from two tables . . .**

   A. You create a query for each table and then glue the two queries together.

   B. You create a query that contains field lists for both tables and include fields from both tables in the design grid.

   C. You copy the records from both tables to a word-processing document and edit the information together.

   D. You create a report for each table and then make a query that combines the two reports.

   E. You give up and hire a consultant.

2. **What is an inner join?**

   A. A relationship among three different tables.

   B. A relationship between tables stored in different databases.

   C. A relationship between two tables in which queries will include only records that match in both tables.

   D. A relationship between two tables in which queries will include all the records from one table and only the matching records from the other table.

   E. A yoga position.

3. **In the classic musical *Brigadoon*, Gene Kelly plays . . .**

   A. A dancer who appears on Broadway only one day every hundred years.

   B. A disaffected New York businessman who gets killed accidentally in the Scottish Highlands.

   C. A pirate king.

   D. A disaffected New York businessman who falls in love with a woman from a Scottish town that appears only one day every hundred years.

   E. The bagpipe.

Notes:

4. **To create a query that combines the information from two tables . . .**

   A. Delete all the information from one table, type it into the other table, and create a query that uses information from the table that results.

   B. Add more than one field list to the top of the query in Design view and then drag fields from both tables to the design grid.

   C. Add every single table in the database to the top of the query in Design view and then drag a few choice fields to the design grid.

   D. Put both tables into your food processor with the "grate and chop" blade installed. Process until combined.

   E. Use the Simple Query Wizard. (***Hint:*** Try running the Simple Query Wizard in the US Senate database to see whether it can create multitable queries.)

5. **You can use a calculated field in the design grid of a query to do which of the following?**

   A. Display the first few characters of a text field.

   B. Add one numeric field to another.

   C. String multiple text fields together with other text that you specify.

   D. Determine a date 15 days from now.

   E. All of the above.

Unit 9 Exercise

on the CD

1. Open the US Senate database.

2. Create a query that uses information from the Senators and Parties tables.

3. Design the query to produce a list of senators with the full name of the party that each senator belongs to.

4. Sort the list by last name, without showing the Last Name field in the query results.

5. Display your results in Datasheet view.

6. Save the query as Senators with Party Affiliations.

Changing the Design of Your Database

Objectives for This Unit

✓ Adding new fields to a table

✓ Adding the new fields to forms that display records from the table

✓ Adding the new fields to reports that display records from the table

✓ Changing the size, type, or other characteristics of a field

✓ Deleting fields from forms and reports

Prerequisites

▶ Creating a database by using the Database Wizard (Lesson 2-1)

▶ Creating queries (Lesson 4-1)

on the CD

▶ US Senate database (US Senate.mdb)

Wizards are amazing things, and we're glad that Microsoft made lots of them. The Database Wizard does a beautiful job of creating databases; don't get us wrong. Access comes with a wonderful assortment of templates that the Database Wizard can use to create a wonderful assortment of databases that you can use. It's just that, well, sometimes you want to do things your *own* way.

After you make a database — with or without the help of the Database Wizard — you aren't stuck with the way the tables are designed. You don't have to live with the original choice of fields in each table or the sizes and types of the fields — not at all! You can change the design of any table in your database, adding, deleting, and modifying fields as needed to make the database work the way you want. Just be careful that you completely understand the relationships involved in any tables that you change; one seemingly small modification on your part, and the whole complex scheme can collapse.

table design can be changed

heads up

Warning: This unit describes how to change the design of a table, along with the queries, forms, and reports that work with that table. But before you start, here are a few dire warnings that you should pay close attention to:

- Make a backup copy of your database before you start making major changes to it. In Windows Explorer or My Computer, copy the database to another folder under a different name. If you foul up the database with your changes, you can always delete the fouled-up version and go back to using the copy you made.

- Don't mess with the fields that relate one table to another. For example, if the Senate ID field in the Senators table relates to the Senators ID field in the Committee Members table, don't make any changes to the Senator ID field in either table. If you do, you may break the connection between the two tables and many things in your database will stop working. Even if you make the changes in both tables, you may also need to change all kinds of tricky settings in queries, forms, and reports that refer to the relationships between the tables.

- If you delete a field from a table, you'd better delete it from all the queries, forms, and reports in which the field appears. You're better off just leaving any unused fields alone and not deleting them. An empty field doesn't take up much space in a database: Access is smart enough not to store many blank spaces in each record in which the field is empty.

After you make up your mind to make some changes to a table in your database (and you make a backup copy), you are ready to try making some changes to your database.

This unit lets you try out some changes on a sample *Dummies 101* database (which is especially risk free because this is the last unit in the book and the last time you need that database!) to see how involved some simple adjustments can be. With our guidance, you'll make the following changes to the US Senate database:

on the test

- **Adding a field:** After you add a field to a table, add the field to the form(s) that you use for entering, editing, and looking at the information in that table, too. You also need to add the field to any queries that use information from the table, as well as to reports that print information from the table (or information from queries based on the table).

- **Changing the size or type of a field:** Each field in a table is defined as text, number, Date/Time, Yes/No, or some other kind (you'll see the full list of possible types in Lesson 10-1). If you change a field's size or type, you'd better take a look at the forms and reports that include that field, to make sure that the field looks okay on them. For example, if you make a text field a great deal longer, you'd better adjust the forms and reports that display the field so that they allow more space for the field.

- **Deleting a field:** Actually, we recommend that you avoid deleting fields from tables unless you are *absolutely sure* that the field isn't used to link one table to another and that the field isn't used for sorting or selecting the records in a form or table. Only after you've thoroughly checked all the relationships and functions of a particular field should you delete it.

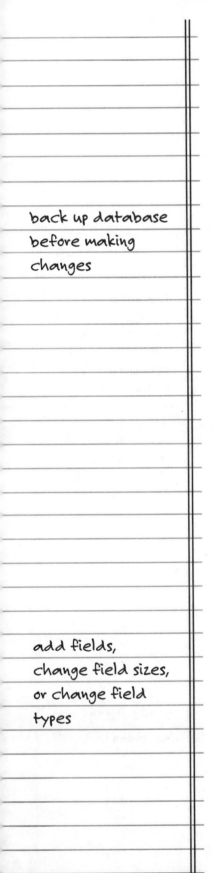

back up database
before making
changes

add fields,
change field sizes,
or change field
types

In Lesson 10-1, you'll make some changes to the Addresses table in the US Senate database (the one you used in Units 8 and 9). In the rest of the lessons in this unit, you'll make the corresponding changes to the queries, forms, and reports in the database.

don't delete fields; just ignore

Adding, Deleting, or Changing Fields in a Table

Lesson 10-1

The Addresses table stores a great deal of fascinating information about your close friends in the U.S. Senate. But what if you want to store some information that's not already there? For example, a field indicating whether a senator has the Sierra Club's seal of approval would be a nice addition. And how about a field that records whether a senator is single or married, to remind you to investigate spouses' activities. (Maybe you also want to add a field for the instrument that the senator plays, if any, because you've heard that the U.S. Senate is thinking of organizing its own rock band.)

Not a problem! A project, yes — but not a problem. In this lesson, you'll make some changes to the Senators table, adding the new fields and typing some values into them.

on the test

When you add a new field to a table (or change an existing field), you must tell Access the following:

Notes:

- **Field name:** Make sure that the name isn't already used in that table (although you can use a field name that's used in a different table in the same database). Field names can contain spaces. Although the Database Wizard doesn't usually use them, we like to, for readability.

field names can contain spaces

- **Data type:** What kind of information will the field contain? Table 10-1 lists the data types from which you can choose.

- **Description:** (Optional) The description can include what the field, contains, it's purpose, and how it's used. This information is for your reference only; Access doesn't understand a word you type in the description.

- **Other properties:** Access needs different information about the field, depending on which data type you pick. For example, for text fields you must tell Access the maximum number of characters to be stored in the field. For numbers, you have to tell Access how big the numbers may be and whether they may contain fractions.

- **Position:** This point is minor, but you can decide where in the series of fields in the table you want this field to appear. The position in the table determines the position in the datasheet (at least, until you start moving columns around in the datasheet). The position in the table doesn't control where the field appears in forms or reports, though.

Notes:

Table 10-1	Types of Fields in Access Tables
Data Type	**What It's For**
Text	Letters, numbers, words, or anything up to 255 characters long. If you store numbers in a text field, you can't total them up. For text fields, you also specify a field size — that is, the maximum number of characters that the particular field will hold. You can sort records on their text fields.
	Use text fields for numbers that are codes, like phone numbers and zip codes.
Memo	The same as a text field but for much longer chunks of text. Memo fields can be longer than 255 characters (in fact, they can hold more than 64,000 characters!), but you can't sort records based on what's in a memo field.
Number	Numbers that you may want to total up or do calculations with. If the numbers represent money, use a currency field instead.
Date/Time	Dates, times, or both. You can tell Access what format to display dates and times in, too. Do you want 25 Dec 1996? 12/25/96? December 25, 1996?
Currency	Money, bucks, greenbacks. Access knows that currency amounts can't have more than two digits after the decimal point. (It won't calculate prices with fractions of cents, for example.)
AutoNumber	A number field that Access numbers automagically. After you add a record to the table, Access automatically assigns a number to the new record. The first record is numbered 1, the second 2, and so on.
Yes/No	Yes or no, on or off, true or false. A Yes/No field can contain only one of two values. The cool thing about Yes/No fields is that they appear as little check boxes on forms (checked = Yes, not checked = No).
OLE Object	Field used by programmer types to link information from other types of files to a record in a table. Forget about this field type!
Hyperlink	Link to a World Wide Web page, intranet page, or even information in another file on your hard disk.
Lookup Field	Field that looks up information from another table. Useful for fields that contain codes.

To make changes to your table, you use Design view, which looks like Figure 10-1. The top half of the window lists the fields in the table. (Scroll down to see the rest of them, if all the fields don't fit.) Each row of this table represents one field in the Senators table. One of the fields is selected; it's got a little triangle pointing at it from the left margin of the field list. Primary key fields have a tiny little key icon in the left margin.

key icon indicates primary key field

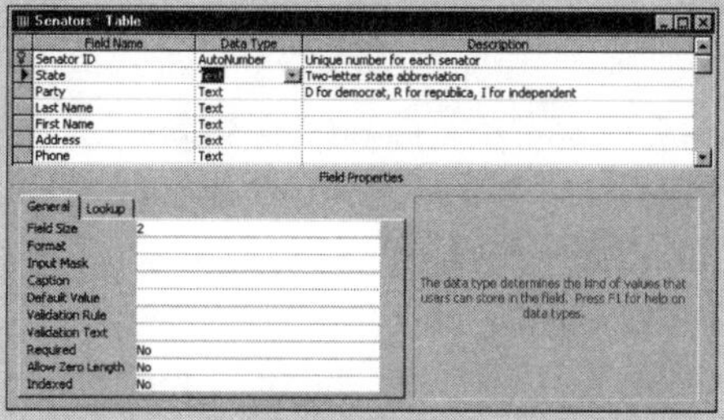

Figure 10-1: In Design view of a table, you can add fields, delete fields, and change the name, type, and other properties of fields.

Figure 10-1

The bottom half of the Design view window is called the Field Properties box, and it lists the properties of the selected field. For example, in Figure 10-1, the State field is selected in the top half of the window, and the bottom half shows the properties of the State field.

In Design view, you can

field properties of selected field appear in lower part of window

- ◗ Add a field to the table by typing information about the new field on a blank row of the design grid. Then you need to add the new field to your queries, forms, and reports.

- ◗ Change the name of a field by editing its Field Name entry. Be sure to change its name in all the queries, forms, and reports, too. Access doesn't update field names automatically.

- ◗ Change the type, description, or properties of a field by changing the entries for the field. If you make a field larger or smaller, you may need to enlarge it or shrink it on forms and reports where it appears.

- ◗ Delete a field by deleting its row from the design grid. Be sure to delete the field from all the queries, forms, and reports where it appears (after checking that deleting the field won't affect the rest of the database). Unless you're sure that the field isn't used to relate the table to another table or to sort or group a query, form, or report, we recommend leaving unused fields alone.

In this lesson, you'll add fields to the Senators table.

Adding fields to a table

Open the Senators table in the US Senate database and make some changes!

1 **In the US Senate database, click the Tables tab in the database window.**

You see the list of tables in the database. Review Lesson 8-2 if you're wondering about the purpose for any of them.

Notes:

use Yes/No field
when only two
values are possible

to add field, add
rows in Design view

Insert Rows button

2 **Click the Senators table and then click Design.**

You see the Senators table in Design view, as shown in Figure 10-1.

3 **Use the ↓ key to move down the list of fields and look at each field's properties in the bottom half of the window.**

Or click the row for each field to move down the list. Don't change the properties of the fields.

4 **Click the Field Name column of the first blank row after the Web Page row to begin entering a new field.**

You'll add the Environmentalist field, to store information about whether or not the Sierra Club approves of each senator's record. A senator gets either a thumbs-up or thumbs-down rating, so you can use a Yes/No field for this purpose.

5 **In the Field Name column, type** Environmentalist. **Then press Tab.**

Your cursor appears in the Data Type column of the Environmentalist row. Access guesses that you want this field to contain text — good guess, but wrong!

6 **Set the Data Type to Yes/No by clicking the list button at the right end of the column and choosing Yes/No from the menu that appears.**

The properties of the new field appear in the bottom half of the window. You can change the Format property from Yes and No to True and False or On and Off, but Yes and No works nicely for this field.

How about adding the other field, Marital Status, right above the Environmentalist field?

7 **Choose Insert⇨Rows from the menu bar or click the Insert Rows button on the toolbar.**

Either way, a new, blank row appears between the Web Page and Environmentalist rows.

8 **In the Field Name column, type** Marital Status **and press Enter or Tab.**

This field stores a code for whether the senator is single, married, divorced, separated, or living with someone. Access suggests Text as the type — sounds okay to us! But look at the Field Size property in the Field Properties box in the lower half of the window; one-character code should be plenty long for this field.

9 **Click the Field Size box in the Field Properties part of the window and change the 50 to 1.**

That's all you need to type for the Marital Status field. You're done with this task!

You've added two new fields to the Senators table. Good work; you're a database designer now!

Looking at your revised table

Switch from Design view to Datasheet view to see the results of your changes and to enter a little data.

1 **Click the View button (the left-most button on the toolbar) or choose View⇨Datasheet from the menu bar.**

Access says that you must save the table design before you can see it in Datasheet view.

2 **Click Yes to save your changes.**

You see the table in Datasheet view. Looks like a normal datasheet, and it is. What's special about it is the two new columns (fields) way over to the right.

3 **Press the Tab key a bunch of times to scroll the datasheet to the right so that you can see the two new fields.**

The Environmentalist field contains a little check box because it's a Yes/No field. None of the boxes is checked because the default for a Yes/No field is No.

You could enter values for the Marital Status field now and click the Environmentalist box for "green" senators, but wouldn't it be easier to make these changes on a form rather than the datasheet? Also, you need to come up with a list of standard codes for marital status (*M* for married, and so on) so that you enter them consistently. Don't enter any codes now until you've created a table of the valid codes to use.

4 **Close the Senators table window.**

Great! Your Senators table now has two new fields. You can use the steps you learned in this lesson to add fields to any table.

Tip: Anytime you're looking at a table in Datasheet view, you can click the View button (the left-most button on the toolbar) to switch to Design view. After looking at or modifying the design of the table, you can click the View button again to switch back to Datasheet view.

Recess

Modifying the design of a table can be dangerous, but sometimes the task must be done. And now you know how to do it!

If you need to take a breather, close your database and take a walk. While you are at it, drink a glass of water. Then come back and add your new fields to the queries, forms, and reports in your database.

View button

Yes/No fields start as No

☑ **Progress Check**

If you can do the following, you've mastered this lesson:

❑ Add a field to a table.

❑ Pick the appropriate data type for a field.

❑ Change the properties of a field.

❑ Review changes you've made by switching between Design view and Datasheet view.

Lesson 10-2

Adding a Related Table to Your Database

The new Marital Status field in the Senators table contains a code for whether the senator is married. Instead of having to remember the codes for married, single, separated, and so on, wouldn't you prefer to choose the codes from a list?

A *lookup table* — a table used only to provide a list of values for a field in another table — is not hard to create. In this lesson, you'll create a new table called Marital Statuses to contain a list of the codes you'll use in the Marital Status field. Then you'll tell Access to use the Marital Statuses table to provide a list of valid entries for the Marital Status field in the Senators table.

Anytime you plan to use codes, be sure to store the list in a table in your database. Then tell Access to use this table to validate the codes you enter in other tables.

The new table, Marital Statuses, will have a one-to-many relationship with the Senators table. One marital status can apply to none, one, or many senators. One senator can have only one marital status.

Making a lookup table

on the CD

1 **In the US Senate database, open the database window and click the Tables tab.**

You see your list of tables.

2 **Click the New button in the database window.**

When the Tables tab is selected, this button creates a new table. You see the New Table window, shown in Figure 10-2.

3 **Click Design View on the list in the New Table window and click OK.**

You see a totally blank Design view of a table. It's time to enter a field name.

4 **In the first row of the table, type** Marital Code **in the Field Name column and press Enter or Tab.**

Access guesses that this new field is a text field with a size of 50 characters.

5 **Press F6 to jump down to the Field Properties box (or click in the Field Size box). Change the Field Size to 1.**

This is the one-letter code that will match codes entered in the Marital Status field in the Senators table. To enable you to remember what the codes mean (is *S* for single or separated?), make another field for the definitions of the codes.

6 **In the second row of the field list, type** Marital Description **in the Field Name column and press Enter or Tab.**

7 **Press F6 to jump down to the Field Properties box (or click in the Field Size box). Change the Field Size to 20.**

Twenty characters is long enough for the definition of each code.

---

lookup table = table containing list of valid entries for field in another table

F6 jumps between field list and Field Properties

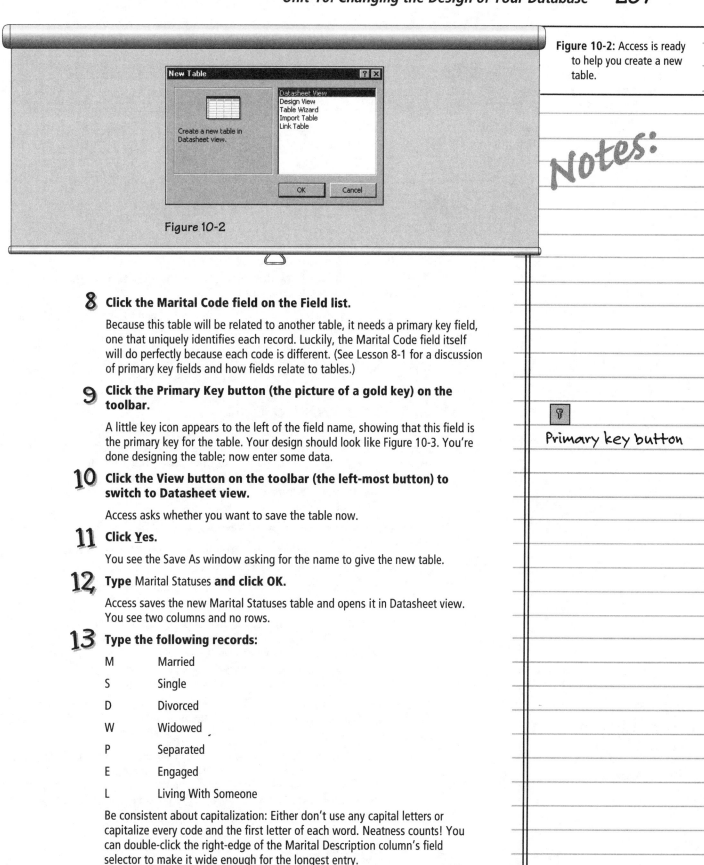

Figure 10-2

Figure 10-2: Access is ready to help you create a new table.

Notes:

8 Click the Marital Code field on the Field list.

Because this table will be related to another table, it needs a primary key field, one that uniquely identifies each record. Luckily, the Marital Code field itself will do perfectly because each code is different. (See Lesson 8-1 for a discussion of primary key fields and how fields relate to tables.)

9 Click the Primary Key button (the picture of a gold key) on the toolbar.

A little key icon appears to the left of the field name, showing that this field is the primary key for the table. Your design should look like Figure 10-3. You're done designing the table; now enter some data.

10 Click the View button on the toolbar (the left-most button) to switch to Datasheet view.

Access asks whether you want to save the table now.

11 Click Yes.

You see the Save As window asking for the name to give the new table.

12 Type Marital Statuses and click OK.

Access saves the new Marital Statuses table and opens it in Datasheet view. You see two columns and no rows.

13 Type the following records:

M	Married
S	Single
D	Divorced
W	Widowed
P	Separated
E	Engaged
L	Living With Someone

Be consistent about capitalization: Either don't use any capital letters or capitalize every code and the first letter of each word. Neatness counts! You can double-click the right-edge of the Marital Description column's field selector to make it wide enough for the longest entry.

Primary key button

Figure 10-3: Here's the design for the new Marital Statuses table, which will contain a list of valid codes for the Marital Status field in the Senators table.

Figure 10-4: Here's how the lookup properties look for the Marital Status field.

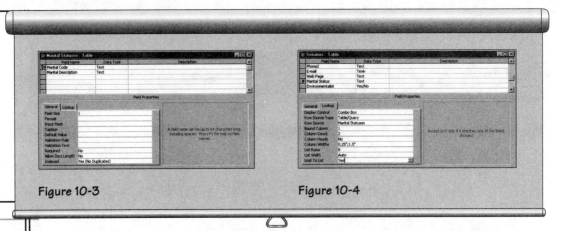

Figure 10-3   Figure 10-4

Notes:

14 **Close the Marital Statuses window, clicking <u>Y</u>es to save the layout of the table if you changed it.**

You see the list of tables in the database window, and there's your new Marital Statuses table.

You've created a new table! Okay, the table has only two fields, but you did it entirely yourself.

Making the lookup field

Now go back to the Marital Status field in the Senators table and tell Access to use the Marital Statuses table as a way to enter codes in the Marital Status field.

1 **In the database window, click the Senators table and click the <u>D</u>esign button.**

You see the Senators table in Design view.

2 **Press Ctrl+↓ and then ↑ to scroll down to the Marital Status field. Click in the row for the field.**

3 **In the Field Properties box in the lower half of the Senators window, click the Lookup tab.**

The list of properties changes, and you see one property: Display Control. This property tells Access what kind of control (that is, what kind of box or button) to use in datasheets and forms to display this field. Currently, this property is set to Text Box so that this field appears as a plain old text box when you use the table in Datasheet view or create a new form. Boring!

4 **Click in the Display Control box, click the list button at the right end of the Display Control box, and choose Combo Box from the menu that appears.**

Text boxes, list boxes, and combo boxes are all boxes (or *controls* in Access lingo) for displaying and entering information in a field. A text box is just a blank box you can type into. Combo boxes and list boxes both display a list of possible entries so that you don't have to type the entries. The two types look very similar, but combo boxes have some extra options, so we always use them.

Display Control = type of box that displays field information

As soon as you change the Display Control property, a whole bunch of properties appear, as shown in Figure 10-4. You've told Access that Marital Status should appear as a combo box on the Senators datasheet so that when you click the list button in the Marital Status field you'll see a little list of valid marital statuses.

Access needs to know where the list of Marital Statuses will come from. The Row Source Type property is set to Table/Query, indicating that the list of Marital Statuses is stored in a table or a query. (It's in the Marital Statuses table, right?)

5 **For the Row Source property, type** Marital Statuses. **Or click the list button at the right end of the Row Source box and choose Marital Statuses from the list of tables and queries that appears.**

The Bound Column property tells Access which column from the Marital Statuses table contains the list of Marital Statuses. Field number 1 in the Marital Statuses table contains the list of codes, so 1 is a good choice.

6 **Set the Column Count property to 2.**

This value means that when the combo box appears, it'll show both the codes and their meanings because the second column in the Marital Statuses table contains descriptions of what the codes mean. You need to tell Access how wide to make each column in the combo box, too.

7 **In the Column Widths property, type** .25;1.5 **very carefully. Then press Enter.**

That is, type **.25** to tell Access to make the first column (with the one-letter code) a quarter-inch wide. Then type a semicolon between the width of the first and second column. Then type **1.5** to make the second column (with the descriptions) an inch-and-a-half wide. When you press Enter, Access adds inch marks ('') after the measurements.

The other property of interest is the last one, Limit To List. Because it is set to No, Access lets a database user type in additional Marital Statuses if the Marital Status that the user wants isn't on the list. That's probably not a good idea; we've entered all possible situations. (We think!)

8 **Set the Limit To List property to Yes.**

That's it; the settings should look like Figure 10-4.

9 **Click the View button on the toolbar to see this table in Datasheet view and click Yes to save the table.**

10 **Tab across the Senators datasheet until you get to the Marital Status column.**

The fastest way to get there is to press ↓ to move to the next record and then ← twice to move to the second-to-last field of the preceding record. When your cursor arrives in the column, a list button appears at the right edge of the column, indicating that this is a combo box, not an ordinary text box.

11 **Click the list button at the right end of the Marital Status column and choose a marital status from the menu that appears.**

Hey! That list of codes looks familiar; it's the list that you typed in the Marital Statuses table a minute ago. The Marital Statuses are sorted alphabetically because the Marital Status field is a primary key. (Access likes to keep primary key fields in order.) The descriptions don't quite all fit, but enough appears for you to know what each code means.

combo boxes and list boxes provide list of valid entries

set Column Width and Column Count to control appearance of combo box list

Limit To List = don't allow other values for this field

❑ **Progress Check**

If you can do the following, you've mastered this lesson:

❑ Create a lookup table.

❑ Give a field a combo-box control.

❑ Link a field to a lookup table.

12 **Press Esc to dismiss the list of marital status codes or choose the one for Jeff Sessions (he's married). Then close the Senators window.**

Wow — the Marital Status field works great! But wait: The new fields (Marital Status and Environmentalist) don't appear on the Senators form, and they don't appear in the queries, either. In the next lesson, you'll add the new fields to the queries already in the database, and in Lesson 10-4, you'll update your forms to include the new fields.

Lesson 10-3   # Adding New Fields to Queries

After you've added fields to a table, take a look at the queries in your database and see which should include the new fields. For each query, think about whether you'd like your new fields to appear in the query or in reports that use the query as a record source. (By *record source,* we mean the table or query that contains the information to be displayed in the form or report.)

If you used the * entry on the Field list to add all the fields in the table to the design grid, Access adds any new fields that you create, too. (See Lesson 7-3 for more details on using * with the design grid.) For queries that should include the new fields, open each query in Design view and check whether the field will be added automatically as part of a * entry; if it won't be added automatically, you need to add the field yourself.

*queries with * in*
design grid
automatically
include new fields

Of course, some queries may not need to include information from the new fields. For example, in the US Senate database, the Inactive Senators query (the one you made in Unit 9) doesn't need to include the Marital Status field, now does it? If none of the new fields is needed in the query, you don't have to do a thing to the query.

What if you deleted fields from a table on which a query is based? You'd better delete the fields from the query, or you'll see an error message the next time you open the query or any form or report that uses the query as its record source. If you changed the name of a field, you need to change the name in all the queries, for the same reason.

In this lesson, you'll add the new fields in the Senators table — Marital Status and Environmentalist — to some queries in the US Senate database.

on the CD

1 **In the US Senate database, open the database window and click the Queries tab.**

You see a list of the queries in the database.

2 **Click the Senators from One State query in the database window and then click Design.**

You see the query in Design view, as shown in Figure 10-5. This query selects records from the Senators table for a specific state. (See the sidebar "Making queries that ask questions" for an explanation of the Criteria entry for the State field in this query.) You'd like the Environmentalist and Marital Status fields to appear on this query.

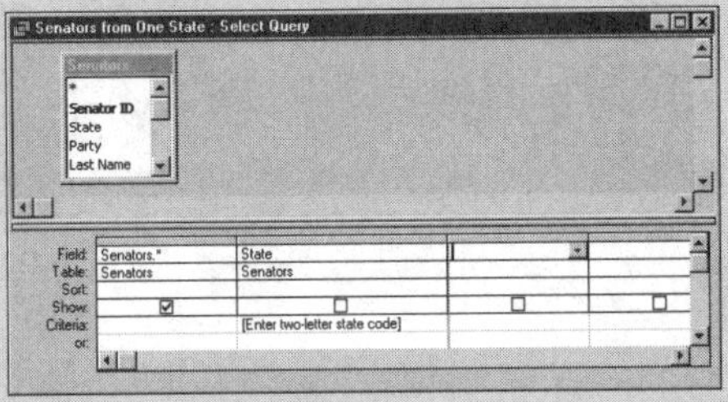

Figure 10-5

Figure 10-5: This query will automatically to include the new fields in the Senators table.

extra credit

Making queries that ask questions

What if you want a query that displays the two senators for a given state? You could make 50 such queries, one for each state, and choose the query for the state you want to see. But there's a much easier way.

You can create a *parameter* in a query — that is, a piece of information that is missing from the query and that gets filled in when the query runs. In Figure 10-5, the Criteria for the State field is `[Enter two-letter state code]`.

Usually, stuff inside square brackets is a field name. But if you enter something that *isn't* a field name, Access creates a parameter by that name. When you run the query (that is, display it in Datasheet view), Access prompts you for the value of the parameter. When you open the Senators from One State query, you see a window that asks `Enter two-letter state code` with a box for you to fill in the code. When you click OK, Access replaces the parameter with the code you typed, finds senators from the state you entered, and displays the results as usual.

Parameters are an easy, powerful way to make useful queries!

But wait! The Field entry in the first column of the design grid is Senators.* — that is, all the fields in the Senators table, including the fields you just added.

3 **Click the View button (the left-most button on the toolbar) to see the results of the query.**

Access asks you for the state whose senators you want to see. (That's what that mysterious Criteria entry in the State column does.)

4 **Type VT for Vermont — or the code for your own state — and then press Enter.**

The query results appear.

5 **Scroll the datasheet to the right until you see the Marital Status and Environmentalist fields.**

Notes:

Figure 10-6: You can add your new fields to this query by double-clicking the field names.

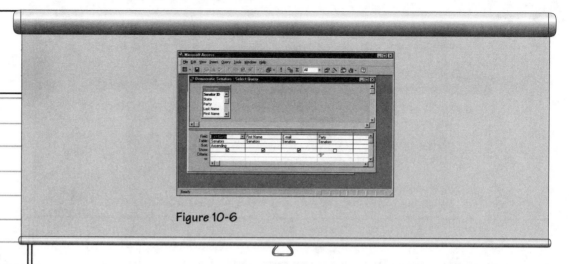

Figure 10-6

You can scroll the datasheet to the right by pressing the Tab key to move the cursor from column to column or by clicking the horizontal scroll bar at the bottom of the window. All the new fields appear in the datasheet because the * entry in the design grid is automatically updated to include all fields.

6 Close the Senators from One State query.

You didn't make any changes to the query; it updated itself!

7 Click the Democratic Senators query in the database window and then click <u>D</u>esign.

You see the Design view, shown in Figure 10-6. The query shows a list of Democratic senators with their e-mail addresses. You'd like to add the Environmentalist field to this query.

8 Double-click the Environmentalist field on the field list in the top half of the query.

You'll have to scroll down the Senators field list to find the Environmentalist field. Access adds the field name to the Field row of the first blank column in the design grid. You may have to scroll the design grid to the right to see the new column.

9 Click the View button (the left-most button on the toolbar) to see the new results of this query.

The query now includes the Environmentalist field in its own column. None of the Environmentalist check boxes is checked, though, because you haven't entered any information in the Environmentalist field yet.

10 Close the Democratic Senators query and click <u>Y</u>es when Access asks whether to save your changes.

After you add new fields to a table, update your queries to add the fields where needed. If you have deleted fields from a table, be sure to delete the fields from all your queries.

☑ Progress Check

If you can do the following, you've mastered this lesson:

❑ Add a field to an existing table.

❑ Check that new fields are added automatically to queries that use the * field name in the design grid.

❑ Add new fields to queries that aren't automatically updated.

Adding New Fields to a Form   Lesson 10-4

When the Database Wizard creates a database, a beautiful form appears for each table in the database. If you make your own database, you can use the AutoForm button to make acceptable forms for your tables. In the US Senate database, the Senators form contains all the fields in the Senators table and makes seeing, entering, or changing information in the records easy. But what about the two fields you just added to the Senators table: Environmentalist and Marital Status?

To add fields to a form (or to make any other changes to a form), you use — what else? — Design view for forms! When you open the Senators form in Design view, it looks like Figure 10-7. The form is divided into one or more sections:

- **Form Header:** Information that appears at the top of the form, like the title of the form

- **Page Header:** Information that appears at the top of each page of the form when the form is printed (or on-screen in Print Preview)

- **Detail:** Information from one record in the form's record source; a form can display one Detail section at a time, showing one record, or several Detail sections, showing several records at the same time

- **Page Footer:** Information that appears at the bottom of each page of the form when the form is printed (or on-screen in print Preview), like a page number

- **Form Footer:** Information that appears at the bottom of the form, like totals or counts of the information on the form

Most forms don't have page headers and footers because most people use forms only on-screen and don't bother to specify what should print at the tops and bottoms of pages. Many forms don't have form headers or footers, either (the Senators form shown in Figure 10-7 doesn't). But all forms have a Detail section because that's the part of the form that displays information from the fields in the record source.

The Detail section is where you need to add new fields to the form or delete fields that you've deleted from a table. You see things called *controls* in Design view: Controls are labels, text boxes, lines, check boxes, and anything else that can appear on a form (or report, as you'll see in the next lesson). When designing a form, you create, move, and modify controls on the form. To add a field to a form, you create a new control that displays the field. Depending on the type of the field, you can create a text-box control, a check-box control, or other types of controls.

add new fields to forms used to edit table records

Detail section is only required section of a form

Figure 10-7: Design view of a form shows the controls that appear on the form.

Figure 10-8: This Properties window shows the properties of the entire Senators form.

Figure 10-9: The Toolbox gives you buttons for creating all kinds of controls on your form.

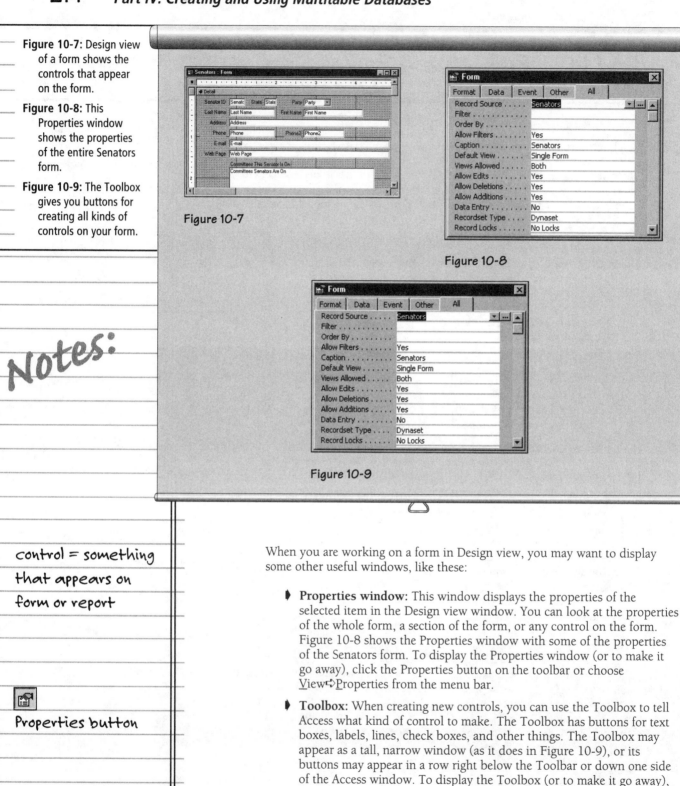

Figure 10-7

Figure 10-8

Figure 10-9

Notes:

control = something that appears on form or report

Properties button

When you are working on a form in Design view, you may want to display some other useful windows, like these:

▶ **Properties window:** This window displays the properties of the selected item in the Design view window. You can look at the properties of the whole form, a section of the form, or any control on the form. Figure 10-8 shows the Properties window with some of the properties of the Senators form. To display the Properties window (or to make it go away), click the Properties button on the toolbar or choose View⇨Properties from the menu bar.

▶ **Toolbox:** When creating new controls, you can use the Toolbox to tell Access what kind of control to make. The Toolbox has buttons for text boxes, labels, lines, check boxes, and other things. The Toolbox may appear as a tall, narrow window (as it does in Figure 10-9), or its buttons may appear in a row right below the Toolbar or down one side of the Access window. To display the Toolbox (or to make it go away), click the Toolbox button on the Toolbar or choose View⇨Toolbox from the menu bar.

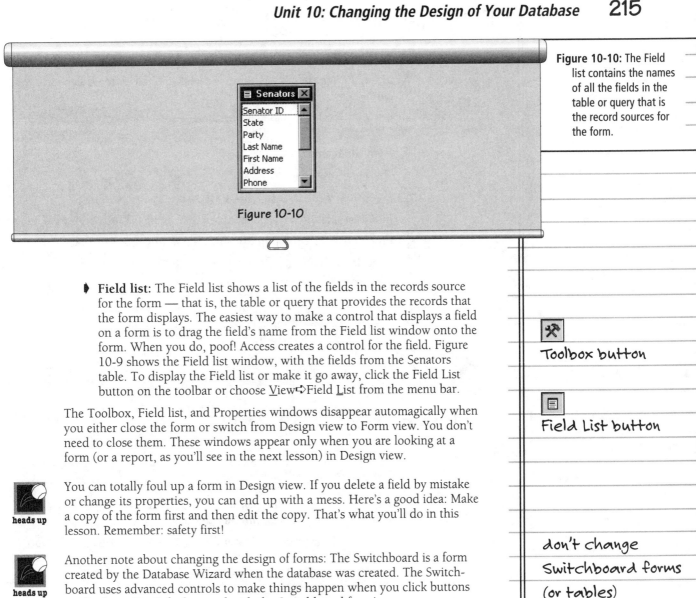

Figure 10-10

▶ **Field list:** The Field list shows a list of the fields in the records source for the form — that is, the table or query that provides the records that the form displays. The easiest way to make a control that displays a field on a form is to drag the field's name from the Field list window onto the form. When you do, poof! Access creates a control for the field. Figure 10-9 shows the Field list window, with the fields from the Senators table. To display the Field list or make it go away, click the Field List button on the toolbar or choose View⇨Field List from the menu bar.

The Toolbox, Field list, and Properties windows disappear automagically when you either close the form or switch from Design view to Form view. You don't need to close them. These windows appear only when you are looking at a form (or a report, as you'll see in the next lesson) in Design view.

heads up

You can totally foul up a form in Design view. If you delete a field by mistake or change its properties, you can end up with a mess. Here's a good idea: Make a copy of the form first and then edit the copy. That's what you'll do in this lesson. Remember: safety first!

heads up

Another note about changing the design of forms: The Switchboard is a form created by the Database Wizard when the database was created. The Switchboard uses advanced controls to make things happen when you click buttons on the form. Don't fool around with the Switchboard form!

Copying a form

Before starting to fool around with the Senators form, be smart and make a copy. To copy a form, click the Forms tab in the database window. Then select the form, press Ctrl+C to copy the form to the Windows Clipboard, and press Ctrl+V to paste a copy of the form back into the database. Access asks what you want to call the copy of the form. For example, you can make a copy of the Senators form and call it Senators Backup.

After you've copied the form, if you mess it up while editing it, you can always delete the messed-up copy and rename the Senators Backup form as Senators.

Toolbox button

Field List button

don't change
Switchboard forms
(or tables)

copy form using
Ctrl+C, then Ctrl+V

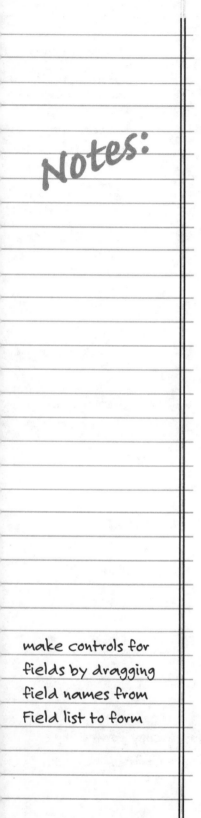

Notes:

on the CD

1 **In the US Senate database, open the database window and click the Forms tab.**

You see a list of the forms in the database.

2 **Click the Senators form and then press Ctrl+C (or choose Edit⇨Copy from the menu bar).**

Nothing seems to happen.

3 **Press Ctrl+V (or choose Edit⇨Paste from the menu bar).**

The Paste As dialog box appears, asking what to call the copy of the form.

4 **Type Senators Backup in the Form Name box and click OK.**

Access inserts a copy of the form in your database, and the form name appears in the database window.

Now you've got a copy of the Senators form, in case your editing goes wrong. If you foul up the Senators form, you can delete it and then rename the Senators Backup form as Senators.

heads up

Tip: You can use the same techniques — copying, deleting, and renaming — with tables, queries, and reports, too!

Adding fields to a form

You are now ready to update the Senators form so that it includes the two new fields: Environmentalist and Marital Status.

1 **In the database window, with the Forms tab selected, click the Senators form and click the Design button.**

You see the Senators form in Design view, which looks like Figure 10-7. Your Design view window may be bigger than the one we show; you can resize the window by dragging its edges around. Make the Design view window big enough to show the whole form.

2 **If the Field list doesn't appear, click the Field List button on the toolbar.**

You're going to use the Field list to create controls for the new fields.

3 **Scroll down the Field list until you find the Environmentalist field.**

Space is available for the Environmentalist field on the first row of controls, just to the right of the Party field.

4 **Using your mouse, drag the name of the Environmentalist field from the Field list onto the form, dragging it to a position just to the right of the Party field. If you don't like where the control for the Environmentalist field ended up, press the Delete key and try this step again.**

make controls for
fields by dragging
field names from
Field list to form

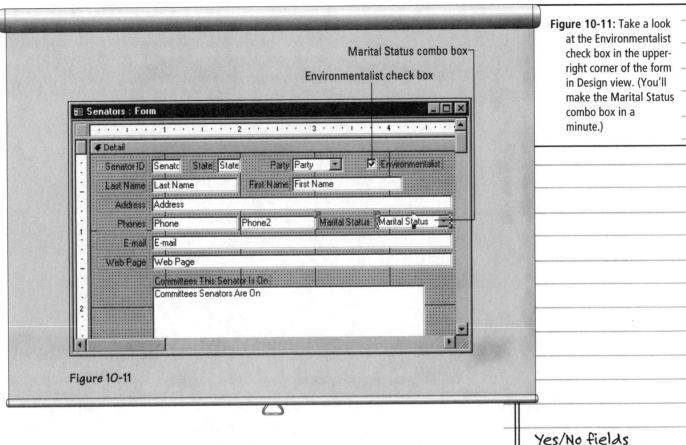

Marital Status combo box

Environmentalist check box

Figure 10-11

Figure 10-11: Take a look
at the Environmentalist
check box in the upper-
right corner of the form
in Design view. (You'll
make the Marital Status
combo box in a
minute.)

A check box appears, with little gray boxes all around it, and the label `Envi-`
`ronmentalist` appears to its right (see Figure 10-11).

Alternatively, you can move the control around on the form: Click the little gray
box at the upper-left corner of the control and drag the control to a new
location.

Voilà! You've created a check box on the form that you can click for senators
who are endorsed by the Sierra Club (if you care).

5 **Click the View button (the left-most button on the toolbar) to see**
how the form looks in Form view (or choose View⇨Form View from
the menu bar).

You see the form, with the new Environmentalist control in the upper-right
corner, as shown in Figure 10-12.

6 **If the form doesn't look the right size, choose Window⇨Size to Fit**
Form from the menu bar.

This command is available only when you are looking at a form in Form view.
When you give this command, Access adjusts the window to exactly fit the
form. The Environmentalist check box appears where you created it.

7 **Click the Environmentalist check box to make this senator pro-**
environmental protection; then click it again to remove the check.

A check appears in the box. If you click the box again, the check disappears.
Isn't this easier than typing Yes and No in a text box?

Yes/No fields
appear as check
boxes on forms

Window→Size to
Fit Form adjusts
size of form

Figure 10-12: New fields appear on your form, and they look great!

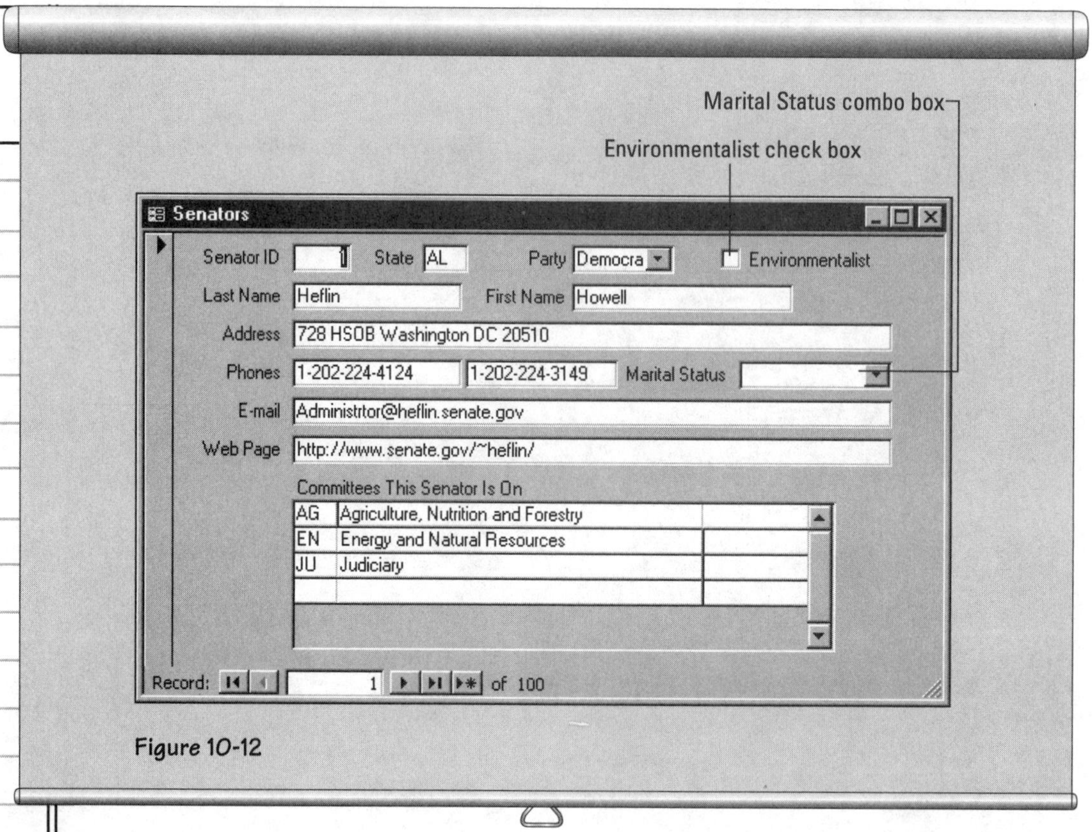

Marital Status combo box

Environmentalist check box

Senators				_ □ ×

Senator ID [1] State [AL] Party [Democra ▼] ☐ Environmentalist

Last Name [Heflin] First Name [Howell]

Address [728 HSOB Washington DC 20510]

Phones [1-202-224-4124] [1-202-224-3149] Marital Status [▼]

E-mail [Administrtor@heflin.senate.gov]

Web Page [http://www.senate.gov/~heflin/]

Committees This Senator Is On

AG	Agriculture, Nutrition and Forestry	▲
EN	Energy and Natural Resources	
JU	Judiciary	
		▼

Record: [◄◄] [◄] [1] [►] [►►] [►*] of 100

Figure 10-12

8 **Switch back to Design view by clicking the View button again (or by choosing View⇨Design View from the menu bar).**

If you don't like where the Environmentalist check box appears, click it to select it and then drag it to a new location or delete it and go back to Step 4.

Where would you like to put the combo box for the Marital Status field? It would fit nicely on the fourth row of fields, if you moved the Phone2 field a little to the left and removed its label.

9 **Click the Phone2 label (not the box) and press the Delete key.**

The Phone2 label disappears, leaving an unlabeled box. Move the Phone2 box over next to the Phone box so that it'll be clear that the two boxes are for phone numbers.

to delete label and leave box, select label and press Delete key

10 **Click the Phone2 box and drag it to the left so it is snug up against the Phone field.**

To move the Phone2 box, drag the little box in the upper-left corner of the box. Just leave a tiny space between the box for the Phone and Phone 2 fields. Hmm . . . how about changing the Phone label to say Phones so that both boxes are obviously for phone numbers?

drag field box to better location

11 **Click the Phone label (not the box) and then click again. The label area turns white, and a cursor appears in it.**

Now you can edit the label.

12 **Edit the label to say Phones. Then press Enter.**

Now there may be space to the right of the Phone2 box for the Marital Status combo box.

13 **Drag the Marital Status field from the Field list to the form to create a combo-box control for the field.**

Put the new Marital Status box well to the right of the Phone2 box. The left-hand edge of the Marital Status box appears in the location where you moved the mouse. If necessary, drag the Marital Status box around until its right edge lines up with the right edge of the Address box.

The Marital Status label overlaps the Phone2 box — and looks lousy.

14 **Move the Marital Status label to the right by clicking in the label area and then clicking and dragging the little box in its upper-left corner.**

You should be able to fit the label between the Phone2 and Marital Status boxes. If necessary, adjust the size and position of the label by clicking it and dragging the little gray boxes on its edges.

15 **Click the Marital Status label box once to select it and then again to edit the text of the label. Delete the colon at the end of the label and press Enter.**

None of the other labels have colons at the end, so this colon looks strange. You may have to try editing the label a few times before you get the text right because the label is so hard to read while you are editing it. The Marital Status control should look like the one in Figure 10-11 (more or less).

When you create the Marital Status box, Access may have widened the form to make room for it. If so, move the right edge of the form back to its original position at five inches wide.

16 **Scroll the form window to the right so that you can see the right edge of the form. Looking at the ruler along the top of the form window, see whether the right edge is positioned at a width more than five inches. If so, click the right edge of the form and drag leftward until it is at the five-inch mark.**

The form doesn't *have* to be exactly five inches wide, but it looks good that way.

17 **When the control looks good, press Ctrl+S (or choose File⇨Save from the menu) to save your changes so far.**

It would be a shame to lose your work if the power went off!

18 **Switch to Form view by clicking the View button (or choosing View⇨Form from the menu bar).**

There's your Marital Status control (see Figure 10-12)! You can tell it's a combo box by the list button at the right end of the control. You can click the list button to see the menu of valid marital statuses.

19 **If the form window is too big, choose Window⇨Size to Fit Form from the menu bar.**

You may want to switch back to Design view to make further adjustments. You can switch back and forth between Design view and Form view as needed until the form looks right.

Notes:

to edit label, click once, then again

move label by dragging its upper-left corner

Figure 10-13: Change the order in which the cursor moves from field to field in the Tab Order dialog box.

Figure 10-13

Controlling how the cursor moves

You have one more task before you are done with this form. You need to tell Access to include your two new controls (for Environmentalist and Marital Status) in the tab order for the form. The *tab order* is the order in which the cursor visits the boxes on the form when you press the Tab or Enter key. You use the View⇨Tab Order command on the menu bar to see the Tab Order dialog box, shown in Figure 10-13.

1 **Switch back to Design view one last time and choose View⇨Tab Order from the menu bar.**

You see the Tab Order dialog box, shown in Figure 10-13. You use this window to tell Access how your cursor should move around in the form as you press Tab after entering or editing each field.

2 **Make sure that the Detail option is selected.**

You need to fix the tab order in the Detail section of the form, which is where you added controls.

You can drag the field up and down the list to control the order in which the cursor moves to the fields. Or you can let Access come up with a good order.

3 **Click the Auto Order button.**

Access looks at the form and rearranges the fields on the Tab Order dialog box so that the cursor moves from field to field across each row of fields and then down to the next row of fields. Sounds good to us!

4 **Click OK.**

The Tab Order dialog box disappears. Now when the cursor is in the Party field and you press Tab, the cursor moves over to the Environmentalist field instead of skipping over it.

Margin notes (handwritten):

tab order = order in which cursor moves from field to field

View→Tab order to change tab order

Auto Order adjusts tab order automatically

save changes to form

5 **Close the Senators form window and click <u>Y</u>es when Access asks whether you want to save your changes.**

Of course, if you accidentally made hash out of the form, you can close it and click <u>N</u>o to leave the form the way it was before you started this lesson!

The two fields that you added to the Senators table now appear on the Senators form as well, so seeing, adding, and editing the information in the new fields is easy.

Recess

This lesson was intense. You learned how to make changes to the guts of the Access database. Take a breather! In the next lesson, you'll use the information that you just learned to make the same sort of changes to reports.

extra credit

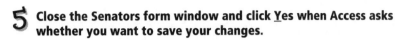

Creating a form with the Form Wizard

You've changed an existing form, but how about making a brand-new form? Making a new form isn't that hard because you can get help from the Form Wizard (who else!). To make a new form, click the Forms tab in the database window and click the <u>N</u>ew button. When you see the New Form window, click Form Wizard and

click OK. The Form Wizard asks you a series of questions about what fields you want on your form and how they should appear.

After the Form Wizard creates the form, you can always make further refinements by using Design view.

☑ **Progress Check**

If you can do the following, you've mastered this lesson:

❑ Look at a form in Design view.

❑ Display the Field list for a form.

❑ Create a new control on a form.

❑ Move a control around on a form.

❑ Adjust the size of a control.

❑ Delete the label for a control.

❑ Review your changes by switching between Form view and Design view.

❑ Correct the order in which the cursor moves from field to field.

Adding New Fields to a Report

Lesson 10-5

In Access, reports are similar to forms. Both are arrangements of the information from your tables: Forms arrange the information on-screen, and reports arrange it on paper.

To make changes to a report, you've probably already guessed that you use Design view. In fact, you can probably already guess that you click the Reports tab in the database window, select the report to change, and click the <u>D</u>esign button! And Design view for reports looks a great deal like Design view for forms; you see controls, a Field list, a Properties window, and a Toolbox. You can add a field to a form by dragging the field name from the Field list to the report, just as you did with forms in Lesson 10-4.

report design works like form design

In the Design view of a report, you may see the following sections, separated by horizontal bars:

◗ **Report Header:** Information that appears at the top of the report, such as the title of the report, or a cover page

◗ **Page Header:** Information that appears at the top of each page of the report, like the title of the report

◗ **Detail:** Information from one record in the report's record source

◗ **Page Footer:** Information that appears at the bottom of each page of the report, like the page number

◗ **Report Footer:** Information that appears at the bottom of the report, such as totals

You can use the same buttons to display the same windows — the Field list window, the Properties window, and the Toolbox — that you saw for designing forms in Lesson 10-4.

In this lesson, you'll change the Alphabetical Senator Listing so that it includes the marital status of each senator.

on the CD

1 **In the US Senate database, open the database window and click the Reports tab.**

You see a list of the reports in the database. Actually, only one report appears — you'll make some more.

2 **Click Alphabetical Senator Listing, press Ctrl+C, and press Ctrl+V. Type** Alphabetical Listing with Marital Status **and click OK.**

You're making a copy of the Alphabetical Senator Listing report; you'll modify the copy of the report so that it includes the Marital Status field.

3 **Click Alphabetical Listing with Marital Status (if it's not already selected) and then click the Design button.**

You see the report in Design view, as shown in Figure 10-14. The report looks a great deal like a form in Design view, doesn't it? The Detail section of the report specifies what the report should print for each record in the record source (the table or query that supplies the records to be printed).

First, change the title in the Report Header section from Alphabetical Senator listing to Alphabetical Listing with Marital Status.

4 **Click the box that says Alphabetical Senator Listing in the Report Header section of the report once. Then click the label again once to edit its text.**

If you double-click the label (or any control on a report or form) by mistake, Access displays the Properties window with information about the control. You can close the Properties window by clicking its Close button.

When you single-click a selected control, a cursor appears, and Access lets you edit the text in the control.

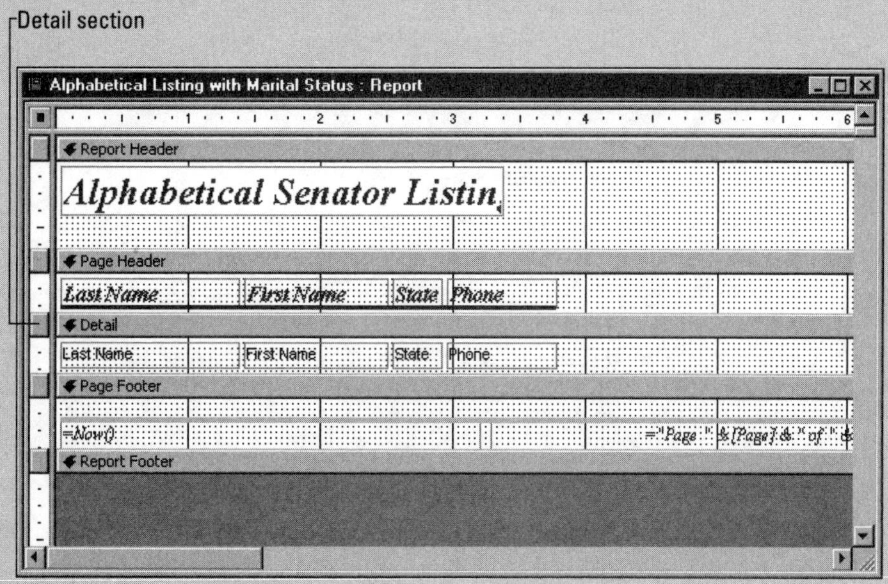

Detail section

Figure 10-14: You are ready to add a field to this report using Design view.

Detail section

Alphabetical Listing with Marital Status : Report

Alphabetical Senator Listin

Report Header

Page Header

Last Name   *First Name*   *State*   *Phone*

Detail

Last Name   First Name   State   Phone

Page Footer

=Now()   ="Page " & [Page] & " of " &

Report Footer

Figure 10-14

5 **Using the Backspace and Del keys, edit the title until it reads Alphabetical Listing with Marital Status (or whatever title you think would be appropriate). Then press Enter.**

Access changes the text. Next, you'll add the Marital Status field to the Detail section of the report that displays information from the Senators table.

6 **If the Field list doesn't appear (a little list of the fields in the record source for the report), click the Field List button.**

The Field list appears in its own little window.

7 **Scroll down the Field list until you find the Marital Status field. Click the Marital Status field name and drag it to the Design view window, in the Detail section, just to the right of the Phone box.**

Access creates a combo-box control for the Marital Status field (because you set up the Marital Status field in the Senators table to use a combo box). When you print a report, a combo box looks just like a text box.

Unfortunately, Access also creates a label to the left of the combo box, which looks just terrible.

8 **Click the Marital Status label that Access just created and press the Delete key.**

That looks better! If you didn't line up the Marital Status control neatly with the other controls in the Detail section of the report, you can now use the mouse to drag the control around to the right location.

Now you need a column heading for the Marital Status column.

Notes:

Field List button

Toolbox button

Label button

☑ Progress Check

If you can do the following, you've mastered this lesson:

❑ Make a copy of a report as a backup in case your changes mess up the original.

❑ Delete a label from a report.

❑ Add a field and a label to a report.

❑ Adjust the appearance of controls on a report.

9 **If you don't see the toolbox window (see Figure 10-9), click the Toolbox button on the toolbar.**

You can use one of the buttons on the toolbox to create a label as the column heading. You can get rid of the Field list if it's in the way; just close its window.

10 **Click the Label button on the toolbox, the left-hand button on the second row of buttons.**

The Label button is for making labels, and it has *Aa* on it.

11 **Move the cursor to where you want the upper-left corner of the label to be, just to the right of the Phone label in the Page Header section of the report. Then hold down the mouse button and drag the pointer to where you want the lower-right corner of the label to be, trying to outline a label box about the same size and shape as the Phone label.**

Don't worry if it isn't perfect. You can adjust the size by clicking the little boxes along the edges of your new label box.

12 **In the label box you just made, type** Marital Status **and press Enter.**

Access uses the same type as it uses in the other label boxes. Looks good!

13 **Click the Print Preview button (the left-most button on the toolbar).**

Access switches the window to Print Preview so you can see how the report looks. Not bad! The Marital Status column is blank unless you've entered marital status codes for any senators.

14 **Close the report, saving your changes.**

Editing reports works a great deal like editing forms: You delete, create, and modify controls in Design view and then see how your changes look.

Bravo! You've completed all the lessons in this book! You no longer qualify as an Access novice; you know the ropes. You're a qualified database user now!

Unit 10 Quiz

For each of the following questions, circle the letter of the correct answer or answers. Remember, each question may have more than one right answer.

1. **Which of the following kinds of changes can you make to your database?**

   A. Adding fields.

   B. Deleting fields.

   C. Changing field sizes.

   D. Adding new queries.

   E. Deleting reports you never use.

2. **You use Design view to . . .**

    A. Tinker with tables.

    B. Quickly modify queries.

    C. Fool around with forms.

    D. Redesign reports.

    E. Doodle in the margins of your database.

3. **In *Peter Pan*, Peter takes Wendy, John, and Michael . . .**

    A. Over the rainbow.

    B. To Neverland.

    C. For a long ride off a short pier.

    D. Away forever.

    E. Out for ice cream.

4. **Which of the following are types of Access fields?**

    A. Text.

    B. Number.

    C. Date/Time.

    D. Yes/No.

    E. Graphic.

5. **You can use the Windows Clipboard to copy . . .**

    A. Forms.

    B. Reports.

    C. Tables.

    D. Databases.

    E. Boxes on a form or report.

6. **Properties are . . .**

    A. Pieces of real estate.

    B. Monopoly cards.

    C. Settings that affect a field in a table or a control on a form or report.

    D. Elements that appear in the Properties window.

    E. Displayed when you click the Properties button.

Unit 10 Exercise

on the CD

1. In the US Senate database, create a table named States, with one field, State Code (the two-letter abbreviation). Make the State Code field the primary key field.

2. In Datasheet view, type the 50 state codes. Refer to the codes in the Senators table to find out what they are, sorting the Senators datasheet by the State field.

3. Modify the Senators table, making the State field a lookup field. Use the Lookup tab in the Field Properties part of the Design view of the table. Tell Access to look up the state codes in the States table you just created. You can leave the Column Count at 1 so that you don't have to enter anything for the Column Widths.

4. Save the changes to your Senators table and look at it in Datasheet view. Take a look at the State field and try out its combo box.

Part IV Review

Unit 8 Summary

- **Related tables:** Tables that contain records connected by having the same value in one field in each table (*primary key field* and *foreign key field*). Using related tables avoids the storage of duplicate information.

- **One-to-many relationship:** One record in one table (the *master table*) has no, one, or many matching records in the other table (the *detail table*).

- **Many-to-many relationship:** One record in either table has no, one, or many matching records in the other table. Access stores a many-to-many relationship in a separate table that has one-to-many relationships with the two tables.

- **Relational lookup:** Looking up the record in the master table that matches a record in the detail table.

- **Referential integrity:** Each record in a detail table must have a matching record in the master table.

- **Designing databases with multiple tables:** 1. State the problem. 2. Identify the data. 3. Decide what type of information each field contains. 4. Review the data, eliminating unnecessary items. 5. Organize the information into groups of related items (tables and fields). 6. Choose a primary key field (or combination of fields) for each table. 7. Link the tables, adding fields and tables as needed. 8. Make final adjustments.

- **Creating a multitable database:** Use the Database Wizard and choose any template except the Address Book. Or create new tables in an existing database or make a database from scratch.

- **Creating and reviewing relationships:** Choose Tools⇨Relationships to display the Relationships window. To see details of a relationship, double-click the join lines between tables.

Unit 9 Summary

- **Creating queries using multiple tables:** Include a field list for each table in the upper half of the Design view for the query. Access draws join lines between related tables. Then drag fields to the design grid as usual.

- **Calculated fields:** Column in the query that is created by entering an expression in the Field row of the query's design grid. Name the calculated field by typing the name and a colon before the expression.

- **Expression:** Formula using field names (in square brackets, which Access will add for you), operators (+ for addition, - for subtraction, * for multiplication, / for division, and & for text concatenation), numbers, text (in quotes), or other items to tell Access how to create a calculated field.

- **Show box:** Clear check mark from Show box in design grid to omit column from query results. Click the Show box to enter or clear the check mark.

- **Selecting fields that are blank or nonexistent:** Type **In Null** in Criteria row.

- **Inner join:** Queries include only records for which values exist in both related tables.

- **Outer join:** Queries include records for which no matching record exists in one of the tables.

- **Choosing the join type:** To choose between an inner and an outer join, double-click the join line between field lists in Design view of the query or in the Relationships window.

Unit 10 Summary

- **Preparing to make changes to your database:** Make a backup copy of the database before making changes to its design, in case you make a mistake or simply change your mind. To copy a database, use My Computer or Windows Explorer.

Part IV Review

- **Adding a field:** In Design view for the table, add a row for the field that you want to add. Specify the type of information that the field will contain.

- **Changing the size or type of a field:** In Design view of the table, change the Data Type or Field Size for the field.

- **Deleting a field:** In Design view of the table, delete the row for the field. But we don't recommend deleting fields that might be on queries, forms, and reports or that might be used to link the table to other tables.

- **Field name:** Name of the field. You can use the same field name in different tables but not more than once in the same table. Names can contain spaces. Neatness and consistency count!

- **Data type:** What link of information the field will contain: Text, Memo, Number, Currency, AutoNumber, Date/Time, Yes/No are among the data types available.

- **Opening a table in Design view:** Click the Tables tab in the database window and then click the Design button.

- **Effects of design changes:** Changes to the design of a table are not automatically made to the queries, forms, and reports that use information from the table. You must make the necessary corrections to these queries, forms, and reports.

- **Creating new tables:** Click the Tables tab in the database window and then click the New button. Type the fields, one per row. Select one or more fields to be the primary key; then click the Primary Key button on the toolbar. Press F6 to switch between the field list and Field Properties.

- **Lookup field:** Text field that can accept only values that appear in another table, the lookup table. The lookup table (or master table, the "one" side) and the table with the lookup field (detail table, the "many" side) have a one-to-many relationship. To create a lookup field, first create the master table containing the list of possible values. Then in Design view of the detail table, select the field that relates the tables, click the Lookup tab in the Field Properties part of the Design view window, set the Display Control to Combo Box, and set the Row Source to the name of the master table.

- **Change the fields in a query:** Open the query in Design view. To add fields, drag them from the Field list to the design grid. To delete a field from a query, select the column for the field and press Delete. The * entry in the design grid automatically updates to include new fields and omit deleted fields.

- **Changing the fields in a form or report:** Open the form or report in Design view. Each field is represented by a *control,* where the field appears. Field controls usually appear in the Detail section of the form or report. To add a control for a field, drag the field from the Field list. To delete a field, select its control and press Delete.

- **Refining form design:** To move controls, click and drag. To control the order in which the cursor moves from field to field in a form, choose View⇨Tab Order to see the Tab Order dialog box. To add a label, click the Label button on the Toolbox and drag the location for the label with the mouse; then type the label text. Choose Window⇨Size to Fit Form to adjust the size of the window that displays the form.

- **Copying tables, queries, forms, or reports:** Select the table, query, form, or report in the database window, press Ctrl+C to copy it to the Windows Clipboard, and press Ctrl+V to copy it back into the database. Access asks for a new name for the copy.

Part IV Test

The questions on this test cover all the material presented in Part IV, Units 8, 9 and 10.

True False

T   F   1. Related tables must contain the same fields in the same order.

T   F   2. A master table is on the "one" side of a one-to-many relationship.

T   F   3. In the movie version of *Gone with the Wind,* the footage of the city of Atlanta in flames was created by burning the old sets from *King Kong.*

T   F   4. To make a multitable query, you use the New⇨Multiple Query command.

T   F   5. An expression is something to yell at Access when it's adding strangely.

T   F   6. The expression [First Name] & " " & [Last Name] creates a calculated field consisting of each person's first and last names separated by a space.

T   F   7. The difference between an inner join and an outer join has to do with which records are included in queries that include the two joined tables.

T   F   8. Never back up your databases; extra copies just waste disk space.

T   F   9. Currency fields are just like number fields, except that they're specifically designed for storing amounts of money.

T   F   10. To make a field for which you can choose a value from a list of possible values, you need to be able to program.

Multiple Choice

For each of the following questions, circle the correct answer or answers. Remember, a question may have more than one right answer!

11. **Which of the following types of relationships can be represented in Access?**

    A. One-to-one relationship.

    B. One-to-many relationship.

    C. Many-to-many relationship.

    D. Table-to-table relationship.

    E. The knee bone's connected to the thigh bone relationship.

12. **Which of the following are steps in designing a database?**

    A. Think about what the database will be used for.

    B. Determine what type of information will be in each field (text, number, date, and so on).

    C. Group the fields into tables.

    D. Make sure that each table has a primary key field.

    E. All of the above.

13. **How many senators make up the United States Senate?**

    A. 50.

    B. 100.

    C. 435.

    D. 535.

    E. None of the above.

14. **Concatenation is . . .**

    A. Adding two numbers together.

    B. Relating two tables together.

    C. Stringing two text values together.

    D. Adding a field to a table.

    E. None of the above.

15. **When you add a field to a table, Access . . .**

    A. Automatically adds the field to all queries that use the table as a record source.

    B. Automatically adds the field to queries that use the table as a record source and have an * in the Field row of the design grid.

    C. Doesn't make any changes to your queries.

    D. Automatically adds controls for the field to all forms and reports that use the table as a record source.

    E. Doesn't make any changes to forms and reports.

Matching

16. **Match each of the following buttons with its name:**

    A.   1. View button in Design view

    B.   2. Maximize button

    C.   3. Insert Rows button

    D.   4. Primary Key button

    E.   5. Relationships button

17. **Match the term with its definition:**

    A. Master table   1. Line representing relationship between tables

    B. Foreign key field 2. Table on "one" side of one-to-many relationship

    C. Detail table   3. In detail table, field that contains values from primary key field in master table

    D. Join line   4. Field that uniquely identifies each record in table

    E. Primary key field 5. Table on "many" side of one-to-many relationship

18. **Match the operator with its name:**

    A. +   1. Addition

    B. /   2. Subtraction

    C. -   3. Multiplication

    D. &   4. Division

    E. *   5. Concatenation

Part IV Lab Assignment

In this lab, you add a States table in the Dickens Address Book 7 database by importing it from another database. Then you use the States table to validate entries in the StateOrProvince field in the Addresses table. No more guessing at state codes!

Step 1: Open the Dickens Address Book 7 database and import the States table from the States database.

on the CD

The States database contains only one table — States — which is a list of two-letter U.S. state, district, and territory abbreviations. To import the table into the Dickens Address Book 7 database, choose File➪Get External Data➪Import from the menu bar, choose the States.mdb database in the *Dummies 101 Access 97* folder, choose the States table, and click OK.

(This list of states and provinces and their abbreviations comes from the U.S. Postal Service's Web site at http://www.usps.gov and Canada Post Corporation's Web site at http://www.mailposte.ca.)

Step 2: Take a look at the States table.

Step 3: Modify the design of the Addresses table, changing the StateOrProvince field from a text field to a lookup field.

Tell Access to display the StateOrProvince field as a combo box, displaying two columns from the States table, with column widths 0.25 inch and 1 inch.

Step 4: Look at the Addresses table in Datasheet view to see how the combo box looks.

Not bad! The combo box is a little narrow, but it's wide enough so you can tell which state you're selecting.

Extra Credit: To make the combo box wider, switch back to Design view, look at the field properties for the StateOrPrivince field, and change the List Width setting from Auto to 2 inches. Then change the Column Widths setting to 0.25 inch and 1.5 inches.

Step 5: Change the StateOrProvince control on the Addresses form from a text box to a combo box.

Make a copy of the form first, just in case.

In Design view of the Addresses form, select the text box for the StateOrProvince field and delete it. Display the Field list if it's not already visible. Drag the StateOrProvince field from the Field list to the form, dropping it where the text box used to be. Access creates a combo box for the field. Move the control around if necessary.

Choose View⇨Tab Order from the menu to fix the tab order for the StateOrProvince field. Because you deleted the original field and made a new one, the cursor moves to the list field dead last. Move the StateOrProvince field upward on the list until it appears between the City and PostalCode fields.

Switch to Form view to see how the new StateOrProvince combo box looks.

Step 6: In the Relationships window, create a relationship between the Addresses and States tables.

Add the Addresses and States tables to the Relationships window. (Don't add the Switchboard table, which contains information used by the Main Switchboard and Report Switchboard forms.)

Relate the two tables by dragging the State Code field from the States field list over to the StateOrProvince field on the Addresses field list. Click the Enforce Referential Integrity box so that Access checks state codes before adding addresses.

If Access displays an error message, saying that one or more records in the Addresses table violate the referential integrity rule you want to set up, you've got a typo or two in the StateOrProvince field of the Addresses table. Minimize the Relationships window while you open the Addresses table in Datasheet view and check for bogus state abbreviations. After you fix any errors, try creating the relationship again.

Step 7: You're done!

Celebrate your graduation from *Dummies 101: Access 97 For Windows!* Exit Access before starting to celebrate — you wouldn't want to delete anything while partying!

Part I Test Answers

Question	Answer	If You Missed It, Try This
1.	True	Review Lesson 2-3.
2.	False	Review Lesson 2-1, in which you make a terrific database without programming.
3.	False	Review Lesson 2-2. (We hate the use of social security numbers as primary keys!).
4.	True	Review Lesson 2-1.
5.	False	Review Lesson 2-1.
6.	True	Review Lesson 1-3.
7.	False	Review Lesson 1-2.
8.	False	Review Lesson 2-4.
9.	True	Review Lesson 2-2.
10.	True	Review Lesson 2-3.
11.	A, C	Review Lesson 2-2.
12.	A, B	Review Lesson 2-3.
13.	C, D	Review Lesson 2-3.
14.	A, B, C, D, E	Review Lesson 1-3.
15.	A-1, B-5, C-2, D-3, E-4	Review Lessons 2-1, 2-2, 2-3, and 2-4.
16.	A-4, B-3, C-5, D-1, E-2	Review Lesson 2-2.

Part II Test Answers

Question	Answer	If You Missed It, Try This
1.	False	Review Table 3-1.
2.	True	Review Lesson 3-1.
3.	True	Review Lesson 3-1.
4.	False	Review Lesson 3-2.
5.	True	Review Lesson 3-2.
6.	True	Review Lesson 3-4.
7.	False	Review Lesson 3-5.
8.	False	Review Lessons 4-1 and 4-2.
9.	True	Review Lesson 4-2.
10.	True	Review Lesson 5-3.
11.	C	Review Lesson 3-2.
12.	A, B, E	Review Lesson 3-5.
13.	B, D	Review Lesson 4-1.
14.	E	Review Lesson 4-3.
15.	C	Read it!
16.	A-2, B-4, C-5, D-1, E-3	Review Lessons 3-1, 3-3, 3-5, 4-1, and 5-4.
17.	A-2, B-2, C-3, D-4, E-1	Review Lesson 3-5 and Table 3-1.
18.	A-4, B-3, C-2, D-5, E-1	Review Lesson 4-3.
19.	A-5, B-2, C-1, D-4, E-3	Review Lesson 4-2.
20.	A-5, B-3, C-2, D-1, E-4	Watch *Star Wars* again.

Part III Test Answers

Question	Answer	If you Missed It, Try This
1.	False	Review Lesson 6-1.
2.	True	Review Lesson 6-3.
3.	True.	Review Lesson 6-1.
4.	True.	See *The Wizard of Oz* again.
5.	False.	Review Lesson 7-4.

6.	True.	Review Lessons 7-1 and 7-2.
7.	True.	Review Lesson 7-2.
8.	False.	Review Lesson 7-2.
9.	False.	Review Lesson 7-3.
10.	True.	Review Lesson 7-5.
11.	A, B, D, E	Review Lesson 6-2.
12.	A, B, C, D	Review Lesson 6-3.
13.	A, B, C, D, E	See Lesson 6-1.
14.	B, C, D	The Panama Canal runs northwest to southeast, with the Caribbean on the northwest end. Check your atlas.
15.	A, B, C, E	Review Lesson 7-2.
16.	A, B, D, E	Review Lesson 7-4.
17.	C	Review Lesson 7-5.
18.	A-2, B-3, C-1, D-5, E-4	Review Lessons 4-1, 6-2, 6-3, and 6-4.
19.	A-4, B-5, C-1, D-2, E-3	Rent some classic movies!
20.	A-1, B-5, C-4, D-3, E-2	Review Lessons 6-1, 6-2, 6-3, and 6-4.

Part IV Test Answers

Question	Answer	If You Missed It, Try This
1.	False	Review Lesson 8-1.
2.	True	Review Lesson 8-1.
3.	True	Or so we hear.
4.	False	Review Lesson 9-1.
5.	True	But you'll also find another definition in Lesson 9-2.
6.	True	Review Lesson 9-2.
7.	True	Review Lesson 9-3.
8.	False	Review introductory text at the beginning of Unit 10.
9.	True	Review Table 10-1 in Lesson 10-1.
10.	False	Review Lesson 10-2.

11.	A, B, C	Review Lesson 8-1.
12.	E	Review Lesson 8-1.
13.	B	There are two from each state. (See the Senators file in the US Senate database.)
14.	C	Review Lesson 9-2.
15.	B, E	Review introductory text at the beginning of Unit 10.
16.	A-5, B-2, C-4, D-1, E-3	Review Lessons 8-3, 9-2, 10-1, and 10-2.
17.	A-2, B-3, C-5, D-1, E-4	Review Lessons 8-1 and 8-3.
18.	A-1, B-4, C-2, D-5, E-3	Review Table 9-1 in Lesson 9-2.

Appendix B

• • • • • • • • • •

About the CD

This appendix lists the files on the *Dummies 101* CD in the back of this book, explains how to install the files so that they are ready for you to use, and lists which lesson covers each file. Most files on the CD are Access 97 databases, along with a few files in other formats that you'll use when you learn to import information into Access. In the Introduction, we explain how to install the files you'll be using in the book, but this appendix reviews everything you need to know about the CD.

heads up

Before you can use the files on this CD, you install them in a folder on your hard disk. After installing the files, wait until you get to the lesson that introduces each file before using it. If you open a database and make changes before you get to the lesson in which you use the database, the steps in the lesson may not work! If it's too late and you've already messed up a file, don't panic — you can reinstall a file from the CD-ROM by following the installation instructions again.

Also note that this CD doesn't contain the Access 97 program itself. You've got to buy that from Microsoft. Access 97 (also known as Access Version 8.0) comes as part of Microsoft Office 97 Professional. Check your hard disk — you may have it installed (click Start and choose <u>P</u>rograms to see what programs are available). If you have Access 7.0 (which comes with Microsoft Office 95) or an earlier version of Access, you won't be able to read these databases, which were created using Access 97.

System Requirements

To use the files on this CD, you need

- ▶ Windows 95 installed on your machine.

- ▶ Microsoft Access Version 8 or Microsoft Office 97 Professional installed on your computer.

- ▶ A CD-ROM player.

- ▶ At least 3MB of free space on your hard disk.

If you need more information on PC or Windows 95 basics, check out *PCs For Dummies,* 4th Edition, by Dan Gookin, or *Dummies 101: Windows 95* by Andy Rathbone, both published by IDG Books Worldwide, Inc.

What's on the CD

Here's a list of all the files on the CD along with the lesson in which you first make the acquaintance of each file:

Dickens Address Book 2.mdb	Lesson 2-3
Dickens Address Book 4.mdb	Lesson 4-1
Dickens Address Book 5.mdb	Lesson 5-4
Dickens Address Book 7.mdb	Lesson 7-1
Dickens Books.mdb	Part II Lab Assignment
Dickens Extras.htm	Lesson 5-2
Dickens Extras.mdb	Lesson 5-1
Dickens Extras.txt	Lesson 5-3
Middlebury Tours.mdb	Lesson 1-1
More Dickens Extras.htm	Unit 5 Exercise
States.mdb	Part IV Lab Assignment
US Senate.mdb	Lesson 6-1

In addition, the file readme.txt includes the same information you are reading in this appendix.

Putting the Exercise Files on Your Hard Drive

The exercise files are sample documents and databases that you use while following along with the lessons in the book. You need to put these files on your hard drive. After you're done with the book, you can remove the files easily (see "Removing the Exercise Files" at the end of this appendix).

If you have problems with the installation process, you can call the IDG Books Worldwide, Inc., Customer Support number: 800-762-2974 (outside the U.S.: 317-596-5261).

on the CD

With Windows 95 up and running, follow these steps:

1 **Insert the Dummies 101 CD (label side up) into your computer's CD drive and wait about 30 seconds to see whether Windows 95 starts the CD for you.**

Be careful to touch only the edges of the CD. The CD drive is the one that pops out with a circular drawer.

If your computer has the Windows 95 AutoPlay feature, the installation program begins automatically and you see the a window telling you that the program is about to start the installation. If the program does not start after 30 seconds, go to Step 2. If it does, go to Step 4.

2 **If the installation program doesn't start automatically, click the Start button on the Windows 95 Taskbar and choose Run from the menu that appears.**

3 **In the dialog box that appears, type** d:\setup.exe **(if your CD drive is not drive D, substitute the appropriate letter for** d**) and click OK.**

You see a window telling you that the installation program is about to install some icons you can use to finish the installation.

4 **Click OK.**

The installation program creates a folder on your desktop containing two icons, one for finishing the installation and one for uninstalling the files later. The same two options have also been added to a new Dummies 101 menu on your Start⇨Programs menu (the menu you see when you click the Start button on the Taskbar and choose Programs).

You see a window asking if you'd like to use the CD now, that is, whether you want to go ahead and install the exercise files for the book from the CD.

5 **Click Yes.**

You see the End-User License Agreement window, with a bunch of legalese.

6 **Read the license agreement and click Agree if you don't have a problem with it.**

You see the Dummies 101: Access 97 For Windows installation window.

7 **Click Install Exercise Files.**

Another message appears, asking whether you want to go ahead and copy the exercise files to your hard disk.

8 **Click OK to continue with the installation or click Cancel if you want to stop.**

If you click Cancel, you can install the files later by repeating these steps.

You see a window asking where to install the exercise (sometimes known as *practice*) files on your computer. To make the installation and the exercises in this book as simple as possible, let the installer place the exercise files in the recommended location. If you really want to put the files somewhere else, you can change the location by following the on-screen instructions (make sure that you remember where you put them if you change the location).

Unless you change the location, the exercise files are installed in the C:\My Documents\Dummies 101 Access 97 folder.

9 **Click OK to install the files in the folder shown.**

The installation program copies the exercise files to your computer. You see a little window telling you that the installation is done and referring you to the book for how to use the exercise files.

10 Click OK to make the little window go away.

You see the Dummies 101: Access 97 For Windows installation window again (the one with the Dummies man).

11 Click the Exit button in the lower right corner of the window.

A window appears asking if you really, really want to exit.

12 Click Yes.

Tip: If at some point you accidentally modify an exercise file and want to reinstall the original version, just follow the steps in this appendix again. The installation program will copy the original files over the exercise files you've been using, restoring them to their pristine, pre-use state. If you want to save your modified version of any of the files, either move the file to another folder before reinstalling the original or tell the exercise file installer to place the replacement files in a different folder in Step 8.

heads up

Remember that you need to have Access 97 for Windows installed on your computer in order to open and edit the exercise files. Access 97 for Windows is *not* included on the CD.

Using the exercise files

You'll find detailed instructions on how to access the exercise files in Unit 1, where you first need to open a file. Please wait until you read Unit 1 to open the files.

Removing the exercise files

After you have been through the book and no longer need the exercise files, you can remove them by running the uninstallation program that comes on the CD. When you installed the files from the CD, you installed the uninstallation program, too (how farsighted of you!). If you want to keep any of the files, be sure to move them to another folder before deleting the Dummies 101 Access 97 folder.

Here's how to uninstall the exercise files. (While the program is at it, it'll also delete the Dummies 101 - Access 97 icons from your desktop and remove the Dummies 101 - Access 97 commands from your Start menu. Nice!)

1 Click the Start button on the Windows 95 Taskbar and choose Programs⇨Uninstall Dummies 101 Access 97 CD.

You see the Uninstall Dummies 101 - Access 97 for Windows window.

2 Leave the Automatic option selected and click Next.

3 Click Finish.

The program uninstalls everything and exits. You're done!

Index

IDG BOOKS WORLDWIDE, INC.
END-USER LICENSE AGREEMENT

Read This. You should carefully read these terms and conditions before opening the software packet(s) included with this book ("Book"). This is a license agreement ("Agreement") between you and IDG Books Worldwide, Inc. ("IDGB"). By opening the accompanying software packet(s), you acknowledge that you have read and accept the following terms and conditions. If you do not agree and do not want to be bound by such terms and conditions, promptly return the Book and the unopened software packet(s) to the place you obtained them for a full refund.

1. **License Grant**. IDGB grants to you (either an individual or entity) a nonexclusive license to use one copy of the enclosed software program(s) (collectively, the "Software") solely for your own personal or business purposes on a single computer (whether a standard computer or a workstation component of a multiuser network). The Software is in use on a computer when it is loaded into temporary memory (i.e., RAM) or installed into permanent memory (e.g., hard disk, CD-ROM, or other storage device). IDGB reserves all rights not expressly granted herein.

2. **Ownership**. IDGB is the owner of all right, title, and interest, including copyright, in and to the compilation of the Software recorded on the disk(s)/CD-ROM. Copyright to the individual programs on the disk(s)/CD-ROM is owned by the author or other authorized copyright owner of each program. Ownership of the Software and all proprietary rights relating thereto remain with IDGB and its licensors.

3. **Restrictions on Use and Transfer.**

(a) You may only (i) make one copy of the Software for backup or archival purposes, or (ii) transfer the Software to a single hard disk, provided that you keep the original for backup or archival purposes. You may not (i) rent or lease the Software, (ii) copy or reproduce the Software through a LAN or other network system or through any computer subscriber system or bulletin-board system, or (iii) modify, adapt, or create derivative works based on the Software.

(b) You may not reverse engineer, decompile, or disassemble the Software. You may transfer the Software and user documentation on a permanent basis, provided that the transferee agrees to accept the terms and conditions of this Agreement and you retain no copies. If the Software is an update or has been updated, any transfer must include the most recent update and all prior versions.

4. **Restrictions on Use of Individual Programs**. You must follow the individual requirements and restrictions detailed for each individual program in Appendix B of this Book. These limitations are contained in the individual license agreements recorded on the disk(s)/CD-ROM. These restrictions may include a requirement that after using the program for the period of time specified in its text, the user must pay a registration fee or discontinue use. By opening the Software packet(s), you will be agreeing to abide by the licenses and restrictions for these individual programs. None of the material on this disk(s) or listed in this Book may ever be distributed, in original or modified form, for commercial purposes.

5. **Limited Warranty.**

(a) IDGB warrants that the Software and disk(s)/CD-ROM are free from defects in materials and workmanship under normal use for a period of sixty (60) days from the date of purchase of this Book. If IDGB receives notification within the warranty period of defects in materials or workmanship, IDGB will replace the defective disk(s)/CD-ROM.

Dummies 101 CD-ROM Installation Instructions

Here's how to install the exercise files from the Dummies 101: Access 97 For Windows CD-ROM onto your hard disk. You need a CD-ROM drive and about 3MB of space on your hard drive. You also need to be running Windows 95. See Appendix B for the details on the CD.

If you have problems with the installation process, you can call the IDG Books Worldwide, Inc. Customer Support number: 800-762-2974 (outside the U.S.: 317-596-5261).

on the CD

With Windows 95 up and running, follow these steps:

1 Insert the Dummies 101 CD (label side up) into your computer's CD drive and wait about 30 seconds to see whether Windows 95 starts the CD for you.

Be careful to touch only the edges of the CD. The CD drive is the one that pops out with a circular drawer.

If your computer has the Windows 95 AutoPlay feature, the installation program begins automatically and you see the a window telling you that the program is about to start the installation. If the program does not start after 30 seconds, go to Step 2. If it does, go to Step 4.

2 If the installation program doesn't start automatically, click the Start button on the Windows 95 Taskbar and choose Run from the menu that appears.

3 In the dialog box that appears, type d:\setup.exe (if your CD drive is not drive D, substitute the appropriate letter for d) and click OK.

You see a window telling you that the installation program is about to install some icons you can use to finish the installation.

4 Click OK.

You see a window asking if you'd like to use the CD now.

5 Click Yes to make the End-User License Agreement window appear.

6 Read the license agreement and click Agree to make the Dummies 101: Access 97 For Windows installation window appear.

7 Click Install Exercise Files.

Another message appears, asking whether you want to copy the exercise files to your hard disk.

8 Click OK to continue with the installation, or click Cancel if you want to stop.

You see a window asking where to install the exercise files on your computer. To make the installation and the exercises in this book as simple as possible, let the installer place the exercise files in the recommended location. Unless you change the location, the exercise files are installed in the C:\My Documents\Dummies 101 Access 97 folder.

9 Click OK to install the files in the folder shown.

The installation program copies the exercise files to your computer. You see a little window telling you that the installation is done and referring you to the book for how to use the exercise files.

10 Click OK to make the Dummies 101: Access 97 For Windows installation window reappear.

11 Click the Exit button. The program asks is you really, really want to exit.

12 Click Yes.

You don't have to do anything with the files yet — we tell you when you need to open the first file (in Unit 1).

heads up

Remember that you need to have Access 97 for Windows installed on your computer in order to open and edit the exercise files. Access 97 for Windows is *not* included on this CD.